Process Consultation Revisited

Building the Helping Relationship

Edgar H. Schein
Sloan School of Management
Massachusetts Institute of Technology

An imprint of Addison Wesley Longman, Inc.

Reading, Massachusetts • Menlo Park, California • New York • Harlow, England
Don Mills, Ontario • Sydney • Mexico City • Madrid • Amsterdam

Executive Editor: Michael Roche
Assistant Editor: Ruth Berry
Production Supervisor: Louis C. Bruno, Jr.
Senior Marketing Manager: Julia Downs
Senior Marketing Coordinator: Joyce Cosentino
Print Buyer: Sheila Spinney
Composition and Prepress Services: Pre-Press Co., Inc.
Printer and Binder: Courier Westford
Cover Printer: Lehigh Press

This book is in the Addison-Wesley Series on Organization Development.
Consulting Editors: Edgar H. Schein and Richard Beckhard

Library of Congress Cataloging-in-Publication Data

Schein, Edgar H.
Process consultation revisited: building the helping relationship / Edgar H. Schein.
p. cm.
ISBN 0-201-34596-X
1. Business consultants. 2. Social psychology. I. Title.
HD69.C6S283 1998
658.4'6—dc21 98-24926
CIP

2 3 4 5 6 7 8 9 10—CSW—02010099

Series Foreword

The Addison-Wesley Series on Organization Development originated in the late 1960s when a number of us recognized that the rapidly growing field of "OD" was not well understood or well defined. We also recognized that there was no one OD philosophy; hence, one could not at that time write a textbook on the theory and practice of OD, but one could make clear what various practitioners were doing under that label. So the original six books in the OD Series launched what became a continuing enterprise, the essence of which was to allow different authors to speak for themselves rather than to summarize under one umbrella what was obviously a rapidly growing and highly diverse field.

By the early 1980s, OD was growing by leaps and bounds and expanding into all kinds of organizational areas and technologies of intervention. By this time, many textbooks existed that tried to capture core concepts in the field, but we felt that diversity and innovation continued to be the more salient aspects of OD. Accordingly, our series had expanded to nineteen titles.

As we moved into the 1990s, we began to see some real convergence in the underlying assumptions of OD. As we observed how different professionals working in different kinds of organizations and occupational communities made their cases, we saw that we were still far from having a single "theory" of organizational development. Yet, some common premises were surfacing. We began to see patterns in what was working and what was not, and we were becoming more articulate about these patterns. We also started to view the field of OD as increasingly connected to other organizational sciences and disciplines, such as information technology, coordination theory, and organization theory.

In the early 90s, we added several new titles to the OD Series to describe important new themes: Ciampa's *Total Quality* illustrates the important link to employee involvement in continuous improvement; Johansen et. al.'s *Leading Business Teams* explores the important arena of electronic information tools for teamwork; Tjosvold's *The Conflict-Positive Organization* shows how conflict management can turn conflict into constructive action; and Hirschhorn's *Managing in the New Team Environment* builds bridges to group psychodynamic theory.

In the mid 1990s, we continued to explore emerging themes with four revisions and three new books. Burke took his highly successful *Organization Development* into new realms with more current and expanded content; Galbraith updated and enlarged his classic theory of how information management lies at the heart of organization design with his new edition of *Competing with Flexible Lateral Organizations*; and Dyer wrote an important third edition of his classic book, *Team Building*. In addition, Rashford and Coghlan introduced the important concept of levels of organizational complexity as a basis for intervention theory in their book *The Dynamics of Organizational Levels*; in *Creating Labor-Management Partnerships*, Woodworth and Meek take us into the critical realm of how OD can help in labor relations—an area that has become increasingly important as productivity issues become critical for global competitiveness; In *Integrated Strategic Change*, authors Worley, Hitchin and Ross powerfully demonstrate how the field of OD must be linked to the field of strategy by reviewing the role of OD at each stage of the strategy planning and implementation process; and finally, authors Argyris and Schön provided an important link to organizational learning in a new version of their classic book entitled *Organizational Learning II: Theory, Method, and Practice*.

Now, as we continue to think about the field of OD and what it will mean in the 21st century, we have added several titles that reflect the growing connections between the original concepts of OD and the wider range of the applications of these concepts. Rupert Chisholm's book *Developing Network Organizations: Learning from Practice and Theory,* explores and illustrates the link between OD and building community networks. In their new book called *Diagnosing and Changing Organizational Culture*, Cameron and Quinn explore one model and technique of how to get at the crucial concept of culture and how to make this concept relevant for the practitioner. Finally, the theme of process consultation has remained central in OD, and we have found that it continues to be relevant in a variety of helping situations. In *Process Consultation Revisited: Building the Helping Relationship*, Schein has completely revised and updated this concept by focusing on process consultation as a general model of the helping process; his new volume pulls together material from previous work and also adds new concepts and cases.

Our series on Organization Development now includes over thirty titles. We will continue to welcome new titles and revisions as we explore the various frontiers of organization development and identify themes that are relevant to the ever more difficult problem of helping organizations to remain effective in an increasingly turbulent environment.

New York, New York Richard H. Beckhard
Cambridge, Massachusetts Edgar H. Schein

Other Titles in the Organization Development Series

Diagnosing and Changing Organizational Culture
Kim S. Cameron and Robert E. Quinn 1999 (0-201-33871-8)
This book helps managers, change agents, and scholars to understand, diagnose, and facilitate the change of an organization's culture in order to enhance its effectiveness. The authors present three forms of assistance for readers: (1) validated instruments for diagnosing organizational culture and management competency, (2) a theoretical framework for understanding organizational culture, and (3) a systematic strategy and methodology for changing organizational culture and personal behavior. This text is a workbook in that readers can complete the instruments and plot their own culture profile in the book itself. They can also use the text as a resource for understanding and leading a culture change process.

Developing Network Organizations: Learning from Theory and Practice
Rupert F. Chisholm 1998 (0-201-87444-X)
The interorganizational network is rapidly emerging as a key type of organization, and the importance of the network is expected to increase throughout the 21st century. This text covers the process of developing these complex systems. The author uses in-depth description and analysis based on direct involvement with three diverse networks to identify critical aspects of the development process. He explains relevant concepts and appropriate methods and practices in the context of developing these three networks, and he also identifies ten key learnings derived from his direct involvement with the development process.

Organizational Learning II: Theory, Method, and Practice
Chris Argyris and Donald A. Schön 1996 (0-201-62983-6)
This text addresses how business firms, governments, non-governmental organizations, schools, health care systems, regions, and whole nations need to adapt to changing environments, draw lessons from past successes and failures, detect and correct the errors of the past, anticipate and respond to impending threats, conduct experiments, engage in continuing innovation, and build and realize images of a desirable future. There is a virtual consensus that we are all subject to a "learning imperative," and in the academy no less than in the world of practice, organizational learning has become an idea in good currency.

Integrated Strategic Change: How OD Builds Competitive Advantage
Christopher G. Worley, David E. Hitchin, and Walter L. Ross 1996 (0-201-85777-4)
This book is about strategic change and how firms can improve their performance and effectiveness. Its unique contribution is in describing how

organization development practitioners can assist in the effort. Strategic change is a type of organization change that realigns an organization's strategy, structure and process within a given competitive context. It is substantive and systemic and therefore differs from traditional organization development that produces incremental improvements, addresses only one system at a time, or does not intend to increase firm-level performance.

Team Building: Current Issues and New Alternatives, Third Edition
William G. Dyer 1995 (0-201-62882-1)
One of the major developments in the field of organization redesign has been the emergence of self-directed work teams. This book explains how teams are most successful when the team becomes part of the culture and structure or systems of the organization. It discusses the major new trends and emphasizes the degree of commitment that managers and members must bring to the team-building process. It is written for managers and human resource professionals who want to develop a more systematic program of team building in their organization or work unit.

Creating Labor-Management Partnerships
Warner P. Woodworth and Christopher B. Meek 1995 (0-201-58823-4)
This book begins with a call for changing the social and political barriers existing in unionized work settings and emphasizes the critical need for union-management cooperation in the present context of international competition. It demonstrates the shift from confrontational union-management relationships toward more effective and positive systems of collaboration. It is written for human resource management and industrial relations managers and staff, union officials, professional arbitrators and mediators, government officials, and professors and students involved in the study of organization development.

Organization Development: A Process of Learning and Changing, Second Edition
W. Warner Burke 1994 (0-201-50835-4)
This text provides a comprehensive overview of the field of organization development. Written for managers, executives, administrators, practitioners, and students, this book takes an in-depth look at organization development with particular emphasis on the importance of learning and change. The author not only describes the basic tenets of OD, but he also looks at OD as a change in an organization's culture. Frameworks and models like the Burke-Litwin model (Chapter 7), as well as numerous case examples, are used throughout the book to enhance the reader's understanding of the principles and practices involved in leading and managing organizational change.

Competing with Flexible Lateral Organizations, Second Edition
Jay R. Galbraith 1994 (0-201-50836-2)
This book focuses on creating competitive advantage by building a lateral capability, thereby enabling a firm to respond flexibly in an uncertain world.

The book addresses international coordination and cross-business coordination as well as the usual cross- functional efforts. It is unique in covering both cross-functional (lateral or horizontal) coordination, as well as international and corporate issues.

The Dynamics of Organizational Levels: A Change Framework for Managers and Consultants
Nicholas S. Rashford and David Coghlan 1994 (0-201-54323-0)
This book introduces the idea that, for successful change to occur, organizational interventions have to be coordinated across the major levels of issues that all organizations face. Individual level, team level, inter-unit level, and organizational level issues are identified and analyzed, and the kinds of intervention appropriate to each level are spelled out.

Total Quality: A User's Guide for Implementation
Dan Ciampa 1992 (0-201-54992-1)
This is a book that directly addresses the challenge of how to make Total Quality work in a practical, no-nonsense way. The companies that will dominate markets in the future will be those that deliver high quality, competitively priced products and service just when the customer wants them and in a way that exceeds the customer's expectations. The vehicle by which these companies move to that stage is Total Quality.

Managing in the New Team Environment: Skills, Tools, and Methods
Larry Hirschhorn 1991 (0-201-52503-8)
This text is designed to help manage the tensions and complexities that arise for managers seeking to guide employees in a team environment. Based on an interactive video course developed at IBM, the text takes managers step by step through the process of building a team and authorizing it to act while they learn to step back and delegate. Specific issues addressed include how to give a team structure, how to facilitate its basic processes, and how to acknowledge differences in relationships among team members and between the manager and individual team members.

Leading Business Teams: How Teams Can Use Technology and Group Process Tools to Enhance Performance
Robert Johansen, David Sibbett, Suzyn Benson, Alexia Martin, Robert Mittman, and Paul Saffo 1991 (0-201-52829-0)
What technology or tools should organization development people or team leaders have at their command, now and in the future? This text explores the intersection of technology and business teams, a new and largely uncharted area that goes by several labels, including "groupware"—a term that encompasses both electronic and nonelectronic tools for teams. This is the first book of its kind from the field describing what works for business teams and what does not.

The Conflict-Positive Organization: Stimulate Diversity and Create Unity
Dean Tjosvold 1991 (0-201-51485-0)
This book describes how managers and employees can use conflict to find common ground, solve problems, and strengthen morale and relationships. By showing how well-managed conflict invigorates and empowers teams and organizations, the text demonstrates how conflict is vital for a company's continuous improvement and increased competitive advantage.

Change by Design
Robert R. Blake, Jane Srygley Mouton, and Anne Adams McCanse 1989 (0-201-50748-X)
This book develops a systematic approach to organization development and provides readers with rich illustrations of coherent planned change. The book involves testing, examining, revising, and strengthening conceptual foundations in order to create sharper corporate focus and increased predictability of successful organization development.

Power and Organization Development: Mobilizing Power to Implement Change
Larry E. Greiner and Virginia E. Schein 1988 (0-201-12185-9)
This book forges an important collaborative approach between two opposing and often contradictory approaches to management: OD practitioners who espouse a "more humane" workplace without understanding the political realities of getting things done, and practicing managers who feel comfortable with power but overlook the role of human potential in contributing to positive results.

Designing Organizations for High Performance
David P. Hanna 1988 (0-201-12693-1)
This book is the first to give insight into the actual processes you can use to translate organizational concepts into bottom-line improvements. Hanna's "how-to" approach shows not only the successful methods of intervention, but also the plans behind them and the corresponding results.

Process Consultation, Volume 1, Second Edition: Its Role in Organization Development, Second Edition
Edgar H. Schein 1988 (0-201-06736-6)
How can a situation be influenced in the workplace without the direct use of power or formal authority? This book presents the core theoretical foundations and basic prescriptions for effective management.

Organizational Transitions: Managing Complex Change, Second Edition
Richard Beckhard and Reuben T. Harris 1987 (0-201-10887-9)
This book discusses the choices involved in developing a management system appropriate to the "transition state." It also discusses commitment to

change, organizational culture, and increasing and maintaining productivity, creativity, and innovation.

Stream Analysis: A Powerful Way to Diagnose and Manage Organizational Change
Jerry I. Porras 1987 (0-201-05693-3)
Drawing on a conceptual framework that helps the reader to better understand organizations, this book shows how to diagnose failings in organizational functioning and how to plan a comprehensive set of actions needed to change the organization into a more effective system.

Process Consultation, Volume II: Lessons for Managers and Consultants
Edgar H. Schein 1987 (0-201-06744-7)
This book shows the viability of the process consultation model for working with human systems. Like Schein's first volume on process consultation, the second volume focuses on the moment-to-moment behavior of the manager or consultant rather than the design of the OD program.

Managing Conflict: Interpersonal Dialogue and Third-Party Roles, Second Edition
Richard E. Walton 1987 (0-201-08859-2)
This book shows how to implement a dialogue approach to conflict management. It presents a framework for diagnosing recurring conflicts and suggests several basic options for controlling or resolving them.

Pay and Organization Development
Edward E. Lawler 1981 (0-201-03990-7)
This book examines the important role that reward systems play in organization development efforts. By combining examples and specific recommendations with conceptual material, it organizes the various topics and puts them into a total systems perspective. Specific pay approaches such as gainsharing, skill-based pay, and flexible benefits are discussed, and their impact on productivity and the quality of work life is analyzed.

Work Redesign
J. Richard Hackman and Greg R. Oldham 1980 (0-201-02779-8)
This book is a comprehensive, clearly written study of work design as a strategy for personal and organizational change. Linking theory and practical technologies, it develops traditional and alternative approaches to work design that can benefit both individuals and organizations.

Organizational Dynamics: Diagnosis and Intervention
John P. Kotter 1978 (0-201-03890-0)
This book offers managers and OD specialists a powerful method of diagnosing organizational problems and of deciding when, where, and how to

use (or not use) the diverse and growing number of organizational improvement tools that are available today. Comprehensive and fully integrated, the book includes many different concepts, research findings, and competing philosophies and provides specific examples of how to use the information to improve organizational functioning.

Career Dynamics: Matching Individual and Organizational Needs
Edgar H. Schein 1978 (0-201-06834-6)
This book studies the complexities of career development from both an individual and an organizational perspective. Changing needs throughout the adult life cycle, interaction of work and family, and integration of individual and organizational goals through human resource planning and development are all thoroughly explored.

Matrix
Stanley M. Davis and Paul Lawrence 1977 (0-201-01115-8)
This book defines and describes the matrix organization, a significant departure from the traditional "one man-one boss" management system. The authors note that the tension between the need for independence (fostering innovation) and order (fostering efficiency) drives organizations to consider a matrix system. Among the issues addressed are reasons for using a matrix, methods for establishing one, the impact of the system on individuals, its hazards, and what types of organizations can use a matrix system.

Feedback and Organization Development: Using Data-Based Methods
David A. Nadler 1977 (0-201-05006-4)
This book addresses the use of data as a tool for organizational change. It attempts to bring together some of what is known from experience and research and to translate that knowledge into useful insights for those who are thinking about using data-based methods in organizations. The broad approach of the text is to treat a whole range of questions and issues considering the various uses of data as an organizational change tool.

Preface

I originally wrote *Process Consultation* in 1969 out of a sense of frustration that my colleagues did not really understand what I did when I worked with clients in organizations. I now have a new sense of frustration that my colleagues in consulting and the managers whom I am trying to reach still do not understand the essence of process consultation. It is not a technology or a set of interventions for working with groups, as it was originally stereotyped. It is not just a model for nondirective counseling applied to the organizational setting. It is not an occupation or a full-time job. Rather, it is a philosophy of "helping," and a technology or methodology of how to be helpful.

Help is needed by our friends, spouses, children, colleagues, bosses, subordinates, and even strangers at various times in our lives. It is when we sense that help is needed or we are being explicitly asked for help that the philosophy of process consultation becomes relevant. But, as all professional helpers have learned, it turns out that help is not easy to give, just as it is not easy to admit that one needs help and not easy to receive it when offered. In order to understand process consultation, then, it is necessary to have much more psychological and sociological insight into the dynamics of the helping relationship.

In my earlier editions I took for granted that my readers understood a good deal about giving and receiving help, but it is in this arena that I find my students, clients, and colleagues most lacking. As I started to think about this revision I realized that my 40 years of experience with trying to be helpful had given me some new perspectives about the helping process itself. Therefore, I have reorganized my thinking and instead of writing a third edition of the existing two volumes, I have written a new volume directed specifically at creating a more general model of the helping relationship. Much of the material in this book comes from the previous two volumes, but it is totally reorganized and leaves room for a subsequent volume to deal with most of the material on organizational change, learning, leadership, intergroup dynamics, and other topics relevant to organization development per se. Here, I focus much more on the relationship between the consultant and the client in the face-to-face and small group setting. My intention is to provide a model for all kinds of helping, not just what the organizational consultant does. The therapist, social worker, high school counselor, coach, parent, friend, manager, and anyone else who tries to give help should find this a useful set of ideas, guidelines, and principles.

When someone needs help and asks for it, a difficult dynamic is set up between the helper and the "client," because the helper is automatically invited to adopt an expert role. Implied is that the helper has something that the client is lacking, and the helper is empowered to grant or withhold that something. Not only does this invite helpers to see themselves as experts, but it puts them into an automatic power position vis-a-vis the client. This initial imbalance in the relationship is the source of the psychological dynamics that have to be understood, assessed, and dealt with if help is actually to be provided.

At the same time, the cultural dynamics surrounding what it means to ask for help, to accept help, and to give help, especially when that implies levels of frankness and openness that are not ordinarily culturally sanctioned, make it necessary to understand the sociological dynamics of the helping relationship. In this book I have been able to bring together some broader perspectives deriving from my own background, which includes not only clinical and social psychology but sociology and anthropology as well.

In other words, in this book I try to explore a general theory and methodology of helping based on an understanding of psychological and social dynamics. My choice of concepts and method of presentation reflect 40 years of experience in various kinds of helping situations. It is my hope that the reader will find the concepts and methods described helpful as well.

Cambridge, Massachusetts E.H.S.

Acknowledgments

Many people have influenced my thinking over the years, but none more than Douglas McGregor, Alex Bavelas, and Richard Beckhard. McGregor and Bavelas were both teaching at MIT when I first took a seminar there in 1952, and they functioned as my faculty mentors when I returned there as an Assistant Professor in 1956. I met Dick Beckhard in 1957 and began to work closely with him first in Bethel and later at MIT where he became an Adjunct Professor. Warren Bennis joined our group at MIT in 1958 and also became a close colleague and co-author. What I learned most from these mentors and colleagues is that, in human affairs, it is best not to dictate to others but to help them to discover what they need and then helpfully steer them toward that. One cannot really control people's motives, attitudes, and thoughts; but if one can help them to discover what it is they need, one can at least align and maybe even integrate one's own needs with theirs.

A story about Alex Bavelas has always stuck in my mind. When he taught at MIT in the early 1950s, he would announce at his first class meeting: "I am Alex Bavelas; my office is down the hall. When you have figured out what you want to learn in this class come and see me." He would then walk out and not reappear until some student delegation summoned him. After some weeks of "testing," the students realized he meant it, got to work figuring out what they wanted and needed, and then had a dynamite class for the rest of the semester. I have always thought that this story is prototypical of a philosophy going back to Kurt Lewin and Carl Rogers that the learner must be involved in his or her own learning and that, in the end, one can only help people to help themselves. The spirit of this philosophy has stayed with me as an organizational consultant, and I am grateful especially to Dick Beckhard because he showed me many times how to implement it.

I learned another great lesson from Dick—that managing human affairs is largely a matter of *designing and managing processes.* What helpers really have to become expert in is the design and management of process, especially the *design* portion. In my 15 years of working at Bethel I learned how to design three-, two-, and one-week human relations workshops and conferences. In my consulting I learned how to design educational interventions and workshops. In my teaching I learned how to design learning experiences and group processes. Inability to design is one of the greatest problems that managers, teachers, and consultants face. Dick came to such design skills naturally from his days as a stage manager. He more than anyone has taught me how important design is to having the right outcomes. It is fortunate that he has finally written his own story (*R. Beckhard, Agent of Change,* Jossey-Bass, 1997) so that others can benefit from his insights.

As I started to rethink and rewrite this book, I had the benefit of help from a very different kind of colleague—a younger member of our profession—Otto Scharmer. He was interested in *Process Consultation* and volunteered to read my chapters as I developed them. He shared them with his wife Katrin, also a talented social scientist, and between them they provided detailed feedback on how the book was developing. I am immensely grateful to them for this help and many of their ideas have found their way into the book.

My reviewers Warner Burke, Michael Brimm, and Dick Beckhard made valuable suggestions and provided encouragement. Another colleague and friend, David Coghlan, a Professor at Dublin University, also read the manuscript and made many valuable suggestions that were incorporated. He has played a special role in the evolution of these ideas because of his own seminal work on process consultation and organization development embodied most recently in his books (Rashford, N. S. & Coghlan, D. *The Dynamics of Organizational Levels,* Addison Wesley, 1994, and Coghlan, D. *Renewing Apostolic Religious Life,* Dublin: The Columba Press, 1997).

I have also spent many influential hours wrestling with the meaning of "learning" with my friend and colleague of almost 50 years, Don Michael, whose work on organizational learning and its relationship to planning opened up a field long before the world was ready to recognize and deal with it (Michael, D. *Learning to Plan and Planning to Learn* (2d ed.), Alexandria, VA: Miles River Press, 1997).

My clients over the years have taught me much, and several of them stand out as having been especially helpful to me—Betty Duval of General Foods, Ken Olsen and John Sims of Digital Equipment Corporation, Jurg Leupold of Ciba-Geigy, and most recently Peter Lanahan of ConEdison and Laura Lake of AMOCO. Sharing experiences with them and designing future learning experiences for their client systems have always been great sources of my own learning.

Writing a book is always a highly involving and taxing experience. I am most grateful to my wife Mary for putting up with the endless hours when I am physically present but psychologically absent while I think about some unsolved writing problem. Without her support this book could not have been written.

Edgar H. Schein
Cambridge, MA

Contents

Part I

Process Consultation Defined

In this part of the book the basic concept of process consultation is defined and compared to other major consultation concepts. Process consultation is a philosophy about and attitude toward the process of *helping* individuals, groups, organizations, and communities. It is not merely a set of techniques to be compared to and contrasted with other techniques. Process consultation is the key philosophical underpinning to organizational learning and development in that most of what the consultant does in helping organizations is based on the central assumption that *one can only help a human system to help itself.* The consultant never knows enough about the particular situation and culture of an organization to be able to make specific recommendations on what the members of that organization should do to solve their problems.

On the other hand, once an effective helping relationship with a client system has been developed, the client and consultant together can diagnose the situation and develop appropriate remedies. The ultimate goal of process consultation, then, is the establishment of an effective *helping relationship.* What the helper/consultant needs to know, what skills she needs to develop, what attitudes she needs to hold to build and maintain effective helping relationships, and what she needs to do to implement this philosophy of helping are the primary focus of this book.

The ability to build and maintain a helping relationship is applicable to a large variety of human situations. Such a relationship is central to therapy, to counseling, and to all forms of consulting. But it is not limited to those situations in which helping is the primary function of the relationship. The ability to be an effective helper also applies to spouses, friends, managers vis-a-vis their superiors, subordinates, and peers, parents vis-a-vis their own parents and children, and teachers vis-a-vis their students. Sometimes help is solicited explicitly, sometimes we sense the need for it though the request remains implicit, and sometimes we sense that others need help even when they do not recognize it themselves. The ability to respond at that point, to adopt a helper role when it is solicited or simply when we recognize that it is needed, is a central requirement of being a responsive and responsible human being. The philosophy and methodology of process consultation is therefore central to all human relationships, not only those that are formally defined as helper/client.

In thinking about the following concepts the reader should think in terms of his or her daily life situations at home or at work. I have found that my greatest insights about *helping relationships* have come from family and friendship situations not from the formal consulting situations in organizations. I have also found that if I am in the formal helping situation it can be dysfunctional to think too much in terms of "technique" or "method" instead of focusing on the human reality that exists when people interact with each other in the effort to establish some form of relationship. Just as the artist must learn to see before she can render something, the helper must learn to see what is going on as a relationship forms in which helping becomes possible.

In the chapters that follow, my intention is to help the reader to see more clearly and to provide some concepts and simplifying models of how to think about what is going on. Chapter 1 provides some basic definitions and contrasts three fundamentally different kinds of consulting/helping roles. Chapter 2 digs beneath the surface and articulates some of the psychodynamic issues which arise in the helper and the person being helped. Chapter 3 addresses the implications of these psychodynamics for the issue of how to establish a helping relationship and introduces the concept of "active inquiry." In Chapter 4 we address the issue of how to think about the concept of "client" and identify the different types of client situations that arise, especially in organizational or community consulting. Then, in Part II we begin to examine some of the concepts and simplifying models that will help the consultant to make sense of the human realities that will be encountered as the consultation proceeds.

As I have experienced a variety of different situations in which help was needed, I have come away with some *general principles* that seem to apply across all of those situations. I have articulated those in the various chapters and have put them in bold print to highlight their central importance to learning to think like a helper.

1

What Is Process Consultation?

This book is about the psychological and social processes that are involved when one person tries to help another person. Whether a therapist is helping a patient or working with a group, a parent is helping a child, a friend is helping another friend, or an organizational consultant is working with managers to improve some aspects of the organization, the same fundamental dynamics are involved. What goes on between a helper and the person or group being helped is what I have called *process consultation* or PC for short.

The emphasis is on "process" because I believe that *how* things are done between people and in groups is as—or more important than—*what* is done. The how, or the "process," usually communicates more clearly what we really mean than does the content of what we say. Process, however, is often less familiar to us. We are less skilled in thinking about processes, in observing them in action, and in designing processes that will accomplish what we intend. In fact, we often design or participate in processes that actually undermine what we want to accomplish. To become aware of interpersonal, group, organizational, and community processes is, therefore, essential to any effort to improve how human relationships, groups, and organizations function.

I will describe what PC is and the role it plays in daily life and in organization development, change, and learning. Any form of consultation implies that one person is helping another person, hence the central focus of this analysis will be on deciphering what is helpful and what is not helpful in any given human situation. I will also be looking at PC as one of the key activities that takes place at the beginning of and throughout any organization development (OD) and learning effort. Organization development is typically defined as a planned organization-wide program, but its component parts are usually activities that the consultant carries out with individuals or groups. The mode in which these activities are carried out reflects the assumptions that underlie PC. Recent emphases on organizational learning and organizational change also make it necessary to show how PC relates to those particular activities and to build a model and a theory of helping that relates to all of those organizational processes. The central focus remains on OD, however, because I view organization development to be a general process that incorporates learning and change.

Central to any organization improvement program is the creation of a situation in which learning and change can take place by individuals and/or groups. How, then, does the consultant build readiness for learning and change? How does the consultant function as trainer, teacher, mentor, or coach in facilitating learning and change? How does the consultant work with the key individuals of an organization as part of planning an organization-wide program and/or work as a counselor when anxieties and concerns in key individuals may influence the success of the entire effort?

In dealing with these and other questions I will attempt to show that the mode in which the consultant chooses to operate moment to moment makes a major difference in how helpful the consultation will actually be. The consultant must become able to distinguish among (1) from the consultant's position as an expert, telling the client what to do; (2) selling solutions that the consultant may favor or selling the use of tools that the consultant knows how to use; or (3) engaging the client in a process that will in the end be perceived as helpful to the client by both consultant and client. As we will see, these three modes rest on fundamentally different basic models of what is involved in "helping," and these in turn rest on quite different tacit assumptions about the nature of reality and the nature of help.

The field of consultation has grown remarkably in recent years, yet conceptual confusion still exists about consultants—what they actually do for organizations, how they go about doing it, and what tacit assumptions they hold about giving help. For example, people who label themselves organizational consultants provide information, analyze information using special diagnostic tools, identify and diagnose complex problems, recommend solutions for the problems, help managers to implement difficult or unpopular decisions, give managers support and comfort, or a combination of these activities.

Many analysts of the consultation process argue that the process only works when the client knows exactly what he[1] is looking for and when the consultant can deliver specific recommendations pertaining

[1]"He" or "she" will be used alternately and randomly throughout the text.

to the problem. In such a model when clients are disappointed in the results, *they* are blamed for not having been clear in what they wanted or for being unwilling to do what the consultant recommended. In my experience, however, the person seeking help often does not know what she is looking for and indeed should not really be expected to know. All she knows is that something is not working right or some ideal is not being met, and that some kind of help is therefore needed. Any consultation process, then, must include the important tasks of helping the client figure out what the problem or issue is and—only after that—deciding what further kind of help is needed. Managers in an organization often sense that all is not well or that things could be better, but they do not have the tools with which they can translate vague feelings into the clear insights that lead to concrete actions.

The mode of consultation I will describe in detail deals especially with situations of the kind just described. The consultant operating in the PC mode does not assume that the manager knows what is wrong, or what is needed, or what the consultant should do. For the process to begin constructively the only requirement is that someone wants to improve the way things are and is willing to seek help. The consultation process itself then helps the client to define the diagnostic steps that will lead ultimately to action programs and to concrete changes that will improve the situation.

Models of Consultation and the Tacit Assumptions on Which They Rest

Consultation and helping processes can be distinguished best by analyzing the tacit assumptions they make about the client, the nature of help, the role of the consultant, and the nature of the ultimate reality in which the client and the consultant operate. The three basic models that will be discussed below can be thought of as different modes of operating and are defined by the three different roles consultants can operate in when they help a client. These models also apply to the different ways in which we provide help in our daily life when a child, spouse, or friend seeks our help. The main reason for clearly distinguishing among the three models is that *the helper must choose from one moment to the next which role to be in or which model of helping to use, but all three models imply that help is the primary function of consultation.* The focus on the concept of *helping* is so central throughout this approach to consultation that it must be stated as the first overarching principle of how to deal with others.

PRINCIPLE 1: Always Try to Be Helpful.

Consultation is providing help. Obviously, therefore, if I have no intention of being helpful and working at it, I am unlikely to be successful in creating a helping relationship. If possible, every contact should be perceived as helpful.

The three models rest on very different assumptions about the nature of help in any given situation, however, and they have potentially very different consequences. In any situation where help is sought or offered, we must be clear about what is really going on and what helping role to adopt. We cannot be in all three roles at once, so our only choice is to be conscious of which role we want to be in from one moment to the next. This consciousness rests on our ability to decipher and experience the reality that is operating and on our ability to act on that reality. By *reality* I mean some sense of what is going on inside me, what is going on inside the other person or persons in the situation, and what the nature of that situation is. Wishful thinking, stereotypes, projections, expectations, prior plans, and all other forces that are based on past conceptions or psychological needs rather than here-and-now data tend to get in the way of making a wise choice of how best to help.

This concept of reality also rests on the epistemological assumption that culture and thought create the external reality in which we operate and that we are, therefore, in a perpetual process of jointly deciphering what is going on. Neither the consultant nor the person seeking help can define an objective external reality that exists outside their relationship and cultural context. But together they can approximate how their current assumptions and perceptions create that reality and how they can best deal with that reality in terms of the client's intentions to improve the situation. The second overarching principle that should guide the action of the helper/consultant, therefore, is to always deal with the here-and-now reality.

PRINCIPLE 2: Always Stay in Touch with the Current Reality.

I cannot be helpful if I do not know the realities of what is going on within me and within the client system; therefore, every contact with anyone in the client system should provide diagnostic information to both the client and to me about the here-and-now state of the client system and the relationship between the client and me.

MODEL 1
The Purchase-of-Information or Expertise Model: Selling and Telling

The telling and selling model of consultation assumes that the client purchases from the consultant some information or an expert service that she is unable to provide for herself. The buyer, usually an individual manager or representative of some group in the organization, defines a need and concludes that the organization has neither the resources nor the time to fulfill that need. She will then look to a consultant to provide the information or the service. For example, a manager may wish to know how a particular group of consumers feels, or how a group of employees will react to a new personnel policy, or what the state of morale is in a given department. She will then hire the consultant to conduct a survey by means of interviews or questionnaires and to analyze the data.

The manager may also wish to know how to organize a particular group and may need the consultant to find out how other companies organize such groups—for example, how to organize the accounting and control functions given the capabilities of current information technology. Or the manager may wish to know particular things about competitor companies, such as their marketing strategy, how much of the price of their product is determined by production costs, how they organize their research and development function, how many employees they have in a typical plant, and so on. He will then hire the consultant to study other companies and bring back data about them. Each of these cases assumes that the manager knows what kind of information or service she or he is looking for and that the consultant is able to provide the information or service.

The likelihood that this mode of helping will work then depends on

1. Whether or not the manager has correctly diagnosed his own needs
2. Whether or not he has correctly communicated those needs to the consultant
3. Whether or not he has accurately assessed the capabilities of the consultant to provide the information or the service
4. Whether or not he has thought through the consequences of having the consultant gather such information, or the consequences of implementing the changes that the

information implies or that may be recommended by the consultant

5. Whether or not there is an external reality than can be objectively studied and reduced to knowledge that will be of use to the client.

The frequent dissatisfaction with consultants and the low rate of implementation of their recommendations can easily be explained when one considers how many of the above assumptions have to be met for the purchase model to work effectively. It should also be noted that in this model the client gives away power. The consultant is commissioned or empowered to seek out and provide relevant information or expertise on behalf of the client; but once the assignment has been given, the client becomes dependent on what the consultant comes up with. Much of the resistance to the consultant at the later stages may result from this initial dependency and the discomfort it may arouse consciously or unconsciously in the client.

In this model the consultant is also likely to be tempted to sell whatever she knows and is good at—when you have a hammer the whole world looks like a bunch of nails. Hence the client becomes vulnerable to being misled about what information or service would actually be helpful. And, of course, there is the subtle assumption that there is knowledge "out there" to be brought into the client system and that this information, or knowledge, will be understandable and usable by the client. For example, organizations frequently purchase surveys to determine how their employees feel about certain issues or even to "diagnose" their culture. When the "expert" information comes back in quantitative form, I have observed managers poring over the bar graph data, trying to figure out what they now *know* when they note that sixty-two percent of the employees think the organization has a poor career development system. What kind of information value does such a statement actually have, given the problems of sampling, the problems of questionnaire construction, the semantics of words like *career* and *development,* the ambiguity of whether sixty-two percent is really good or bad outside some broader context, the difficulty of determining what the employees were thinking when they answered the question, and so on? Reality in this situation is an elusive concept.

The PC Alternative. The PC philosophy, in contrast, is to immediately involve both the client and the consultant in a period of *joint diagnosis,* reflecting the reality that neither the client nor the consultant knows enough at this point of initial contact to define the kind of expertise that might be relevant to the situation. The consultant is willing to deal with an individual client or come into an organization without having a clear mission, goal, or defined problem because of the underlying assumption that any person, group, or organization can always improve its processes and become more effective if it can accurately locate the processes that make a difference to its overall performance. No organizational structure or process is perfect. Every organization has strengths and weaknesses. Therefore, the manager who senses that something is wrong because performance or morale is not what it should be should not leap into action or seek specific help until he has a clear idea of the strengths and weaknesses of the organization's present structures and processes.

The main goal of PC is to help the manager make such a diagnosis and develop a valid action plan based on it. Implicit in this goal is the assumption that the client and consultant must both remain in power. Both must share the responsibility for the insights obtained and actions planned. From the PC point of view, the consultant must not take the monkey off the client's back but recognize that *the problem is ultimately the client's* and only the client's. All the consultant can do is to provide whatever help the client needs to solve the problem himself.

The importance of *joint* diagnosis and action planning derives from the fact that the consultant can seldom learn enough about any given organization to really know what a better course of action would be or even what information would really help because the members of the organization perceive, think about, and react to information in terms of their traditions, values, and shared tacit assumptions—that is, their organizational culture and the particular styles and personalities of their key leaders and members[2]. However, the consultant can help the client to become a sufficiently good diagnostician herself and to learn how to manage organizational processes better so that she can solve problems for herself. It is a crucial assumption of the PC philosophy that *problems will stay solved longer and be solved more effectively if the organization learns to solve*

[2]Most of the points on organizational culture and leadership are drawn from my book on this subject and related literature that will be referred to in various chapters (Schein, 1985, 1992).

those problems itself. The consultant has a role in teaching diagnostic and problem-solving skills, but he should not attempt actually to solve the problems himself unless he is certain that he has the requisite information and expertise. The consultant must always deal with the reality revealed by joint diagnostic activities and never trust his own a priori assumptions.

When we examine various other contexts in which help is sought, the same choice must be made between operating in the expert mode or the PC mode. When my child comes to me asking for help with a math problem, when a student comes to me for specific information pertaining to a management problem, when a stranger on a street corner asks me for directions, when a friend asks me what movie I would recommend, when my wife asks me what she should wear to the party, I have to process instantaneously what is really being asked and what kind of response will, in fact, be helpful. What is the reality that is operating in the situation at that moment?

The easiest course is to take each request at face value and apply the purchase of information model—that is, answer the immediate question using one's own expertise. But often the immediate question masks a deeper or hidden issue. Maybe the child wants to spend some time with me and the math problem is the only thing she could think of to get my attention. Maybe the student has a deeper question but is afraid to ask it. Maybe the stranger is really looking for the wrong thing but does not know it. Maybe the friend is really testing whether or not I want to go to a movie with him. Maybe my wife is really trying to point out something about her wardrobe or maybe she is uncomfortable about the party to which we are going.

The danger in answering the immediate question is that it may terminate the conversation and the hidden issue never has a chance to surface. If I am to be helpful, I must inquire enough to determine where the help is really needed, and that implies starting in the PC mode. Only after I have jointly diagnosed the situation with the other party am I in a position to determine whether my expertise or information will, in fact, be relevant and helpful. One preliminary generalization, then, is that *the PC mode is necessary at the beginning of any helping process because it is the only mode that will reveal what is really going on and what kind of help is needed.*

The immediate reality is that, at the beginning of any relationship, the consultant does not know what is really being asked or is needed. It is this state of *ignorance* that is, in fact, the consultant's most important guideline for deciding what questions to ask, what advice to give, or in general what to do next. The consultant must be able to perceive what he or she does not really know, and that process has to be an *active searching out of one's areas of ignorance* because we are so filled with preconceptions, defenses, tacit assumptions, hypotheses, stereotypes, and expectations. To discover our areas of ignorance can be a difficult process of weaving our way through all our preconceptions and overcoming some of our own perceptual defenses. The active word *accessing* therefore articulates the third overarching principle of helping. As we successfully access our areas of ignorance, we can engage in genuine mutual exploration; and as areas of ignorance are removed, more layers of reality are revealed, thus making it possible to define help more accurately.

PRINCIPLE 3: Access Your Ignorance.

The only way I can discover my own inner reality is to learn to distinguish what I know from what I assume I know, from what I truly do not know. I cannot determine what is the current reality if I do not get in touch with what I do not know about the situation and do not have the wisdom to ask about it.

MODEL 2
The Doctor–Patient Model

Another common generic consultation model is that of doctor–patient. One or more managers in the organization decide to bring in a consultant to "check them over," to discover if there are any organizational areas that are not functioning properly and might need attention. A manager may detect symptoms of ill health, such as dropping sales, high numbers of customer complaints, or quality problems, but may not know how to make a diagnosis of what is causing the problems. The consultant is brought into the organization to find out what is wrong with which part of the organization and then, like the physician, is expected to recommend a program of therapy or prescribe a remedial measure. Perhaps leaders in the organization discover that there is a new cure being used by other organizations such as Total Quality Programs, Reengineering, or Autonomous Work Groups, and they mandate that their organization should try this form of therapy as well to improve the organization's health. The consultant is then brought in to administer the program. In this model the client assumes that the consultant operates from professional standards; that the selling is done responsibly, based on good data that the program will provide help for the problem; that the consultant has the diagnostic expertise to apply the program only where it will help; and that the cure will take.

Notice that this model puts even more power into the hands of the consultant in that she diagnoses, prescribes, and administers the cure. The client not only abdicates responsibility for making his own diagnosis—and thereby makes himself even more dependent on the consultant—but assumes, in addition, that an outsider can come into the situation, identify problems, and remedy them. This model is of obvious appeal to consultants because it empowers them and endows them with X-ray vision. Providing expert diagnoses and prescribing remedial courses of action justify the high fees that consultants can command and make very visible and concrete the nature of the help that they claim to provide. In this model the report, the presentation of findings, and the recommendations take on special importance in identifying what the consultant does. For many consultants this is the essence of what they do, and they feel that they have not done their job until they have made a thorough analysis and diagnosis leading to a specific written recommendation.

For example, in one version of this model that is advocated for managers, the consultant uses in-depth interviews and psychological tests as part of a diagnostic phase leading to a formal, written diagnosis and a prescription for the next steps to take. Another common version has the consultant designing and administering opinion and attitude surveys to parts of the organization as a basis for diagnosing problems. The consultant is expected to know what questions to ask, what percentages of positive or negative answers constitute a problem, and what patterns of answers identify areas of potential difficulty in the organization. Sophisticated statistical techniques are often brought into play to bolster the diagnosis and to reassure the client that the consultant is indeed a diagnostic expert.

Perhaps the most common version of this model is for consultants to contract with senior executives to do extensive interviews in the client organization to find out what is going on, base their diagnosis on these data, and then recommend remedial projects to the client who initially hired them. One currently popular version of this process is to assess the competencies that are needed for success in a given job category; to compare the profile of existing competencies to databases drawn from many organizations; and, based on the observed gaps, to prescribe selection, training, and career-development programs to increase the specific competencies that have been identified as lacking.

As most readers will recognize from their own experience, this model is fraught with difficulties in spite of its popularity. All of us, as clients, have experienced how irrelevant a helper's advice or recommendations can be or how offensive it can be to be told what to do, even when we asked for the advice. All of us, as consultants, have had the experience more often than we would care to admit of having our report and recommendation accepted with a polite nod only to have it shelved or, worse, have it rejected altogether with the implication that we did not really understand the client situation at all. Clients often become defensive and belittle our recommendations by pointing out key facts we missed or by informing us that the recommended course of action has already been tried and has failed. Consultants, when operating in this doctor–patient mode, often feel that the clients are to blame—that the clients don't know what they want, that they don't recognize the truth when it is put before them, or that they resist change and don't really want to be helped. To begin to understand these difficulties and to put the PC model into perspective we must analyze some of the implicit assumptions of the doctor–patient model.

One of the most obvious difficulties with this model is the assumption that the consultant can get accurate diagnostic information on her own. In fact the organizational unit that is defined as sick may be reluctant to reveal the kind of information the consultant needs in order to make an accurate diagnosis. Quite predictably, systematic distortions will occur on questionnaires and in interviews. The direction of these distortions will depend on the climate of the organization. If the climate is one of distrust and insecurity, respondents will most likely hide any damaging information from the consultant because of fear of retaliation, something that we have seen repeatedly in the misadventures of whistle blowers. Or respondents may view the interview, survey, or test as an invasion of their privacy and provide either minimal answers or distortions based on what they consider to be the expected or safe responses. If the climate is one of high trust, respondents are likely to view contact with the consultant as an opportunity to get all their gripes off their chests, leading to an exaggeration of whatever problems may exist. In either case, unless the consultant spends a lot of time personally observing the department, she is not likely to get an accurate picture of what may be going on.

An equally great difficulty with this model is that the client is likely to be unwilling to believe the diagnosis or to accept the prescription offered by the consultant. Most organizations probably have drawers full of reports by consultants that are either not understood or not accepted by the client. What is wrong, of course, is that the doctor has not built up a common diagnostic frame of reference with his patient. They are not dealing with a common reality. If the consultant does all the diagnosing while the client waits passively for a prescription, a communication gulf will predictably arise that will make the diagnosis and prescription seem either irrelevant or unpalatable.

Even in medicine, doctors have increasingly realized that patients do not automatically accept diagnoses nor automatically do what the doctor recommends. We see this most clearly in the cross-cultural context, in which assumptions about illness or what should be done about it may differ from culture to culture. We also see this increasingly in the treatment of breast cancer, with the oncologist involving the patient in the crucial choice as to whether to have a mastectomy, a lumpectomy, a program of chemotherapy, or a program of radiation. Similarly, in plastic surgery or in the decision of whether or not to have back surgery, the patient's goals and self-image become crucial variables in determining the ultimate success of the surgery. If we take a medical version of the doctor model of consultation, we had better examine the psychiatric model in which the analysis of resistence and defenses becomes one of the major therapeutic tools.

A third difficulty with this model is that in human systems, indeed in all systems, the process of diagnosis is itself an intervention of unknown consequence. Giving psychological tests to the executive team, conducting attitude surveys in parts of the organization, interviewing people about their perceptions of the organization influence employees by raising questions in their mind of what might be going on in the organization that warrants the introduction of consultants in the first place. Although the consultant may be acting completely innocently, the employee may conclude that management is getting ready to reorganize and lay off people. The consultant may just be doing her scientific best when she gives the tests or surveys, but the employee may feel that his privacy has been invaded or may begin to form defensive coalitions with other employees that alter the relationships within the organization. It is ironic that the elaborate precautions to make survey responses truly anonymous by having those responses mailed to neutral parties presume a level of distrust within the organization that may be a far more significant reality than whatever data the survey itself may reveal.

A fourth difficulty with the doctor–patient model is that even if the diagnosis and prescription are valid, the patient *may not be able* to make the changes recommended. In the organizational context this may in fact be the most common problem. It is often obvious to the outside consultant what should be done, but the culture of the organization, its structure, or its politics prevents the recommendations from being implemented. In many cases the consultant does not even find out about cultural and political forces until recommendations are rejected or subverted, but by then it may be too late to be really helpful.

In other words, the degree to which the doctor–patient model will work will depend on

1. Whether or not the client has accurately identified which person, group, or department is, in fact, sick or in need of some kind of therapy
2. Whether or not the patient is motivated to reveal accurate information
3. Whether or not the patient accepts and believes the diagnosis that the doctor arrives at and accepts the prescription that the doctor recommends
4. Whether or not the consequences of doing the diagnostic processes are accurately understood and accepted
5. Whether or not the client is able to make the changes that are recommended.

The PC Alternative. The process consultation mode, in contrast, focuses not only on *joint* diagnosis but also on *passing on to the client the consultant's diagnostic and problem-solving skills.* The consultant may perceive early in her work what some of the problems in the organization may be and how they might be solved. But she typically will not share her insights prematurely for two reasons: (1) She may be wrong. If she prematurely makes a diagnosis that is incorrect, she may damage her credibility with the client and undermine the relationship. (2) She recognizes that even if she is right, the client may well be defensive, may not listen, may wish to deny what he hears, or may misunderstand what the consultant is saying and thus subvert remedial efforts.

It is a key assumption underlying PC that *the client must learn to see the problem for herself or himself by sharing in the diagnostic process and be actively involved in generating a remedy.* The reason the client must be involved is that the diagnostic process is itself an intervention and any intervention has ultimately to be the responsibility of the client and be owned by him. If tests or surveys are to be administered or if interviews are to be conducted, the client must understand and take responsibility for the decision to conduct these activities. The client must be able to explain to the possibly suspicious subordinate why this is being done and why the consultant is being brought in, or all the difficulties just described may arise.

The consultant may play a key role in helping to sharpen the diagnosis and may provide suggestions for alternate remedies that may not have occurred to the client, but she encourages the client to make the ultimate decision on what diagnostic and remedial actions to take. Again, the consultant does this on the assumption that if she teaches the client to diagnose and remedy situations himself, problems will be solved more permanently and the client will have learned the skills necessary to solve new problems as they arise.

It should also be noted that the consultant may or may not be an expert at solving the particular problems that may be uncovered. The important point in adopting the PC mode initially is that such content expertise is less relevant than are the skills of involving the client in self-diagnosis and helping him to find a remedy that fits his particular situation and his unique set of needs. The consultant must display expertise at giving help and at establishing a relationship with clients that makes it possible to be helpful and that builds a jointly shared reality in which communication is possible. The organizational consultant operating in this mode does not need to be an expert in marketing, finance, or strategy. If problems are uncovered in such areas, the consultant can help the client to find an expert resource and, more importantly, help the client to think through how best to ensure that he will get the help he needs from those experts.

The doctor–patient model, like the purchase-of-expertise model, is constantly applied by us in our daily life. When my child asks me to solve the math problem, I am strongly tempted to make an instant diagnosis of what is wrong and act on it. When my friend asks me about a movie, I make instant assumptions about his entertainment needs and give advice on what movie to see. When my student asks me to recommend some readings pertaining to her research project, I immediately think I know what kind of information she needs and suggest several books and papers. When my wife asks me what she should wear to the party, I instantly think I know what problem she is trying to solve and dispense reactions and advice accordingly. The temptation to accept the power that the other person grants you when he asks for advice is overwhelming. It takes extraordinary discipline in those situations to reflect for a moment on what is actually going on (deal with reality) and to ask a question that might reveal more or encourage the other to tell you more before you accept the doctor role (access your ignorance).

If the consultant is to be helpful, it is essential to ensure that both the other and the consultant understand what problem they are trying to solve and that they have created a communication channel in which they will understand each other so that they can solve the problem effectively and jointly. It is the ultimate purpose of PC to create such communication channels to permit joint diagnosis and joint problem solving.

The fact that *how* we go about diagnosing has consequences for the client system reveals a fourth overarching principle to be added. We must recognize that *everything the consultant does is an intervention.* There is no such thing as pure diagnosis. The common description in many consulting models of a diagnostic stage followed by recommended prescriptions totally ignores the reality that if the diagnosis involves any contact with the client system, the intervention process has already begun. How we go about diagnosing must, therefore, be considered from the point of view of what consequences our diagnostic interventions will have and whether we are willing to live with those consequences.

Principle 4: Everything You Do Is an Intervention.

Just as every interaction reveals diagnostic information, so does every interaction have consequences both for the client and for me. I therefore have to own everything I do and assess the consequences to be sure that they fit my goals of creating a helping relationship.

MODEL 3
The Process Consultation Model

Let me now summarize the main assumptions of what I am calling the process consultation philosophy, or model. The following assumptions may not always hold. When they do hold, when we perceive or sense that the reality is best described by those assumptions, however, then it is essential to approach the helping situation in the PC mode.

1. Clients, whether managers, friends, colleagues, students, spouses, or children, often do not know what is really wrong and need help in diagnosing what their problems actually are. But only they "own" the problem.
2. Clients often do not know what kinds of help consultants can give to them; they need to be helped to know what kinds of help to seek. Clients are not experts on helping theory and practice.
3. Most clients have a constructive intent to improve things, but they need help in identifying what to improve and how to improve it.
4. Most organizations can be more effective than they are if their managers and employees learn to diagnose and manage their own strengths and weaknesses. No organizational form is perfect; hence every form of organization will have some weaknesses for which compensatory mechanisms must be found.
5. Only clients know what will ultimately work in their organizations. Consultants cannot, without exhaustive and time-consuming study or actual participation in the client organization, learn enough about the culture of an organization to suggest reliable new courses of action. Therefore, unless remedies are worked out jointly with members of the organization who do know what will and will not work in their culture, such remedies are likely either to be wrong or to be resisted because they come from an outsider.
6. Unless clients learn to see problems for themselves and think through their own remedies, they will be less likely to implement the solution and less likely to learn how to fix such problems should they recur. The process consultation mode can provide alternatives, but decision making about such alternatives must remain in the hands of the client because it is the client, not the consultant, who owns the problem.
7. The ultimate function of PC is to pass on the skills of how to diagnose and constructively intervene so that clients are more able to continue on their own to improve the organi-

zation. In a sense both the expert and doctor models are remedial models whereas the PC model is both a remedial and a preventive model. The saying "instead of giving people fish, teach them how to fish" fits this model well.

This last point differentiates the models clearly in that the expert and doctor model can be compared to single-loop, or adaptive, learning, whereas PC engages the client in double-loop, or generative, learning. One of the goals of PC is to enable the client to learn how to learn. The expert and doctor models fix the problem; the goal of PC is to increase the client system's *capacity for learning* so that it can in the future fix its own problems.[3]

The helping process should *always begin in the PC mode* because until we have inquired and removed our ignorance we do not, in fact, know whether the above assumptions hold or whether it would be safe or desirable to shift into the expert or doctor mode. Once we have begun this inquiry, we will find that one useful way to decide whether to remain in the PC role or move to one of the other modes is to determine some of the properties of the type of problem being faced by the person seeking help.[4] If both the problem definition and the nature of the solution are clear, then the expert model is the appropriate one. If the problem definition is clear but the solution is not, then the doctor has to work with the patient to develop the right kind of adaptive response using his or her technical knowledge. If neither the problem nor the solution is clear, the helper has to rely initially on process consultation until it becomes clear what is going on,

---

[3]This terminology for learning derives originally from Bateson's concept of *deutero-learning* and Argyris & Schon's description of single- and double-loop learning. Perhaps the most thorough treatment is Michael's "Learning to Plan and Planning to Learn." The distinction between adaptive and generative learning has been explored by Senge in the context of how to think about organizational learning as *capacity building* (Argyris & Schon, 1996; Bateson, 1972; Michael, 1973, 1997; Senge, 1990).

[4]Heifetz in his book *Leadership without Easy Answers* (1994) defines *adaptive work* as something the leader and the follower have to do together if the problem and the solution are not clear. Comparing process consultation to a form of leadership seems entirely appropriate as situations become more complex. "What can authority do when the authority does not know the answer? In those situations, the authority can induce learning by asking hard questions and by recasting people's expectations to develop their response ability. . . . her actions are nothing if not expert, but they are expert in the management of processes by which the people with the problem achieve the resolution." (pp 84–85, Heifetz, 1994).

what help is needed, and how it is best obtained. The decision whether a technical fix or an adaptive response will be needed will then depend on the degree to which the client or learner will have to change attitudes, values, and habits.

Process Consultation Defined

With these assumptions in mind, we can define PC:

Process Consultation is the creation of a relationship with the client that permits the client to perceive, understand, and act on the process events that occur in the client's internal and external environment in order to improve the situation as defined by the client.

Process consultation focuses first on building a relationship that permits both the consultant and client to deal with reality, that removes the consultant's areas of ignorance, that acknowledges the consultant's behavior as being always an intervention, all in the service of giving clients insight into what is going on around them, within them, and between them and other people. Based on such insight, PC then helps clients to figure out what they should do about the situation. But at the core of this model is the philosophy that clients must be helped to remain proactive, in the sense of retaining both the diagnostic and remedial initiative because only they own the problems identified, only they know the true complexity of their situation, and only they know what will work for them in the culture in which they live. This can be stated as a fifth overarching principle.

PRINCIPLE 5: It Is the Client Who Owns the Problem and the Solution.

My job is to create a relationship in which the client can get help. It is not my job to take the client's problems onto my own shoulders, nor is it my job to offer advice and solutions for situations in which I do not live myself. The reality is that only the client has to live with the consequences of the problem and the solution, so I must not take the monkey off the client's back.

The events to be observed, inquired about, and learned from are the actions that occur in the normal flow of work, in the conduct of meetings, in the formal or informal encounters between members of the organization, and in the more formal organizational structures. Of particular relevance are the client's own actions and their impact on other people in the organization, including their impact on the consultant. As counselors and therapists have found in other domains, one of the most powerful sources of insight is the interaction between the client and the consultant and the feelings this interaction triggers in both of them.[5]

Implicit in this model is the further assumption that all organizational problems are fundamentally problems involving *human* interactions and processes. No matter what technical, financial, or other matters may be involved, there will always be humans involved in the design and implementation of such technical processes, and there will always be humans involved in the initial discovery that technical fixes may be needed. A thorough understanding of human processes and the ability to improve such processes are therefore fundamental to any organizational improvement. As long as organizations are networks of people engaged in achieving some common goals, there will be various kinds of processes occurring between them. Therefore, the more we understand about how to diagnose and improve such processes, the greater will be our chances of finding solutions to the more technical problems and of ensuring that such solutions will be accepted and used by members of the organization.

Summary, Implications and Conclusions

Process consultation is a difficult concept to describe simply and clearly. It is more of a philosophy or a set of underlying assumptions about the helping process that lead the consultant to take a certain kind of attitude toward his or her relationship with the client. Process consultation is best thought of as one mode of operating that the consultant can choose in any given situation. It is most necessary early in the encounter because it is the mode most likely to reveal what the client really wants and what kind of helper behavior will, in fact, be

[5]I was influenced here by the Gestalt movement. My first trainer was the late Richard Wallen, who taught me a great deal about observing what is inside me. Subsequently I was greatly influenced by Ed Nevis, who applied Gestalt principles to organizational consulting (Nevis, 1987). In my graduate training and early career, I was heavily influenced by the work of Kurt Lewin and the work of Gestalt psychologists like Koehler and Koffka.

helpful. If it turns out that the client wants simple information or advice and the consultant is satisfied that she has relevant information and advice, she can safely go into the expert or doctor role. However, when she switches into that mode, she must be aware of the assumptions she is making and recognize the consequences of encouraging the client to become more dependent on her. She must also be careful not to take the problem onto her own back.

What the consultant must be really expert at, then, is sensing from one moment to the next what is going on and choosing a helping mode that is most appropriate to that immediate situation and that will build a helping relationship. *No one of these models will be used all the time. But at any given moment, the consultant can operate from only one of them.* The experienced consultant will find herself switching roles frequently as she perceives the dynamics of the situation to be changing. We should, therefore, avoid concepts like "*the* process consultant" and think more in terms of *"process consultation"* as a dynamic process of helping that all consultants, indeed all humans, find to be appropriate at certain times.

Though PC is increasingly relevant in today's organizational world, it is important to see how the model applies as well to our daily relationships with friends, spouses, children, and others who from time to time may seek our help. Ultimately what is being described here is a philosophy and methodology of the helping process and an attempt to show its relevance to organization development and learning. Central to this philosophy is a set of operating principles. All told there are ten such principles, five of which have been identified and discussed so far:

1. **Always try to be helpful.**
2. **Always stay in touch with the current reality.**
3. **Access your ignorance.**
4. **Everything you do is an intervention.**
5. **It is the client who owns the problem and the solution.**

If the consultant/helper can operate consistently from these principles, the specific roles of when to give information, when to be a doctor, and when to remain in the process consultant role sort themselves out naturally. However, accessing ignorance and dealing with reality are not easy. These are learned skills that require conceptual models, training, and insight based on experience. In the remaining chapters of this book I will focus especially on some simplifying conceptual models to help the consultant/helper to make sense of the realities that he or she faces.

Case Examples

Case examples will be used in several different ways throughout the text. At times illustrations and even longer cases will be inserted into the text where they are needed to provide concrete examples. At other times they will be placed at the end of the chapter to give the more practice-oriented reader an opportunity to dig into cases in greater depth. If the general material is clear, the reader can skip these cases.

Case 1.1: Designing and Participating in the Annual Meeting at International Oil

This case is intended to illustrate a number of the tactical complexities of staying in the process consultant mode and, at the same time, to make clear the contrast between the different modes. The reader will also note that the content of the case illustrates what is really meant by process, *in that the interventions dealt almost exclusively with* how *things were done, not the actual content of what the group was working on.*

The company is a large multinational oil and chemicals concern with headquarters in Europe. I knew a number of the people in the corporate management development group and had met one of their senior executives, Steve Sprague, years ago in an MIT executive program. My involvement resulted from the fact that some senior executives developed the desire to look at their own corporate culture and how it might or might not fit the strategic realities of the next decade. Several members of the corporate management development staff knew that I had just published some papers and a book on organizational culture.

I received a phone call from a man in the corporate staff group who was helping to design the annual three-day off-site meeting for the top forty executives of the company. The proposition was to come in for two days, listen to their internal discussions, and then lecture about culture, weaving in examples from their own discussion to provide feedback on their own culture. I was not to be actively involved at the very beginning and end of the meeting, so this was defined initially as primarily an educational intervention during the second day of the meeting. Although the overt purpose of this educational intervention was to present some formal material to the executives, a covert purpose was to involve them in thinking more realistically about their own culture and its consequences.

I was interested in this company and wanted to learn more about various company cultures, so this seemed like an ideal match. I agreed to the terms as originally stated and was then told that further briefing on the meeting would be provided by Sprague, who had become an executive vice president reporting directly to the chairman of the company. We arranged a meeting in New York during his next trip to the United States. Sprague agreed that my time and expenses were from this point on billable at my usual rates.

At the meeting Sprague talked at length about the strategic situation of the company, saying that it was critical at the annual meeting to take a real look at whether the direction on which the company had embarked still made sense, whether it should be slowed down or speeded up, and how to get the commitment of the top group to whatever was decided. I also learned at this point that Sprague was in charge of the overall design of the three-day meeting and that he not only wanted to brief me but wanted to review the entire design with me.

The initial call had focused on my lecturing on culture, but Sprague was now asking me to be an expert resource to help design the annual meeting and was making himself the primary client. I found myself switching roles from process consultant to design expert because we were discussing the design of a meeting, a topic about which I obviously knew more than he, and we both understood this switch in role and made it explicit.

We reviewed the design of each component of the meeting in terms of Sprague's goals, and the idea emerged that for me to function as a process consultant throughout the meeting might be helpful. Since my schedule permitted attending the whole meeting, it was decided by Sprague, with my agreement, to have me play several roles throughout. I would give a short input on culture and strategy early in the meeting and define my role as one of trying to see how these topics would relate to each other as the meeting unfolded. I would do my session on culture on day 2, and, most importantly, I would run the session on day 3, during which the whole group would draw out what areas of consensus they had reached about future strategic options.

These areas of consensus would deal with the business strategy, but it would be easier for me to test for such consensus than it would be for any of the insiders to do so; it would also free the chairman to play an advocacy role. It therefore made sense to both of us to have me play the consensus-tester role, and I judged that Sprague knew the personality of the chairman well enough that an outsider's assuming such a role would also be acceptable to him. Sprague's insight throughout the discussion reassured me that he had a good grasp of the issues and knew the climate of the organization well. In any case there was no time to meet the chairman, so I had to accept this role on faith.

My participation during the three days worked out as planned. The chairman was comfortable with having me present as an outside resource on process because he felt that this would permit him to focus more on the content, the strategic issues the group was wrestling with. It permitted him a degree of freedom that he ordinarily did not feel because he had played the role of consultant as well as chairman in prior meetings. He explained my role to the other executives and took ownership of the decisions to have me present in my multiple roles.

The active interventions I made focused heavily on task process. *For example, I occasionally attempted to clarify an issue by restating what I thought I had heard, asking clarifying questions, restating goals, testing consensus when conclusions seemed to be reached, and keeping a summary of areas of consensus for purposes of my formal input sessions. When it was time to present my feedback on culture, I gave some formal definitions and descriptions of culture as a set of basic assumptions but then asked the group to provide the content. Several members of the group asked more pointedly how I perceived and evaluated their culture, but I had found from past experience that it was best to remain speculative about this because even if I provided an answer that was technically correct, it might arouse defensiveness or denial. I kept emphasizing that only insiders really could understand the key cultural assumptions and invited members of the group to provide the answers.*

On the final day I formally tested consensus by structuring the areas of discussion that had been covered and inviting the group to state conclusions, which I then wrote down on flip charts to make them explicit to everyone. My playing this up-front role made it possible for the chairman to be much more active in providing his own conclusions without using his formal power to override the conclusions of others. I sharpened many of the issues based on my listening during the three days and challenged the group in areas where the participants seemed to want to avoid being clear. In this role I was partly process consultant and partly management expert in giving occasional editorial comments on the conclusions being reached.

For example, the group talked of decentralizing into business units, but doing so would take power away from the units currently based in different regions. The business unit headquarters were all in the home city, so they were really centralizing as much as decentralizing. I pointed out the implications of this for various other kinds of policies, such as the movement of people across divisional or geographic lines.

The event terminated on a high note and the decision was made to revisit the results several months later. I met with Sprague to review results and learned that both he and the chairman felt that things went as expected. They felt that bringing me in as an outside resource had helped very much, both at the level of process and content.

Lessons. The consultant must be prepared to operate in whatever mode is most appropriate, given the realities of the moment. At the outset in any client relationship, the consultant must start in the process mode to discover what the client's realities are and what the consultant's relevant skills are for dealing with those realities. New roles evolve as the relationship evolves and as the client system changes. Diagnosis and intervention are completely interwoven.

Case 1.2: Suspended Team Building in Ellison Manufacturing

This case is intended to illustrate several elements in process consultation. I won't dwell here on how I got into the following situation, but I want to highlight the issue of joint ownership of the process, of the client's owning the problem, of the fact that everything we do, even the most innocent inquiries, are interventions with unknown consequences, and of the importance of accessing our ignorance and dealing with reality.

I had been working with the plant manager of a local plant for some months in a one-on-one counseling relationship. He wanted to think out a strategy for developing more trust among his managers and between labor and management in the plant. After several once-a-month sessions, he concluded that taking his senior management team (his immediate subordinates) to a two-day off-site meeting to build them into a team was a logical next step to take. He scheduled a working lunch with me and his organization development advisor to design the two-day meeting and to plan what my own participation in that meeting would be.

At the beginning of the lunch, I decided I needed some general information about the setting and the people, so I asked, "Who will actually attend the meeting, as you see it, and what are their roles?" (This question exemplifies what I mean by accessing my ignorance. I could not help with the planning if I did not know who would be attending the meeting and in what roles.) The plant manager started down his list of subordinates, but when he got to the third name he hedged and said, "Joe is my financial person, but I am not sure he will make it; I have some reservations about his ability and have not yet decided whether or not to keep him or to transfer him." I then asked if there were any others in the group about whom he had reservations, and he said that there was one other person who had not yet proved himself and might not end up on the team.

At this point, all three of us at the lunch meeting had the same insight, but the plant manager himself articulated it. He said, "I wonder if I ought to be having this team-building session if I'm not sure about the membership of two of the people." I asked what he thought would happen if we went ahead but then he later fired one or both of them. He concluded that this would undermine the team building and that it was not really fair to the two people about whom he was unsure.

After discussing the pros and cons of having the team-building session at all until he had made up his mind about the marginal people, we decided to postpone the meeting until he had decided, and we all breathed a huge sigh of relief that this issue had surfaced at this time rather than later.

Lessons. The crucial information came out in response to an innocent question and the inquiry process allowed the plant manager himself to reach the conclusion to cancel based on his own thinking through of the issues. He regarded the lunch as a most helpful intervention even though we ended up canceling the team-building effort for the time being.

Case 1.3: The Unnecessary Management Meeting at Global Electric

Dealing with current and emerging realities means that the consultant must be prepared to do less as well as more. This case illustrates how useless it is to think in terms of selling services, given what may be going on in the client system.

I was asked to attend a large Swiss multinational organization's annual management conference to help the president develop a senior management committee. The divisions were operating in too isolated a fashion and, if we could use my educational input as an excuse to bring a small group together regularly, that group could gradually begin to tackle business problems.

The contact client was the director of management development and training, who briefed me during several meetings on the company's situation. They badly needed to find a vehicle to start the autonomous division managers' meeting but felt that such meetings would not work without an outsider to serve as both the excuse for the meeting—that is, the planned seminar—and as the facilitator. So an educational intervention made sense, even though the real goal was to build a more collaborative management team.

After our planning had proceeded and a date had been set some months hence, we scheduled a meeting with the president at the headquarters in Europe to discuss the details of the project. The meeting with the president revealed a somewhat different issue. He was worried that two of his key division managers were fighting all the time and undercutting each other. One of these was too dominant and the other too subservient. What he hoped to do was to bring them together in a group situation in which some feedback to both of them would "correct" their weaknesses. I was a bit skeptical about the potential of the group to do this, but he was prepared to go slowly. We decided that a seminar discussing career anchors and different management styles, a seminar similar to one that had worked well in another Swiss-German company, would serve their needs (Schein, 1985).

Two months before the seminar, I received a call from the contact client saying that they were terribly sorry but the seminar had been canceled and he would explain later. I was to bill them for any time lost; they did not know whether or not they would do the seminar later. I learned what had actually happened when I visited another client who knew the Swiss company's people well, the adventures of the Swiss company's having become a topic of discussion among others in the industry.

I heard that the president had become so upset at the "weaker" manager that he had replaced him, and with that replacement most of the difficulties that had motivated the seminar seemed to have disappeared. I also learned from my contact client that my long interview with the president had partially precipitated this decision. Our meeting had made him rethink carefully what he was doing and why. He had noted my skepticism about what the group could do and so chose a different remedial course.

Lessons. Though the consultation process was brief and seemingly terminated before it began, it appears that the interventions made with the president during the planning of the educational intervention produced a level of insight that led the president to fix the problem in a way that he thought more appropriate. The consultant cannot know from one moment to the next which interventions will be crucial in producing the help that the client needs, but in this case my expertise on groups and my raising the question about whether or not the group could fix an interpersonal problem between key players apparently was decisive.

Conclusion: Complexities in Defining the Consultant Role

What these examples have illustrated is the difficulty of defining the emerging realities in a dynamic client situation, and the need to switch roles as new data emerge. Not only does the client shift in unpredictable ways, but with each intervention, new data are revealed that alter what it means to be helpful. Frequently the consultant has to switch to the expert mode, but then he must be able to switch back smoothly to the process consultant mode.

Many descriptions of the consultation process emphasize the need for a clearly articulated contract from the outset. The reality for me has been that the nature of the contract and who the client is with whom I should be doing the contracting shift constantly, so that contracting is virtually a perpetual process rather than something one does up front prior to beginning the consultation.

The consultant should also be clear, many models say, about precisely who the client is. I am always very clear about who the contact client is when I am first called or visited, but once I have begun to work with the contact client and we have defined a next step, the client base starts to expand in unpredictable ways.

Exercise 1.1: Reflecting on How You Help

The purpose of this exercise is to make you aware of the possibility of playing different roles when you are cast in the helper role. You can do steps 1, 2, and 6 by yourself (20 minutes), or, if you are in a workshop setting, you can work with a partner to do all 6 steps (1 hour).

1. Think back over the last several days and identify two or three instances of someone's asking for your help or advice.
2. Reconstruct the conversation in your own mind and identify what role you took in response to the request for help. What did the other person want? How did you respond? Could you have responded differently from the way you did respond? Does your response fall clearly into one of the models of consultation described—expert, doctor, process consultant?
3. Pair up with another person if you are in a workshop setting and recount your cases to get a reaction from the other on what they observe in your behavior.
4. Analyze their response to your story from the point of view of what role they took in response to your story and how you reacted to it.
5. Reverse roles and respond to your partner's story, and then analyze how you responded and what reactions that elicited in your partner.
6. Reflect on the roles that you seem to take naturally and spontaneously when someone seeks your help and ask yourself whether those roles are appropriate as you look back on the situation. Are there other roles that you should learn to take?

2

The Psychodynamics of the Helping Relationship

Consultation is defined in the dictionary as *seeking advice or professional counsel,* a definition that fits very well with the purchase of expertise or the doctor–patient model described in Chapter 1. Process consultation (PC) as a philosophy recognizes that the more fundamental purpose of seeking advice or counsel is to get *help* with a perceived problem. We seek counsel in order to solve problems that cannot be solved alone. And we hope that the counsel or advice will be helpful. But, as we all know from our own experience, advice and counsel are often *not* helpful, resulting in resistance or defensiveness on the part of the person seeking help. In order to understand this resistance, we must delve into the psychodynamics of the helping relationship and examine what conditions must be met for help to be successfully provided.

One must also distinguish the helping relationship from various other kinds of relationships that can develop between people—such as those between givers and receivers, teachers and students, friends, spouses, and superiors and subordinates. In each of these cases, help may be one of a number of issues in the relationship, but many interactions between people also involve the exchange of things other than help.

A way of sorting out this domain is to examine the explicit and implicit psychological contract between helpers and those being helped, call them "clients." What does each party expect to give and to receive, and what psychological conditions must be met for the exchange to occur successfully? For example, mutual trust, mutual acceptance, and mutual respect may all be necessary for a helping relationship to work. If that is the case, how does one achieve these conditions? The first step is to understand clearly the psychological forces that operate when one person asks another for "help."

The Initial Status Imbalance in Helping Relationships

Many cultures emphasize self-reliance and put a value on solving one's own problems. For a person to seek help and make herself temporarily dependent on another person is a de facto confession of weakness or failure, particularly in Western, competitive, individualistic societies. At the beginning of a helping relationship, the two parties are in a tilted or imbalanced relationship with the helper being "one-up" and the person seeking help being "one-down." Because of this one-downness, one can anticipate that the client will consciously or unconsciously have one or more of several possible reactions, each designed to equilibrate or "level" the relationship.[1]

Possible Reactions and Feelings in the Client

1. *Resentment and defensiveness (Counter-dependency)* manifested in the client looking for opportunities to make the consultant look bad by belittling her advice, challenging her facts, and pulling her down so that the client regains a sense of parity.

   "Your idea won't work because of ______."

   "I've already thought of that and it won't work."

   "You don't really understand. The situation is *much* more complex."

2. *Relief* at having finally shared the problem and the frustration with someone else who may be able to help.

   "I'm really glad to be able to share this problem."

   "It feels great to know that someone else might be able to help."

   "I'm so glad that you really understand what I'm going through."

---

[1]This topic has been of great interest to the more psychoanalytically oriented consultants and has been written about extensively. The work of Hirschhorn (1988, 1991) is most helpful in this area. An excellent summary from the psychoanalytic point of view can be found in Jean Neumann's contribution to the *Proceedings of the International Consulting Conference* (1994).

3. *Dependency and subordination* manifested in looking primarily for reassurance, advice, and support.

   "What should I do now?"

   "What I'm planning is ______. Don't you agree that is the right course to pursue?"

   "I'm so glad that someone else can now give me advice on what to do."

4. *Transference* of perceptions and feelings onto the present consultant, based on past experiences with helpers. Transference may appear as any of the above reactions but is based on deeper and unconscious projections that initially neither the consultant nor the client is aware of. For instance, the consultant may be perceived as a friendly or unfriendly parent or as similar to a loved or hated teacher from the past.

The sense of being one-down applies not only to one's self-perception but can be even more strongly felt in relation to others in the organization. In many companies, seeking the help of a consultant is tantamount to admitting that you cannot do your own job. During my quarterly visits to a European company where I worked as a consultant for five years, I would occasionally be taken to lunch in the executive dining room. There I encountered some of the individual executives with whom I had worked on various projects and discovered that they avoided my eyes and walked past me as if they did not know me. My host explained that clearly they did not want their colleagues to see that they had spent time with me because that would be a loss of status. The counterpart of this kind of feeling is the embarrassed looks that are sometimes exchanged between the patient leaving the psychiatrist's office and the others in the waiting room, leading some psychiatrists to have side doors that permit privacy of entry and exit.

Reactions and Feelings in the Helper

The client's feelings of resentment, relief, comfort, and dependency are very likely to *seduce the consultant into accepting the higher status and power position that the client offers.* The consultant's one-upness may then lead to several kinds of feelings and actions.

1. *Using the power and authority* that one has been granted to dispense *premature* wisdom and, thereby, putting the client even further down.

"Simple, just do the following things ________"

"You don't really have a problem; let me tell you what I did in a situation just like that; it was *really* a tough one."

"I have just the answer for you. I have been in that situation many times."

2. *Accepting and overreacting to the dependence* usually manifested by giving support and reassurance even where it may be inappropriate.

   "You poor guy; I really feel sorry for you; it's really a tough one."

   "You are really in a bind. Do whatever makes sense to you."

   "I'm sure what you are planning will work out; if it doesn't it won't be your fault."

3. *Meeting defensiveness with more pressure.*

   "I don't think you understood my suggestion; let me explain what I really have in mind."

   "I understand your reluctance to try it, but let me explain why my suggestion will really work."

   "You aren't hearing me. This will work. Trust me. Try it out."

4. *Resisting entering the relationship* because giving up the power position of being one-up requires the consultant to be influenced and make some changes in her perceptions of the situation.

   "Well, I don't really know how to help, but you might try this _______"

   "You might try the following _______, but if it doesn't work we'll have to reschedule because I'm very short of time.

   "Have you talked this over with _________? He might be able to help."

5. *Counter-transference* or the projection by the helper onto the client of some feelings and perceptions that re-create past consultant/client relationships. The client may resemble a person in a past relationship, leading the helper to unconsciously react to the present client as he did to the past client.

The helper enters the relationship with a lot of psychological predispositions and cultural stereotypes. Just being asked for help is a tremendously empowering situation, implying that the client endows the helper with the capacity to help, with expert knowledge, with a sense of responsibility not to take advantage of the situation, and with the ability to deliver something of value if the help is being paid for. At the same time, the helper may feel frustration because he often perceives himself as capable of giving so much more than the client seems to want, and disappointment when the self-perceived help is not accepted as helpful. Consultants often feel frustrated that they are available as a helper but no one comes to them, a common situation of inside consultants in organizations. When someone finally asks for help, there is so much relief that the consultant risks overworking the situation and providing much more "help" than may be needed or wanted.

As the relationship evolves, the helper often perceives what may appear to be solutions far earlier than the client can see them or, worse, comes to feel that the client is really stupid, messing up, not seeing the obvious or not getting the message. This results in impatience, anger, and disdain. The most puzzling and frustrating aspect of giving help is often that what you might regard as a brilliant insight or intervention is hardly noticed while some of the most routine questions or observations you make turn out to be highly touted by the client as crucial interventions. It often turns out that fortuitous events made far more difference than carefully calculated interventions, as illustrated by the following brief vignette:

Some years ago I was working with the top team of a young company at their weekly Friday afternoon staff meeting. My job was to help them make the meetings more effective. What I observed was a hardworking group that could never get more than halfway through its 10-plus item agenda in the two hours allotted to the meeting. I tried various interventions aimed at cutting down fruitless arguments or diversions to topics not on the agenda, but to no avail. I realized I had to deal with the reality of how this group worked, but I also realized that I had not really "accessed my ignorance" in the sense that I did not really know why they worked in the way they did. I had been working from a stereotype of how the meeting should go.

At one point, after witnessing many frustrating meetings, I asked in true ignorance where the agenda came from. I was informed that it was put together by the President's secretary, but we all suddenly realized that none of us knew how she constructed it. She was asked to come into the room and revealed that she took items in the order in which they were called in and typed them up neatly for the group's meeting. Without my saying another word, the group immediately decided to change the system by having her produce a tentative list of items which the group would then prioritize so that only the less important items would be tabled or dropped. The quality of the meetings and the sense of progress both dramatically increased. What had helped the group most was my genuinely innocent question about the origin of the agenda.

One of the most difficult aspects of being a helper is finding an audience for a discussion of the helping process itself in which your brilliant interventions, key insights, and disastrous errors can be discussed and analyzed. Often the client is completely unaware of how seamlessly the consultant's interventions have led the client to key insights, and it would hardly be constructive for the consultant to point this out to the client. To get some gratification and acknowledgment, as well as to further help themselves, helpers often build associations with other helpers so that they can analyze their own behavior in a safe, peer environment. There they can share stories about things that worked well and get help with things that are not working well. For this same reason, in working with groups and organizations, it is important to work as part of a helping team that often consists of insiders and outsiders who can share the planning of interventions and then review how they came out.

Given all of these forces, it is small wonder that most consultants instantly accept some form of the expert or doctor role because they think that is what the client really wants. We say to ourselves, "If I don't dispense a brilliant diagnosis and offer sound advice, I am not doing my job, I am not meeting the client's expectations." And "If I am being paid, don't I have to deliver a professional service in the form of information, diagnosis, and recommendations, preferably in written form as proof of my service?"

What then is the problem? What is wrong with this picture? Why not just go ahead and be a doctor or expert? From the PC point of view, what is wrong is that the client's conscious or unconscious sense of vulnerability often makes him unwilling to reveal the deeper layers or full complexity of what is really bothering him until he feels that the helper will be accepting, supportive, and, most important of all, willing to listen. The initial problem presentation is often a test to see how the helper will react, and the real problem will surface only later as mutual trust is established. In the initial meetings the client may be hiding things from himself, and many of these do not surface until the relationship is based on mutual trust.

If the consultant is to be truly helpful, therefore, she must first *create a relationship that reestablishes the client's sense of self-esteem, that equilibrates the status between the client and helper, and that reduces the sense of dependency or counterdependency that the client may initially feel.* If such an equal relationship is not built, the risk remains that the client will not reveal, not hear, reject, become defensive, and in other ways undermine the help offered. Both the client and the helper are then the losers.

Implicit Role and Status Negotiating

To equilibrate the relationship requires insight into the social dynamics of status and role. A subtle but powerful force in any helping relationship is the initial status and role that each party accords to the other, based on cultural norms and personal agendas. When we perceive a problem and feel the need of help, we go through a conscious or unconscious process of sorting out whether to go to a friend, spouse, boss, counselor, psychiatrist, social worker, doctor, lawyer, or some other form of consultant. If we decide to go to a professional, we have to sort out whether we want to go to a stranger or a known person, based on prior experience. If it is the former, how do we select someone whom we can trust to give us good help? In this selection process, we build up a stereotype of what the helper will provide and this stereotype may get in the way of what the helper can actually give.

It is for this reason that so much of the consulting literature emphasizes "contracting" at the beginning of the relationship. However, in the early stages of the relationship neither the helper nor the client really has enough information to develop a firm contract. So a better concept than "contracting" might be "exploring mutual expectations." The helper certainly needs to know what implicit expectations the client has, but unfortunately some of those expectations may be unconscious and not surface until they are violated. For example, clients often implicitly expect that the story they tell will be unequivocally accepted and approved. When the consultant raises questions about something the client did or is thinking about doing, this may initially cause shock and dismay. Only then do both parties realize that approval was expected and wanted.

On the part of the consultant, the implicit expectation may be that the suggestions she makes will be given a fair hearing and she may be shocked and dismayed when the client turns on her and implies that the suggestion was trivial or clearly unworkable. In building the helping relationship, it is important that such feelings be treated as a source of learning, not as a source of disappointment in each other. These feelings have to be treated as a normal process of relationship building and as a further source of insight and learning.

Complicating these social forces are the psychodynamics of transference and countertransference that require the consultant to become highly aware of the client's projections onto the consultant and the consultant's tendency to project onto and misperceive the client's reality. For the consultant, learning to see and deal with reality is initially a process of learning to see and deal with her own internal distortions. It is crucial for consultants to learn how to access their ignorance and overcome their own stereotypes.

The relationship begins to be productive when both parties begin to feel comfortable with each other's relative status and roles. Cultural norms play an important role here in that we regard certain kinds of dependency as more legitimate than others. If you go to a highly reputed counselor, psychiatrist, coach, or consultant you are more prepared to make yourself dependent on that person than if you were sharing a problem with a friend or acquaintance. If you go to your boss with a work problem, you are more prepared to make yourself dependent than if you go to a peer or subordinate with the same problem.

In every society there are norms about what kind of dependency is legitimate and what kind is a loss of face. In Western, competitive, individualistic society almost any kind of dependency is viewed as a loss of face, whereas in many Asian cultures one is expected to be dependent upon more senior or higher-ranking individuals. The more egalitarian the society, the more difficult it is to sort out how one should feel about making oneself dependent on another, hence the sorting out of such feelings in Western society is probably more difficult than in some other cultures.

Relationship Building Through Levels of Mutual Acceptance

When the person seeking help and the helper first come together, all of the various factors mentioned previously are at work. How then does the conversation evolve to create a relationship in which the two parties will hear each other, understand each other, and give each other what each needs? The best model for describing this process is to think of it as *a series of mutual tests to see at what level each party can accept the other*. As the client unfolds her story she will be paying close attention to the degree to which the helper is actively listening, understanding, and supporting what she is saying. If the support is consistent and she feels that no matter what she says it will at least be understood, if not always approved, she will experiment with going to a more private level until she feels she might be getting into a level of revelation that would not be acceptable either to the helper or possibly to herself. The consultant must realize that cultural norms will always put some limit on how "open" a conversation can become. There is no such thing as "letting it all hang out." There will always be layers of consciousness that the client will not want to share with even a trusted consultant, and ultimately there are layers of consciousness that we cannot accept in ourselves, and therefore keep them repressed.

The helper, on the other hand, is calibrating how responsive the client is to her prompts, to her questions, to her suggestions, and to her whole demeanor as a helper. She is testing how dependent the client seems to want to be and how willing she (the helper) is to accept that level of dependency. As the client becomes more accepting of the helper, she (the helper) will reveal more of her private thoughts and escalate the conversation to a deeper level. But throughout this process both parties are always testing and alert to any disconfirming feedback. When such disconfirmation occurs, both parties have to recalibrate and rethink the psychological contract—did either party overstep some implicit boundary and create offense? Can the implicit contract be renegotiated or has the relationship reached a level beyond which it cannot move? Or, worse, has the relationship been damaged to the point where feelings of being one-up or one-down are so strong that either the client or the consultant feels they must sever it? As we have all experienced, to build trust takes much more time and energy than to lose it. The essence of building mutual acceptance is therefore to go slowly enough to insure that the movement is toward higher mutual acceptance and more equal status in the relationship. The critical interventions are to let the client tell his story and actively inquire to access and remove the helper's areas of ignorance.

Notice that this process can be viewed as one of *mutual helping*. The helper can create trust by really accepting at every level what the client reveals and possibly changing his own conceptions of what may be going on. In a sense, the helper is dependent on the client for accurate information and feelings, and the helper must be willing to be helped in order for the client to build up the trust necessary to reveal deeper layers. The relationship gradually becomes equilibrated as both parties give and receive help.

Practical Implications

To establish a climate that creates an effective helping relationship, the helper must first remember the previous five overarching principles "Always try to be helpful," "Stay in touch with the current reality," "Access your ignorance," "Treat everything as an intervention" and "Remember that it is the client who owns the problem." We can now add a sixth principle to be observed at all times.

PRINCIPLE 6: Go with the Flow.

All client systems develop cultures and attempt to maintain their stability through maintenance of those cultures. All individual clients develop their own personalities and styles. Inasmuch as I do not know initially what those cultural and personal realities are, I must locate the client's own areas of motivation and readiness to change, and initially build on those.

The helper must try to sense where the client and the relationship are headed and try not to impose too many stereotypes or needs on the situation. If I am really trying to understand the reality of the situation, and am in touch with what I really do not know, and realize that every question or action on my part is an intervention, and know that I am not obligated to take the problem onto myself, it will feel very natural to adopt the idea of going with the flow, letting the client's feelings and my own reactions guide me to next steps rather than falling back on arbitrary rules of how a consultation should evolve.

It helps to be aware of the pitfalls mentioned previously and to keep asking the question—are we working together as a team, is our status equilibrated, are we each giving and getting what is expected? Process-oriented questions such as "Is this conversation being helpful?" "Am I getting a sense of the problem?" "Are we talking about the right set of issues?" can be very helpful to keep you on target.

If we take seriously the point that the client's situation is likely to be complex and that the consultant is quite ignorant of that complexity early in the relationship, it will keep the consultant from making premature evaluations and judgments. It is not just a matter of not blurting them out; rather it is an exercise of realizing how little is known and how inappropriate it is to second-guess the situation or evaluate it. Fairly nondirective interviewing that keeps the client in the driver's seat telling her story is most likely to protect one from such premature judgments and, in the process, make the client feel more valued. Such "active inquiry" is explored in the next chapter.

Summary and Conclusions

I have tried to outline the major psychodynamic issues of the helping relationship by describing and analyzing the initial psychological situation in the person seeking help, in the potential helper, and in the initial interaction between them. The strategic goal is to achieve a psychological state in which there is a workable psychological contract, a situation in which each party gives and receives more or less what each expects, and in which the helper and client begin to feel like a team working together first in diagnosing the client's problem and then jointly exploring the next steps. In order to achieve such a workable psychological contract, both parties must gain some insight into their initial stereotypes of the situation and must engage in a conversation that permits the elements of that stereotype to surface. At the same time, they must provide each other a lot of mutual acceptance and support.

The dilemma of creating a workable helping relationship is that both parties must learn about each other while at the same time creating a safe environment for the client to tell his or her story, because initially the client is more vulnerable and dependent than the helper. Helpers must resist the initial impulse to move into the power vacuum that clients create by admitting a problem, and focus instead on equilibrating the status relationship between themselves and their clients. Helpers must realize that they need the help of the client if they are to get a clear sense of the client's reality and that the helping relationship works best when both parties feel they are helping each other, even as they focus on the client's issues.

The overarching principles to keep in mind at all times are:

1. **Always try to be helpful.**
2. **Always stay in touch with the current reality.**
3. **Access your ignorance.**
4. **Everything you do is an intervention.**
5. **It is the client who owns the problem and the solution.**
6. **Go with the flow.**

The cases presented in the next chapter will illustrate many of the points raised here.

Exercise 2.1 Giving and Receiving Help

The purpose of this exercise is to give you practice in (1) adopting explicitly a "helping" role, (2) observing what the psychological dynamics are between the helper and the client, and (3) focusing on the skill of accessing your ignorance.

1. Ask a friend to share some problem or issue with you.
2. As the friend begins to reveal the problem, make a conscious effort to catalogue in your mind or write down on a pad all the things you do not know in relation to that problem.
3. Try to formulate a set of questions that will reduce your ignorance and then ask them.
4. Make it a point *not* to react to what the friend tells you, with advice, judgments, or emotional reactions, even if he or she asks.
5. After about twenty minutes, discuss together the feelings you were having during the first twenty minutes. Review whether you or the friend were having any of the feelings mentioned in this chapter.
6. Review the areas of "ignorance" to determine how successful you were in overcoming your stereotypes or preconceptions.

3

Active Inquiry and Listening as Status-Equilibrating Processes

It goes without saying that one of the most important things for the consultant to do initially is to listen carefully to the client. Listening is, however, a rather complex activity that can be pursued very actively or very passively. If we are to go with the flow and access our ignorance, it would appear at first glance that we should be fairly passive and attentive to let the client develop the story in his or her own way. But in many situations, the client just asks a question or two and then falls silent with an expectant look. It is at this moment that the consultant must be careful not to fall into the trap of taking on all the power that is offered.

For example, after a lengthy discourse on the strategic issues the organization is facing, the client may ask: "So, how should I organize my executive team?" The consultant, eager to display his areas of expertise, may well be tempted to answer: "Why don't you do some team building with the group. I could develop a team-building seminar for you." Not only will the client possibly not understand what has been offered, but, if her dependency needs win out, she may agree and launch into something that may have nothing to do with her problem. Or, if the feelings of one-downness win out, the client may silently conclude that this consultant is just trying to sell his favorite off-the-shelf product and reject the suggestion even though it might be the answer to her problem. No help has been provided in either case.

If one starts with the philosophy of PC, one would, first of all, be sensitive to the psychological dynamics that are operating when the client first reveals a problem or asks a question and would then engage in a multi-purpose inquiry process whose main purpose would be to rebuild the client's self-esteem and raise her status. Giving the client a sense that she can better understand her own problem (and maybe even figure out what to do next) is the essence of this building and status-raising process. The assumption is that unless the client begins to feel secure in the relationship she will not reveal the pertinent elements of her story anyway, and the helper will be operating with incorrect information. The trick is to be actively in charge of this process while maintaining a supportive, listening posture. The process of creating this situation can be thought of as *active inquiry* which includes but supersedes basic listening.

The active inquiry process has several purposes:

1. To build up the client's status and confidence.
2. To gather as much information as possible about the situation.
3. To involve the client in the process of diagnosis and action planning.
4. To create a situation for the client in which it is safe to reveal anxiety-provoking information and feelings.

Strategically the goal is status equilibration and the building of a team with the client so that (1) diagnostic insights make sense because client and helper are speaking the same language and (2) remedial measures are realistic because the client is processing their validity in terms of his own culture. *Tactically* the implementation of active inquiry involves recognition that the inquiry must be managed in such a way that the client's story is fully revealed and that the client begins to think diagnostically himself. If the client's story does not come out in his own words and using his own concepts, the consultant cannot get a realistic sense of what may be going on. It is all too easy to project into what the client is reporting from one's own prior experience. The helper's initial behavior, therefore, must stimulate the client to tell the story as completely as possible and to listen in as neutral and nonjudgmental a way as possible.

Active but nonjudgmental listening also serves to legitimize the potentially anxiety-provoking revelations of the client. The relationship between helper and client must become what Bill Isaacs[1] calls a safe "container" in which it is possible to handle issues that may be "too hot to handle under ordinary circumstances."

Active inquiry is summarized in Table 3.1.

This process can be stimulated with several kinds of inquiry questions, but they must be carefully framed so as not to interfere

---

[1]The concept of a "container" was developed by Isaacs in relation to creating the conditions for *Dialogue* (Isaacs, 1993). The helping relationship can be thought of as one kind of two-person dialogue. How this plays out and the dynamics of dialogue are spelled out in Chapter 10.

Table 3.1
TYPES OF ACTIVE INQUIRY QUESTIONS

I. *Pure Inquiry*

The client controls both the process and content of the conversation. The role of the consultant is to prompt the story and listen carefully and neutrally.

What is the situation? Can you tell me what is going on? What is happening? Describe the situation. Tell me more. Go on.

II. *Exploratory Diagnostic Inquiry*

The consultant begins to manage the *process* of how the content is analyzed and elaborated but does not insert content ideas, suggestions, advice, or options.

1. *Exploring Emotional Responses*
   How did you feel about that? What was your reaction? How did others feel, react?
2. *Exploring Reasons for Actions and Events*
   Why did you do that? Why do you think that happened? Why did the other do that?
3. *Exploring Actions: Past, Present, and Future*
   What did you do about that? What are you going to do? What did the other do? What will the other do? What options do you have? What should you do?

III. *Confrontive Inquiry*

The consultant shares his or her *own ideas and reactions* about the process and content of the story. By sharing own ideas, the consultant "forces" the client to think about the situation from a new perspective, hence these questions are by definition confrontive.

1. *Process Ideas*
   Could you have done the following . . . ? Have you thought about doing . . . ? Why have you not done . . . ? Have you considered these other options? You could do . . .
2. *Content Ideas*
   Have you considered the possibility that you overreacted? Did that not make you feel angry (anxious, elated, etc.)? Maybe what was going on was really something different from what you thought . . .

---

with the story. "The story" is the client's own perception of what is going on and should be revealed in as unbiased a fashion as possible.

Types of Active Inquiry

Pure Inquiry. Pure inquiry starts with *silence*. The helper should convey through body language and eye contact a readiness to listen, but she need not *say* anything. The client may be prepared simply to start into her story. If silence does not elicit the story, the consultant can choose any of the following prompts as may seem appropriate.

"Tell me what is going on."
"How can I help?"
"So . . . ." (accompanied by an expectant look)
"What brings you here?"
"Can you give me some examples of that?"
"Can you give me some of the details of what went on?"
"When did this last happen?"

The important point is to not prompt with questions that presuppose a problem, because that is precisely what the client may wish to deny. Initially the focus should be merely on *what* is going on so that the client can structure the story in any way that she wants. As we will see, *why* questions stimulate diagnostic thinking, and that may get ahead of the story of what brought the client to the helping situation in the first place. For example, to deal with her feelings of one-downness the client may actually start with an interrogation of the consultant to check out his credentials and say nothing about why she is there. Questions such as "What is the problem?" presuppose a problem, and the client may not be ready to reveal it before getting comfortable in the relationship.

In response to whatever the client begins to report, active inquiry means the usual attentive head-nodding, the occasional grunt or other acknowledgment that the consultant is following the story, and, if needed, further prompts such as "go on," "tell me a bit more about that," and "what happened next?" The goal is not to structure how the client tells his story, but to stimulate its full disclosure in order to help the consultant remove his ignorance and enhance his understanding. Asking for examples is an especially important option because the story often comes out at such an abstract level that it is all too easy to project one's own hypotheses about what is going on and miss what the client is really trying to say.

In listening, it may be helpful, as Robert Fritz advocates[2], to visualize the scene, the characters, the setting, and the action, and to build a mental picture of what is going on. Such active visualization keeps the consultant from drifting off into his own reverie or distracting thoughts and helps the consultant to remember many of the details of what the client is reporting. According to Fritz, active visualization helps the listener to begin to see the realities of the structures in which the client is living.

Inevitably the client's story will slow down or end, and further prompts will not restart the process. In fact, the client may terminate abruptly and ask point blank "What do you think?" or "What should I do about that?" At that moment the consultant must again avoid the trap of becoming the instant expert by answering the question. If the consultant feels that the client is not ready to hear advice or suggestions, she has several process options that keep the client on the hook and working on her own problem. One option is to steer the conversation into diagnostic inquiry.

Exploratory Diagnostic Inquiry. In this form of inquiry the consultant begins to influence the client's mental process by deliberately focusing on issues other than the ones the client chose to report in telling his story. Note that these questions do not influence the *content* of the story, but rather the focus of attention within the story. Three basically different versions of this redirection are available.

1. **Feelings and Reactions**—to focus the client on her feelings and reactions in response to the events she has described.

   "How did (do) you *feel* about that?"
   "Did (does) that arouse any *reactions* in you?"
   "What was (is) your emotional *reaction* to that?"

2. **Hypotheses about Causes**—to focus the client on her own hypotheses about why things might have happened the way they did.

   "*Why* do you suppose that happened?"
   "*Why* did you (she, he, they) react that way?" (after the client has revealed a reaction)
   "*Why* did you (he, she, they) do that?" (after the client has revealed some action)

---

[2]Fritz, 1991.

3. **Actions Taken or Contemplated**—to focus the client on what she or others in the story did, are thinking about doing, or are planning to do in the future. If the client has already reported actions, the consultant can build on that, but often the "story" will not reveal past, present, or future actions either by the client or others in the story.

   "What did you (he, she, they) *do* about that?"

   "What are you going to *do* next?"

   "What did she (he, they) *do* then?"

These categories obviously overlap in any given story and can be explored one at a time or all at once whenever appropriate. However, the consultant must be aware that each question takes the client away from her own thought process into the consultant's thought process and, therefore, constitutes a much stronger intervention than pure exploratory inquiry. Any form of the "How did you *feel* about that?" "*Why* do you think that happened?" or "What will you *do* about that?" question will *change the direction of the client's mental process* because it asks the client to examine some event from a new perspective and with a new lens.

Confrontive Inquiry. The essence of confrontive inquiry is that the consultant inserts his *own ideas* about the process or content of the story into the conversation. Instead of merely forcing the client to elaborate, the consultant now makes suggestions or offers options that may not have occurred to the client.

"Did you confront him (her, them) about that?"

"Could you do ————?"

"Did it occur to you that you, (he, she, they) did that because they were anxious? (in the situation where the client has not revealed any awareness of that emotional possibility)

In all of these cases, what makes the intervention confrontive is that the consultant now is seducing or pushing the client into the consultant's own conceptual territory. Whereas the previous inquiry questions only steered the client through *her own* conceptual and emotional territory, the confrontive intervention introduces new ideas, concepts, hypotheses, and options that the client is now forced to deal with. The helper is now messing with the client's content, not just the process.

The magnitude of this step cannot be overemphasized even if the intervention is a low-key question like "Had you considered your own role in these events?" or "Did that make you angry?" because it either forces or allows the client to now abandon her story and work within the framework provided by the consultant. And, in this process, the great danger is that further information about the reality of the client's situation will be lost because she is now busy dealing with the new concepts instead of revealing what is in her own memory banks. The issue with confrontive inquiry, then, is *when* and *how* to do it.

Constructive Opportunism

In deciding *when* to switch from pure inquiry into the diagnostic or confrontive mode, timing is crucial. Sometimes such a shift will be appropriate within a few minutes of the beginning, and sometimes one has the sense that one should stay in pure inquiry throughout the interaction. Often it is appropriate to jump back and forth among the three modes based on what one is hearing and on the strength of one's own reactions and ideas. There are no simple criteria for deciding when the timing is right for a shift in focus. Ideally the focus should be put on events in the story that offer some potential leverage either for better understanding of the client's issue or problem, or on the kinds of remedial action that might be possible if the problem is obvious. The danger is that one forgets the previous principles—the need to be helpful, to deal with reality, to access one's ignorance, to realize that every question is de facto an intervention, to let the client own the problem, and to go with the flow. The temptation is tremendous to leap in with insights and suggestions, and to project one's own version of reality onto the client.

At the same time, one cannot become just a passive inquiry machine because strong feelings and ideas will arise as one listens. And one's own feelings and ideas may be highly relevant to helping the client understand his or her reality. Going with the flow must, therefore, be balanced by another principle of "constructive opportunism." My major criterion for when to seize an opportunity to shift focus is when the client has said something that has obvious significance to the client's story and that is vivid enough to be remembered by the client. In other words, intervention must be obviously linked to something the client said, not merely to my own thoughts or feelings.

When the timing feels right, the consultant must take some risks and seize an opportunity to provide a new insight, alternative, or way of looking at things. As the case below illustrates, in seizing such opportunities the consultant will sometimes make an error, either in terms of timing or the level of the intervention, leading to rejection by the client and a period of tension in the relationship. At such times the consultant must recognize that the client's reaction reveals not only that the consultant may have erred, but also new data on how the client reacts to certain kinds of input. In other words, everything that happens is data to be learned from.

We make conversational errors all the time in what we say, how we say it, or in the timing of when we say it. Instead of being discouraged by such errors, we need to recognize that they provide opportunities for learning and should therefore be welcomed.[3] We may learn a lesson such as "be more careful in how you state things" or "don't make assumptions, access your ignorance," but we must always go beyond the lesson and ask what the new data reveal about the situation. Thus the learning occurs in two domains; the reaction to the error gives us data about *ourselves* and what we might have done differently, and data about the *client* how he thinks about things and what he is ready for. All of this can be summarized in three further principles.

PRINCIPLE 7: Timing Is Crucial

Any given intervention might work at one time and fail at another time. Therefore I must remain constantly diagnostic and look for those moments when the client's attention seems to be available.

PRINCIPLE 8: Be Constructively Opportunistic with Confrontive Interventions.

All client systems have areas of instability and openness where motivation to change exists. I must find and build on existing motivations and cultural strengths (go with the flow), and, at the same time seize targets of opportunity to provide new insights and alternatives. Going with the flow must be balanced with taking some risks in intervening.

---

[3]Don Michael pointed out long ago in his seminal *Learning to Plan and Planning to Learn* (1973, 1997) that errors should be "embraced" as keys to learning instead of denied and regretted. Fortunately, this important book on organizational learning has being reissued with a new foreword and epilogue because its applicability today is greater than ever.

PRINCIPLE 9: Everything Is Data; Errors Will Always Occur and Are the Prime Source for Learning.

No matter how carefully I observe the above principles I will say and do things that produce unexpected and undesirable reactions in the client. I must learn from them and at all costs avoid defensiveness, shame, or guilt. I can never know enough of the client's reality to avoid errors, but each error produces reactions from which I can learn a great deal about the client's reality.

Elements of the Choice Process

The following case illustrates some elements of this choice process, the importance of timing, and the process of learning from one's errors.

A Case Illustration

A colleague, Jim, wanted some help in figuring out why in his role as a consultant to management he had had a series of four experiences in which his report to management was poorly received, leading to termination of the relationship with those four clients. Jim's task was to advise them on how to organize the information function in their companies. The conversation began with my asking Jim to tell me about these events and prompting him with pure inquiry questions. After about 15 minutes it became obvious to me that he had been operating with his clients entirely from a doctor–patient model. He felt he had made careful diagnoses and given sound recommendations and, therefore, could not understand how these carefully thought-out diagnoses and recommendations could be so quickly dismissed.

In telling the story, he had already revealed many of his reactions, so I did not need to ask about feelings. He felt frustrated and incompetent, and he did not really know what to do. The temptation was strong at this point to short circuit the inquiry process and to share my own reaction and hypothesis that he may have precipitated the defensive responses by his own approach. He had been making formal public reports that were strongly critical of the organization to management groups that often involved more than one hierarchical level. However, I realized that if I did that I would be doing exactly what he had done; that is, to criticize his behavior to his face. This kind of feedback would reinforce his feeling of one-downness and risk his becoming defensive.

I curbed the impulse and instead asked him a diagnostic question: "What is your own theory about why these presentations were not well re-

ceived?" In effect I was asking "Why do you suppose this has happened?"—focusing on the general events and stimulating him to get involved in diagnosing the situation with me. He quickly identified the possibility that the clients did not want to hear negative things about themselves and that their defensiveness was probably legitimate. But he did not extrapolate to the possibility that his own decisions on what and how to report might have stimulated this defensive response. However, his analysis gave me more information on where his blind spots were and activated him to begin figuring out what might have been happening.

The "why" question is a powerful intervention because it often forces the client to focus on something that he had taken entirely for granted and to examine it from a new perspective. By choosing the subject matter of the "why" carefully, the consultant can create a different mental process leading to quite different insights. A major choice is whether to focus the client on why <u>he</u> *did what he did, why* <u>someone else</u> *in the story did what they did, or why* <u>some event</u> *happened that did not involve the client or some specific other person in the story.*

In speculating on why he was getting negative responses, Jim talked about a particularly painful meeting in which his presentation to the executive team led the CEO to challenge him directly right in the meeting, forcing him to admit that he had overstepped his mandate by pointing out how the corporate culture was not aligned with the long-range goals set for the information function. The CEO claimed that at no point had Jim been asked to comment on the culture, a culture with which the CEO identified since he was one of the founders of the company. Jim said he felt very bad about this and apologized publicly to the CEO. But, to his surprise, several other members of the team came to his aid and said that his delving into culture and his behavior in reporting on it had been justified and was even welcomed.

The diagnostic question revealed some new data that had not previously been reported and that were obviously significant. At this point I decided to focus on exploring further the various actions that had been taken by going to <u>action-oriented questions</u>. *This kind of question not only forces further diagnosis but also reveals more about the mental process that the client is going through and what options for action might be entertainable. Action-oriented questions might be prompts like "what did* <u>you</u> *do then?" as contrasted with the pure inquiry question of "what happened next?" or might ask the client to tell about the actions of others. The focus can remain on the past to continue to stimulate the story or can ask about the present or future, i.e. "what do you plan to do next?" or "what are you thinking about doing?" One can also ask about others—What will so and so do?" or, to complicate the process even further, get into what family therapists describe as "circular questions" by asking what others might do in response to some action on the part of the client.4 For example, I could have asked my colleague what would have happened if he had fought the CEO instead of apologizing to him. In this case I decided to focus on the CEO because it was his behavior that seemed most puzzling.*

I asked Jim why the CEO might have acted the way he did. Surprisingly, Jim could not figure out the CEO's behavior. So I shifted gears and asked him why he felt he had to apologize to the CEO; what had he done wrong? I was, in effect, testing my own hypothesis that Jim should first have given the CEO the presentation in draft form and in private to gauge how he would react to the criticisms about the culture. The explanation Jim offered reiterated his own sense of guilt and of having made a mistake, leading me to decide to try a more confrontive intervention. I asked Jim directly why he had not gone to the CEO first with his analysis.

Note that with this question I was for the first time revealing my own thoughts about the situation and what might have happened. This forces the client to think about other elements of the content of the story and is therefore legitimately thought of as "confrontive." These kinds of confrontations can still be couched as questions such as "Had you thought about meeting the CEO privately to share the culture data?" or, to keep the client on the hook, can be in the form of providing more than one alternative such as "Could you have either gone to the CEO or to the group first with a draft of the report?"

The danger of not accessing one's ignorance was revealed in Jim's response to my question, which was a spirited "I did *go to the CEO privately and gave him the same material, but I obviously didn't do a good job or get the message across to him." In fact, what had upset Jim was that the CEO had reacted negatively in public whereas he had said nothing in private.*

I realized at this point that the form of my question was rhetorical. I was really saying that he should have gone to the CEO and was assuming that he had not done so. This was an error on my part because I assumed *that he had not done something instead of simply asking whether or not he had done it. Jim's response revealed my error because he became defensive and again took the blame. But some important new data had surfaced, raising the issue for me of where to go next. I resolved to be more careful in how I ques-*

[4]Borwick, 1983.

tioned someone and reflected on why I had made the error, i.e. time pressure, impatience, or arrogance. At the same time, I learned a great deal more about the events of the case and Jim's tendency to blame himself for not having done a perfect job. I also wondered why he had omitted this crucial event in his story and pondered what this told me about his own mental map of what was and was not important. The pattern of self-blame led to a situation where a more confrontive intervention proved to be genuinely helpful.

After Jim reported that he had met with the CEO privately but that the public outburst occurred anyway, I stated a new hypothesis that the problem may have been that the CEO was embarrassed to have the culture criticized in front of his team. *Jim responded that this might have been the case but that he had assumed the executive team was "together" on this project. Jim seemed insensitive to the status and power differential between the CEO and the rest of the team. He also said forcefully that as a consultant he was* obligated *to report as clearly and validly as possible what he had found in conducting his interviews no matter how the audience was constituted. His own sense of professional expertise seemingly was overriding his ability to sense what was going on in his client system.*

The lesson so far is that errors will occur, that errors are there to be learned from, and that errors in content must be clearly distinguished from errors of timing and presentation. I might have been correct in sensing that something was going on with the CEO, but I erred in when and how I presented my thoughts. I made it more confrontive than necessary by providing a single hypothesis instead of providing several options about the events between Jim and the CEO. I also got enough of a sense that I was somewhat on target in my hypothesis that the issue might have been the public revelation in front of subordinates.

Sensing Status Equilibrium

As the conversation progressed, I noticed that Jim was becoming more comfortable in speculating with me about what might have been going on. He was beginning to broaden his own thinking about the past events even though he was defensive about the particular issue with the CEO. I sensed that the relationship between us was beginning to be equilibrated and that Jim was feeling less dependent and vulnerable, which made it possible to be more confrontive. Once the consultant feels that the relationship is on an even keel the conversation can evolve into much deeper areas without risking defensiveness because the client is now an active learner and welcomes input. "Even keel" does not necessarily mean that the two parties are literally of equal status. What it means is that the implicit contract between them, the level of dependence, the role of the consultant, and the degree to which the client feels accepted, meet their mutual expectations. Both feel comfortable with what they can give and receive.

The signals that this is happening are subtle. The client begins to be more active in diagnosing his own story, the tone of voice changes, and the content becomes more assertive. Self-blame or blame of others declines and objective analysis increases. A sense of being a team with the client emerges in figuring out what went wrong and what might have been the causes. In my conversation with Jim, he began to sound less worried and began to explore more objectively what might have been going on with his four clients. As shown below, this empowered me to become even more confrontive.

Case Illustration (cont.)

The pattern in Jim's story strongly reinforced my sense that he was operating as the "super–expert–doctor–diagnostician" and was so caught up in how to do his very best within that role that he had become quite insensitive to process issues. I decided to test his readiness to face this self-defined expert role by going beyond inquiry and giving him some direct and confrontive feedback. I knew that he understood my distinctions among types of consulting roles so I could be direct.

I said: "In these four situations in which you were rejected, were you really operating as the doctor giving the patient diagnoses and prescriptions in a situation that might have required more of a process role? Why did you not share the process issue of what to report to whom with one or more insiders, even the CEO? Why did you feel that you personally had to make all the decisions about what to report and to whom, and that it had to be in written form with a formal presentation?"

As I launched into this lengthy response I also noticed my own frustration because Jim knows process consultation very well, and I felt he was not using this knowledge. I added "Why is it that consultants continue to feel that they alone must make all of the process decisions and never share those decisions with insiders in the client system? When we have a problem of how to proceed we should share the problem instead of feeling we must make all the process decisions ourselves." All of this was said, though I thought it was risky, because our time was beginning to run out and one of the realities of the situation was that I wanted to get my view across before we had to terminate our meeting.

Jim reacted positively to this outburst and reflected immediately on the question of why he did feel he was acting as a doctor. He was, after all, paid to do the diagnosis and he wanted to do a good job using his own expertise. But he also had the crucial insight that how *he reported,* to whom *he reported, and in* what form *the report would be given were options that should have been discussed with some of his confidants in the organization. Jim was now able to differentiate between (1) being the content expert on the organization of the information function and its relationship to the company culture and (2) being an expert on how to manage the process of feeding back the data in such a way that it would be accepted and be viewed as helpful by the key members of the client system. This insight was immediately applied to the other three cases because Jim now recognized how he had masterminded "perfect" presentations in each case and given little thought to how these presentations might fit into the cultural and political processes of the client systems.*

We parted with a mutual sense that the hour or so spent on this issue brought some new insights. I continued to be puzzled and frustrated about the fact that Jim—who understood process consultation very well—had, nevertheless, fallen completely into the doctor role and could not see this for himself or pull himself out of it.

A major principle that emerged in the feedback and that needs to be added to our nine other principles is "*share the problem*." The consultant often is in a situation where he does not know what to do next or what something means. It is entirely appropriate from a PC point of view to share this with the appropriate insiders or parts of the client system. In Jim's case, he could easily have asked the CEO when he made his private presentation what that CEO thought would be a good next step in feeding back the data to others in the organization. But we get so caught up in our own expertise that we forget to access our ignorance—Jim did not know enough about that organization to know how to give back the report. He should have shared the problem and gathered information about it so that he could deal with the reality as it existed.

PRINCIPLE 10: When in Doubt, Share the Problem.

I am often in the situation where I do not know what to do next, what kind of intervention would be appropriate. It is often appropriate in those situations to share the problem with the client and involve him or her in deciding what to do next.

The Concept of Appreciative Inquiry

The helping process has so far been conceptualized in terms of problems or issues that the client brings to the helper. In an important modification of this point of view, a number of author/consultants have argued for a process of "appreciative inquiry" which puts a more positive frame around "problems."[5] Table 3.2 shows the essence of their argument by noting how a problem focus differs from an appreciative focus. We are all increasingly aware that our mental models and the metaphors we use for deciphering and labeling reality structure what we see and how we think about it. Cooperrider has usefully noted that the "problem focus" is itself a metaphor that predisposes us to thinking in deficit, negative, fixing terms. Often it is more helpful to think in more positive growth terms, focusing on what works well, what ideals we are trying to accomplish, and what visions for the future we have. In a sense appreciative inquiry highlights the difference between "adaptive learning," i.e. fixing the immediate problem and "generative learning," or building the *capacity to learn* so that such problems will not recur.[6] The basic PC philosophy is clearly

Table 3.2
THE CONCEPT OF APPRECIATIVE INQUIRY

Problem-Solving Focus	**Appreciative Inquiry**
"Felt Need"	Appreciating What Is
Identification of Problem	Valuing What is
Analysis of Causes	Envisioning What Might Be
Analysis of Possible Solutions	Dialoguing What Should Be
Action Planning	Innovating What Will Be

Problem Solving is based on the assumption that "reality" is a set of problems to be solved; Appreciative Inquiry is based on the assumption that "reality" is a miracle to be embraced and enhanced.[7]

---

[5]Cooperrider, Bushe, Srivastva, Barrett and others (1987).

[6]This distinction is made by Senge (1990) and builds on the difference noted by many authors between first-order and second-order learning, or learning how to learn (e.g. Bateson, 1972; Argyris and Schon, 1974, 1996).

[7]This diagram is adapted from Barrett and Cooperrider (1990).

geared to generative learning, but such learning often starts with what the client experiences as an immediate problem that requires a fix.

A similar point has recently been made by Marshak in identifying at least four different ways we can think about change, as shown in Table 3.3.[8] The table shows how we can implicitly operate from a physical engineering point of view and think of fixing, moving, or building things; or from a chemical process point of view of catalyzing or changing how things work by mixing the right kinds of people to create good "chemistry"; or from an agricultural biological point of view, in which growth and development are largely under the control of the individuals or groups being helped but the helper can provide nutrients, sunshine, and fertilizer to help natural evolution along.

Table 3.3
METAPHORS FOR CHANGE[9]

Physical/Chemical Metaphors (Fix and Rebuild)	
Machine metaphor	Fix the problem; Re-engineer
Travel metaphor	Move to a new place; Turnaround
Construction metaphor	Build something new; Restructure
Chemical metaphor	Catalyze, Mix, Compound, Crystallize
Biological/Medical Metaphors (Cure and Growth)	
Agricultural metaphor	Grow, Regenerate, Bear fruit, Harvest
Medical metaphor	Cure, Inoculate, Cut, Excise
Psychological/Spiritual Metaphors (Rebirth, Revitalization)	
Psychological metaphor	Provide insight, Change mental models
Spiritual metaphor	Convert, Liberate, Create, Transform
Sociological Metaphors (Regroup, Reorganize)	
Change roles and norms, Change culture	

[8]Marshak (1993).

[9]The categories presented here are a revision and elaboration of a similar set first published by Marshak (1993).

These implicit models may not affect the early inquiry process but most certainly will influence how the consultant pursues diagnostic and confrontive inquiry. It is therefore important for the consultant to be aware of her own metaphors and assumptions. If we start with a problem orientation, we are more likely to follow up with questions that highlight what is wrong; if we start with more of an appreciative orientation, we are more likely to follow up with questions that emphasize what is working, what makes the client feel good, what her goals and ideals are, and where she wants to go. Similarly, our orientation toward machine models of fixing versus biological models of enabling growth will determine how we help clients to diagnose their own situations and the kinds of mental models we provide for thinking about change.

The contrast between the various approaches will be least relevant at the beginning of a helping relationship because it will be *the client's metaphor* that will dictate the situation. Given what we have said about help-seeking in our culture, it is likely that most clients will start with an engineering problem orientation. They will want a fix, and preferably a quick fix. If the consultant works from more of an appreciative inquiry capacity-building position, she will begin to ask more positive health-oriented questions as the relationship evolves and help the client to see the value of appreciating what works instead of bemoaning what does not. At a recent meeting, Cooperrider[10] gave an excellent example.

> A friend who was an internal consultant came to him for help because she had been doing sexual harassment training for decades and was beginning to feel that it was not really helping. Instead of probing in detail why the training might not be helping, he asked the client what she was really after. She admitted that what she really wanted was well-functioning relations at work regardless of gender. He then asked her whether she knew of any cross-gender working pairs or groups that felt they were working well together. They decided to issue a general invitation across the organization for any cross-gender group that felt they were working well together to come forward and discuss their positive experiences. Dozens of such groups volunteered to share their experiences, permitting the consultant to develop a completely new kind of approach to the sexual harassment issue. By analyzing the common properties of relationships that worked, they were able to build an entirely different kind of training program that worked much better.

---

[10]Presentation at the American Academy of Management meeting, Cincinnati, August 12, 1996.

Summary and Conclusions

I have tried to illustrate how some of the problematic dynamics of the helping relationship can be ameliorated by engaging in an active inquiry process that keeps clients in the driver's seat—allowing them to regain status by becoming active problem solvers on their own behalf, to give them confidence that they can decipher their own situation to some degree, and to reveal as much data as possible for both the client and consultant to work with. Active inquiry is more than good listening. It involves understanding the psychological dynamics involved when someone seeks help and understanding the impact of different kinds of questions on the mental and emotional process of the client.

Three levels of inquiry have to be distinguished: (1) Pure inquiry that concentrates solely on the client's story; (2) Diagnostic inquiry that brings in feelings, diagnostic questions, and action oriented questions; and (3) Confrontive inquiry that brings in the consultant's own views of what may be going on.

The choice of when to engage in which level of inquiry depends on the actual situation, the events in the story as they come out, and, most importantly, the consultant's assessment of when the client is no longer feeling one down in the relationship. The actual roles that may emerge for the client and helper will vary with the situation, but the relationship will not achieve equilibrium until the inquiry process has enabled the helper and client to sort out the roles, to demonstrate mutual acceptance and, thereby, create a workable psychological contract between them. In the earliest stages of the relationship, pure inquiry is more relevant because it better brings out the expectations of the client and allows the helper to show acceptance and support. Once the client has become an active problem solver, deeper levels of diagnostic and confrontive inquiry become possible.

In managing the inquiry process, the timing of interventions is crucial and the consultant must balance the need to go with the client's flow with constructive opportunism. In that process the consultant will run some risks and inevitably make errors, but such errors should be welcomed as sources of learning both about the consultant and about the client's total situation and his or her reactions to interventions.

The inquiry process is inevitably guided by the metaphors of change, learning, problem solving, and growth that the client and the consultant bring to the situation. It is important for consultants to be aware of their implicit metaphors and make choices based on the realities of the situation. Whatever metaphors the consultant uses, however, one of the central functions of the inquiry process (beyond what has already been stated) is to create a set of conditions in which the client will feel safe and will be able to reveal anxiety-provoking data. As helpers, whether we like it or not, it is our earliest interventions that begin to set the tone and will determine how the relationship evolves. Accessing our own ignorance by engaging as much as possible in pure inquiry is the safest way to reveal the realities that will have to be dealt with as the relationship progresses.

We can now reiterate the ten general principles of PC that have been identified thus far:

1. **Always try to be helpful.**
2. **Always stay in touch with the current reality.**
3. **Access your ignorance.**
4. **Everything you do is an intervention.**
5. **It is the client who owns the problem and the solution.**
6. **Go with the flow.**
7. **Timing is crucial.**
8. **Be constructively opportunistic with confrontive interventions.**
9. **Everything is data; errors are inevitable—learn from them.**
10. **When in doubt, share the problem.**

As I reflect on various consulting–helping encounters that did not go right from my point of view, inevitably I find that I have violated one of these ten principles. Similarly, when I am stuck and don't know what to do next, I review the ten principles, and sooner or later come to a realization of what should have been done and was not, and what therefore to do next. And if that does not resolve the issue, I go to principle 10 and share the problem.

Case Example

Refusing to Play Doctor in Hansen Laboratories

This case illustrates a clear conflict in expectations and the need for the consultant not only to manage his role carefully but also to have clear professional standards. What I was willing to accept as the strategic goals of the project clearly did not mesh with what the client expected from the consultant; hence the consultation was terminated at an early stage.

One of my former students was a senior manager in a small company that conducted annual meetings of their key managers from all over the world. The company was run by his uncle and the uncle's brother, the president. My former student had proposed both to me and to his uncle that a consultant like me (hopefully I would have time to do it, he said) should attend their next annual meeting to be a facilitator during the discussion periods.

My job, I was told, would be to "bring out" the silent members of the group by asking them confrontive questions about the presentations on future strategy that were to be made by top management. They felt that a process expert like me would be able to bring out these silent people in a way that they could not.

I asked a broad inquiry question—why they thought they needed an outsider for this—and was told that over the past several years the meetings had gone "badly" in the sense that the overseas managers usually failed to participate in the manner that they were expected to. I asked him to describe what went on at these meetings. This general inquiry pushed my contact to begin to think diagnostically and I learned that senior management gave lecture inputs on future strategy to which they wanted reactions, but that the climate they created elicited only compliance. Furthermore, many of the managers who were supposed to respond to and critique the inputs had language difficulties and were in varying degrees of competition with each other. I suspected that it might not be safe to speak up at the annual meeting because one might create a bad impression both with one's peers and with senior management. Moreover, it was not clear whether senior management was serious about wanting to hear what others had to say.

At this point I felt that I could be most helpful by getting the contact client to see for himself that the conditions for participation might not be present and that bringing in an outsider would not fix this problem. I therefore asked a series of confrontive questions about how serious senior management was about wanting participation and about the nature of the climate they were setting up at the meeting. I was wondering whether they first needed to address their own commitment to participation before trying to figure out mechanisms for how to obtain it in others. I said that if they really wanted participation, surely they could communicate that and set up their own mechanisms to draw out the silent managers. I offered to help them design such mechanisms but did not agree that an outside facilitator would help in this situation.

The contact client, my former student, felt that his uncle did not want the responsibility and that the president might not be very good at eliciting participation, hence they wanted to lean on an outsider. However, he believed that both were committed to participation. As I thought about this I concluded that I did not want to get involved in the meeting because too little was clear about what would go on there and how senior executives' feelings would play out. To be helpful in this situation I felt I needed to get the family to see their own problems more clearly.

I asked my student to tell his uncle that I would be willing to meet with him to discuss the design of the meeting and whether or not it made sense to have any outsider present, but this would constitute a consultation visit for which they would pay my hourly rate. My purpose at this point was to test whether or not they were really motivated to work on this problem and to learn more about the uncle.

The uncle did call and set up a two-hour meeting. At the meeting he reiterated all that his nephew had said and urged me to attend the annual retreat. We would all go up to a country hotel on a bus, spend three days, and then return on the bus. I could help loosen up the group during the bus ride, question people at the meeting if they did not speak up, and further facilitate the process on the ride home. When I asked why they thought they could not set up a climate more conducive to participation themselves, the uncle hedged and argued that they did not have the skill, referring again specifically to his brother.

My emotional response was increasing tension and resistance. The situation felt wrong in that the motives did not match the proposed mechanisms. My judgment, based on talking to the uncle, was that they did not really know what they wanted, were probably sending mixed signals, or, possibly very accurate signals that they wanted only compliance. I felt that the consultant in this situation might only make matters worse by stimulating a level of participation that might not be welcome. I gently confronted the uncle with these thoughts and aroused a surprising amount of denial and defensiveness. He had his mind made up that an outside facilitator was the answer. I told him I felt I could not do it and hoped that he would try to solve the problem internally.

As far as I could tell, what was really going on would have made it unwise and possibly even harmful to agree to the next steps that the client was proposing. In effect they wanted a doctor to come in to diagnose and fix a problem that they might have misdiagnosed, and they were not willing to share responsibility for the proposed intervention by doing more process management themselves. There was no way to tell whether getting junior managers to open up would be welcomed by their seniors or would be in the best interests of the lower-level managers.

My help in this case was to bring to the surface all of this so that the nephew and his uncle could themselves gain some insight into these issues. I reinforced my verbal analysis with a long letter spelling out my analysis and concern. I received my check for two hours of consultation but did not get any further communication so I do not know whether my interventions were, in the end, helpful or not. I did feel comfortable in having made confrontive interventions early on in order to bring out further data about the implicit expectations of the client.

Exercise 3.1: Forms of Inquiry Questions

1. Ask a friend or colleague to share some problem with you or, if that is awkward, just to tell you a story about some recent events that happened to him.
2. As the "client" begins to tell the story make a conscious effort to ask *only* pure inquiry questions.
3. Become aware internally how frequently you are tempted to ask why or what someone did, even though you are presumably still trying to get the story in the client's own terms.
4. Make it a point not to shift to diagnostic or confrontive questions, even if you are tempted, until you sense that the client has told you as much as possible in his own terms.
5. Make an internal decision at some point to shift to diagnostic inquiry questions and observe the impact.
6. Make a further decision at some point to shift to confrontive inquiry questions and observe the impact.
7. After about 20 minutes discuss the thoughts and feelings you were each having during the first 20 minutes. Review what impact the different forms of inquiry questions were having on the conversation.

Exercise 3.2: Appreciative Inquiry

1. Ask a friend or colleague to share some problem they are currently experiencing.
2. Get out the story using the active inquiry questions discussed previously.
3. As you get to the confrontive types of inquiry questions where you share your own thoughts, make a conscious effort to cast your own thoughts into positive terms by asking questions that help the client to look less at the "problem" and what is *not* working, and more at what is working, what positive goals are being sought, and what strengths are available to get there.

4. Review the exercise in terms of (a) the impact on the client of the shift to the positive, and (b) what was happening in your own mental process as you attempted to shift from a problem to a more positive perspective.

4

The Concept of Client

Any helping or change process always has a target or a client. In the discussion so far I have referred to clients as if they were always clearly identifiable, but in reality, the question of who is actually the client can be difficult. I sometimes find myself not knowing whom I am working for, or working with several clients whose goals are in conflict with each other. I can often identify "targets" of change, others whose problems I can see clearly and whom I wish to help, but who do not see their own problems and would resist being seen as "clients." I can be working with an individual, with a small or large group, or with a slice of a total organization in a large meeting. I can be aware that the work I am doing with one person or group will have impacts on other persons or groups who are not aware that anything is going on. Ultimately, everything we do when we intervene will have some impact on the larger community and society in which we live.

The ambiguity of whom one is working with applies not only to consultants. The manager dealing with a group of subordinates or peers, the friend dealing with a neighbor family, and the teacher dealing with a class all have, in practice, the same issue—who exactly is the target of influence? Who needs what help? Who is seeking help? The PC *philosophy* in each of these cases remains the same, *to try to be helpful*, but, as we will see, the strategy and tactics will differ according to the client definition. Also, as the consultation process evolves over time, the question of who is *really* the client and what is the problem or issue being worked, becomes more and more complicated. One way to simplify this complexity is to be clear from moment to moment *with whom one is trying to do what.*[1]

[1]Several of the ideas in this chapter were contributed by Otto Scharmer, whose help and feedback were immensely valuable in the writing of this and the previous chapters.

Who? Basic Types of Clients

1. Contact Clients. The individual(s) who first *contact* the consultant with a request, question, or issue.

2. Intermediate Clients. The individuals or groups that *get involved* in various interviews, meetings, and other activities as the project evolves.

3. Primary Clients. The individual(s) who ultimately *own* the problem or issue being worked on; they are typically also the ones who *pay* the consulting bills or whose budget covers the consultation project.

4. Unwitting Clients. Members of the organization or client system above, below, and in lateral relationships to the primary clients *who will be affected by interventions but who are not aware that they will be impacted.*

5. Ultimate Clients. The community, the total organization, an occupational group, or any other group that the consultant cares about and *whose welfare must be considered* in any intervention that the consultant makes.

6. Involved "Non-Clients". Finally, one must note that in any change effort there may be individuals or groups who are aware of what is going on, who do not fit any of the above client definitions, and whose interests may be to slow down or stop the helping effort. In any social and organizational setting there will be political issues, power plays, hidden agendas, and conflicting goals that the helper must be aware of in planning and executing various interventions.

The contact client, the person who initially contacted the consultant, usually introduces the consultant to other people in the organization who, in turn, may work with the consultant to plan activities for still others in the organization. As the project proceeds, the consultant must be careful to distinguish between the client types, especially between primary clients who pay for the work, the unwitting and ultimate clients who will be affected by it, and the nonclients who will resist and attempt to subvert it. The definition of what is helpful may change as one deals with intermediate, primary, unwitting, and ultimate clients, requiring the consultant to use broader mental models that permit thinking about networks, lines of influence, power relations, and the dynamics of larger social systems.

What? Client Roles by Levels of Problems or Issues

As the helping process unfolds, the consultant must also think about a different classification of client roles based on the nature of the problem being addressed. This point has been argued most clearly by Rashford and Coghlan in their 1994 book, *The Dynamics of Organizational Levels.* Building on their framework, we can distinguish seven levels of problems or issues, each of which involves somewhat different individuals or groups as clients.

1. Individual Level. The individual level can be thought of as the "intrapsychic" issues that a given person brings to the helping relationship. In the group or organizational setting this involves what Rashford and Coghlan identify as the fundamental problem of bonding with others, of membership in an organization or community.

The most relevant interventions usually involve individual career or other personal issues and usually occur during individual counseling, coaching, mentoring, and training. In the organizational context the focus is often on helping an individual employee become a more effective participant in the organization. Individual help in any of these forms could be provided to the contact client, to individuals in the intermediate or primary client system, or even to members of the unwitting or ultimate client populations.

2. Interpersonal Level. This level refers to problems or issues that pertain to the relationship between the individual and other members of the organization or client system. The consultant would, in these cases, be working with more than one person at a time or, if working with individuals one at a time, would be working on the *relationship* rather than just the individual's intrapsychic issues. The one-on-one context may remain the same, but the focus of the inquiry would be on the relationship being explored, on the client's roles in various groups, and his effectiveness as a team member. The interventions described for the individual level might well overlap with the interventions most appropriate to this level, but in the individual case, the consultant would focus more on the impact of relationships on the individual, and in the latter case, more on the impact of the individual's behavior on others.

Some typical interventions specifically geared to this level would be role negotiation, mediation, use of a "third party" in conflict resolution, and relationship counseling such as is common in marriage counseling or family therapy. More focused and formal interventions of this sort would, of course, only be used as the consultant–client relationship reached a level where they decided together to formally focus on interpersonal issues.

3. Face-to-Face Group Level. This level shifts to problems or issues that are lodged in how a group or team functions *as a group*. "Face-to-face" implies that the group is conscious of itself as a group even if it is not co-located or does not meet physically on a regular basis. Electronic connections can serve as a surrogate for face-to-face communication if the members think of themselves as working together. In these cases the consultant plays a variety of helping roles from being a nondirective facilitator of meetings to managing the agenda, or even helping to structure the work of the group. The consultant may meet with members individually for purposes of identifying issues or agenda concerns, and those individuals can come from any of the previously mentioned client types, but the focus is on how the group works as a group. Much of the work that goes under the label of "team building" (Dyer, 1995) would fall at this level and the concept of "client" could now be broadened to the entire group.

4. Intergroup Level. This level focuses on problems or issues that derive from the way in which groups, teams, departments, and other kinds of organizational units relate to each other and coordinate their work on behalf of the organization or larger client system. The consultant now has to intervene at the system level and be able to think in terms of large multi-unit interventions.[2] Blake's *Intergroup Exercises* (Blake *et al,* 1989) and Beckhard's *Confrontation Meeting* (Beckhard, 1967) are examples where whole units are involved as "client systems." Alternatively, the consultant may work with the individual leaders of the various departments or groups, or with a smaller group in which the members function as representatives of their units. The configuration of the clients will vary, but the issues addressed at this level will always pertain to improving the *coordination* and *alignment* of the organizational units involved.

[2]An excellent review of such interventions has been published by Alban and Bunker (1996).

Again it needs to be emphasized that such interventions presume the prior building of relationships with members of the client system so that clients know and understand what they are getting into with these larger, systemic interventions.

5. Organizational Level. This level pertains to problems or issues that concern the mission, strategy, and total welfare of the whole client system whether that be a family unit, a department, an organization, or a whole community. Again, whether or not the consultant is working with individual leaders, groups or intergroups will vary, but the focus is on total system-level problems. Examples would be some of the total organizational *Survey Feedback Projects* (Likert, 1961), *Weisbord's Future Search Conferences* (Weisbord and Janoff, 1995), *Open Systems Planning* (Beckhard and Harris, 1987), *Blake and Mouton's Grid OD* (1969, 1989), Worley, Hitchin and Ross's *Integrated Strategic Change* (1996), and some forms of cultural analysis if pursued by top management (Schein, 1992).

6. Interorganizational Level. This level pertains to the coordination, collaboration, and alignment issues that arise as total organizational or community units begin to form consortia or interorganizational networks (Chisholm, 1997). The consultant typically works with large or small groups of representatives and focuses on broader network issues even when working with individuals. What distinguishes this set of issues from the intergroup issues is that the units are autonomous and not necessarily bound by a single larger purpose or political entity. For example, the consultant might be working with a UN committee, a consortium of companies brought together for a purpose like "organizational learning," or a community network trying to create a regional development program.

7. Larger System Level. Finally, this level pertains to problems or issues that involve the wider community or society where the consultant may be working with social networks, organizational sets, or community groups on issues pertaining to the health of larger systems, even the planet in the case of environmentally oriented projects such as "The Natural Step."[3]

---

[3]"The Natural Step" is a program developed by K. H. Robert to make society at all levels conscious of the global environmental problem and what each of us can begin to do about it (Eriksson and Robert, 1991).

My purpose in presenting these typologies is to focus on the inherent complexity of client identification and to note that even though the consultant may be working most of the time in one-on-one or small group situations, the problem focus will differ dramatically as given clients adopt different roles. The different levels of issues also alert us to the fact that the later and often "deeper" interventions that result from the initial diagnostic interventions will have vastly different consequences as they begin to pertain to broader client systems. The reason an organizational attitude survey is considered in most consulting models as an "intervention" while "diagnostic interviews" of a few key executives are usually considered to be "just diagnostic," is because of the broader ramifications of the survey and the problems a survey typically addresses. However, the psychodynamics of the relationship between consultant and client remain essentially the same even as the problem focus shifts levels. What then changes with change in focus?

As the consultant–helper gets beyond individual counseling or group facilitation, the diagnosis of whom to work with, what to focus on, and whose interests to consider in planning next steps or major interventions becomes very complex. To remain in the PC mode, one needs to share this task with whatever part of the client system the consultant is working with at the time. The consultant should not go off and figure out by herself what to do next because she will never know enough about the culture and politics of the larger system to make such decisions. Instead she should involve as much of the intermediate or primary client system as she has access to in planning at what level and by what means to continue helping. It is in this arena that the principle of "Share the Problem" rather than trying to figure everything out for oneself becomes particularly applicable.

One of the ethical dilemmas of helping, whether we are talking about a consultant, a manager helping a subordinate, or a friend helping another friend, derives from the fact that the helper is always dealing with more than one part of the client system; and some parts may not have the same needs or expectations as others (Schein, 1966). In the managerial context we think of these as different "stakeholders" and acknowledge that it is central to the managerial role to balance the interests of these groups. Managers and consultants, therefore, have something to learn from each other on how such multiple relationships can be conceptualized and managed when one intervenes in complex systems.

Having described the general categories of clients and the levels of client issues, I want now to look at the some of the specific issues that arise with each type of client.

Contact and Intermediate Client Issues

The helping process always starts with a contact client who may be thought of as the first person with whom the consultant meets concerning the problem or issue, whether or not that person admits to owning the problem that is to be worked on. If I am to be helpful in terms of the assumptions of PC, I need to know as soon as possible what perceptions and expectations this contact client and others in his organization have of me and my consulting philosophy. I especially do not want to be cast into the expert or doctor role prematurely and, at the same time, I want the contact client to feel helped even if we have only had a brief phone conversation. The principle that every conversation must be felt to be helpful by the other person applies.

Given the prior concerns, I must start with broad exploratory inquiries that identify the realities in the situation and that reduce my ignorance of what is going on (see Chapter 3). What is on the client's mind? Why has the person called or come to visit? Why at this particular time? The reasons contact clients give then provide clues as to their perception, which I can either reinforce or "correct":

- The contact client read a book or paper on my consulting style.
- He was referred by a former or current client.
- He was referred by a colleague who knows my style and areas of interest.
- He became acquainted with me at a workshop in which I did some teaching.
- He heard a lecture or read a paper or book on some topic on which I have written, such as "Career Anchors" (1990) or "Organizational Culture and Leadership" (1992), and perceives some connection between that topic and the problem area.

As I listen to the answers, I calibrate as best I can whether the situation warrants continuing the relationship; that is, whether or not I can be ultimately helpful in the situation. I have to make an assessment of whether the contact client and others in his organization have a willingness and readiness to engage in the kind of joint inquiry and problem solving that the PC model advocates and, if not, whether I have other kinds of expertise that the client needs. I have to discover whether the client's intent is constructive or not, so that I do not unwittingly become a pawn in someone's political game.

But of course I can only discover the answers to these questions through a process of careful questioning that is simultaneously exploratory and helpful. I always have to operate by the overarching principle that whatever I say or do is an intervention which must be perceived (as much as possible) as helpful in the immediate situation. My goal is to have the caller feel that she not only received the information she sought but also got some help in thinking about the problem itself. In most cases, this help would be in the form of questions that the contact client had not previously considered or suggestions of ways that the contact client can go back to her organization with her own helpful interventions and suggestions. One of these might be to suggest that if other potential clients back in the organization want to explore the situation further, I would meet with them for an hour or so to see whether it would make sense to get further involved, and would bill them for that time.

Billing for such an exploratory meeting is warranted because useful insights typically result from such initial meetings and there is often no need for further involvement. The contact client and whomever he involves in that meeting may learn from it what needs to be done next, and those next steps often do not require any further help from the outside consultant. Billing for exploratory meetings has the further function of testing the contact client's motivation to get help, and, third, sends the message that help is available on an "hourly" basis and does not have to involve long projects or elaborate formal contracts.

If the initial contact is perceived to be helpful, the contact client and the consultant *together* will plan the next step, which usually involves intermediate clients or direct involvement with the primary client. In the ideal situation the contact client is the primary client, but primary clients often do not want to expose their issues until the consultant has been "legitimated" by initial contacts. The contact client may be testing whether or not the consultant is the type that would work well with the primary client, and/or the primary client may call for an initial meeting to "test the chemistry" before making a commitment to further work.

In terms of the level of issue, the consultant must be prepared to work at any level and use the initial contacts to begin to gather diagnostic information as to whether the problem will be at the individual, interpersonal, group, intergroup or total system level. As conversations occur, the consultant must not only work on reducing her ignorance but must constantly build the relationship with whichever client she is working with to create a shared diagnostic team, so that next steps can be jointly owned.

The contact client may or may not be the person who has a problem that must be worked on and who ultimately pays for the consultant's services. He or she may even be just an agent for someone else in the organization who either does not want to take the time or is too embarrassed or troubled to seek the help directly. For example, I often get calls from personnel or training departments of companies inquiring on behalf of line managers whether or not I do certain kinds of consulting. The caller admits to having a list of names and making the same inquiry of all the people on it. To give a sensible answer on whether and how I could be helpful, I would need to know what kind of organization, what kind of line manager would pass on such a task to a staff person, and why. I would therefore think of the caller as a contact client and try various exploratory interventions to determine whether or not to proceed further to identify the intermediate or primary client:

> "Can you tell me a bit more about this manager and the situation?"
>
> "What is happening now that makes an outside consultant desirable?"
>
> "How does this manager relate to you in the organization?"
>
> "Can you tell me how you got my name, or why you are calling me in particular?"

My purposes in asking these kinds of questions are (1) to obtain information in order to proceed, (2) to be helpful to the contact client by raising questions that may not have been considered, and, (3) to create the correct initial impression of how my consultation will proceed. Hence the questions also suggest some avenues for the contact client to explore on his own. They help him to structure his next steps. The commonest version of this tactic is to ask the contact client to speculate on why the line manager is asking for help and why he has chosen the particular format of having someone else gather names of potential consultants. That question gets the contact client thinking diagnostically and helps him to own his part of the problem.

As the conversation develops, I may suggest alternative steps for the caller to offer to the potential primary client—a meeting between me and the manager, a direct telephone conversation with the manager, or maybe just some further questions to put to the manager regarding what she may have in mind. If the contact client and I agree that the next step is for this "intermediate client" to call me directly or to set up a meeting, my focus shifts to the creation and management of the intermediate client relationship. This involves setting a schedule, making a time for a call or meeting, deciding on where to meet, who should be at the meeting, how long the meeting should be, and what the purpose of the meeting should be. Note that the questions themselves keep involving the contact client in diagnostic issues and not only help her to own the next steps, but train her in how to start thinking diagnostically herself.

Primary Client Issues

A primary client is a person or group that has a particular problem or issue that has started the process of seeking help. One operational way to define the primary client is to ask whose budget will pay for the consultation. That question often reveals a complexity that the consultant must be careful to diagnose. I have been in the situation where a senior manager was willing to pay for my services if I would help *someone else* in the organization. A specific case, actually my first organizational consulting experience, illustrates the dilemma.

During my second year as an Assistant Professor at MIT I was asked by my mentor, Douglas McGregor, whether a colleague and I would be willing to take on a consulting assignment at a nearby company. Doug did not have the time himself and was anxious to introduce all of us on the faculty to the experience of consulting. (Doug was, by definition, the contact client because he had been approached by the company).

The assignment was to do an interview survey of the technical personnel in the company's research laboratory. According to the VP of Industrial Relations and Personnel there was a morale problem in the lab and the laboratory director was interested in finding out what the employees thought so that the problems could be fixed. It was this VP who knew McGregor personally and had asked Doug to either do the survey or find someone who could. The VP had not only authorized the study but our consulting expenses came out of his budget. He assured Doug that the director of the research labs was on board and was delighted to have the survey done. All of this information came from Doug, our contact client. We never met the VP but we did talk to the director of the lab briefly and learned that he was in favor of doing the interviews and would set-up the process with his technical people.

After some months of careful interviewing, my colleague and I collated the data and wrote a fairly complete report on all of the issues that had been identified by the technical staff. As might have been expected, among the complaints registered were many about the managerial style of the director. We noted these complaints in one section of our report. A feedback session was scheduled with the director during which my colleague and I were prepared to go through all of the data in the report. We requested two hours since there was a lot of information to cover and we wanted to be very thorough in showing how valid the information really was by showing various statistics.

My colleague and I walked into the director's office, presented him with a copy of the report (he was the first person in the company to see it), and started our presentation while he leafed through the report. He immediately spotted the section in which his management style was mentioned, read it over quickly, and then interrupted us in a rather angry manner with a curt "thank you" and dismissed us. We had had no more than 15 minutes with the director and were not invited back either by him or the VP. We never found out what happened to the report that we left with the director.

This case illustrates a variety of errors we made from the point of view of PC, especially from the perspective of client identification. In retrospect, we had never identified or properly targeted our primary client. Was it the VP, was it the Lab Director, or was it even Doug McGregor? Each of them had a stake in the outcome and each had a problem to solve. But by not inquiring further before leaping into action, we never found out what problem we were really addressing in our survey. We did not really know *why* Doug wanted us to do this assignment. We never found out *what* the VP who was willing to pay for it really had in mind. For example, might he have been gunning for the director and saw this as an opportunity to put him down? Was he trying to influence the director's management style and saw the survey as a nice outsider intervention to provide a handle on the situation? Or was he just being supportive of an organization development activity that someone had suggested to him?

We never knew whether the director of the lab really favored the project or whether he was seduced or even "coerced" into it by the VP. Most important of all, we never found out what the director really wanted from the survey. He clearly did not want to hear negative things about his management style. We fell into a whole series of traps with unknown outcomes, by not figuring out who the primary client was and involving that primary client in designing the project. We never found out what happened to the report, to the director, or to the relationship between the VP and McGregor. In retrospect, if we had paid attention to the fact that the project was paid for by the VP, we should have insisted on a session with him to try to learn more about his motives and why he was willing to foot the bill. We should have asked why it was not being charged to the research lab. Our ignorance and our failure to access it led us to a series of interventions whose impact we could never determine.

Once the primary client is clearly identified, the consultant must engage in an active exploratory inquiry process with that individual or group. As the previous case illustrates, one cannot take the word of the contact or intermediate clients on what the primary client might want or need. Getting information directly from the primary client not only guarantees accuracy, but, more importantly, begins to build a relationship that allows the consultant and the primary client to work together to diagnose the situation and develop further interventions. If we remember the principle that it is the client who owns the problem, we can avoid the trap of the consultant starting to make suggestions and interventions based on second-hand information. If the consultant moves ahead on her own, the primary client may be relieved, may become dependent, and create the inappropriate situation of the consultant ending up owning the problem. Therefore, I am willing to be passed on to new primary clients only if the current one I am working with takes joint responsibility with me for the decision, and if the mechanisms we jointly work out for involving the new client make sense to both of us.

Unwitting and Ultimate Client Issues

Unwitting and ultimate clients are the stakeholders whose interests should ultimately be protected even if they are not in direct contact with the consultant. In other words, the helping process should not help a primary client if it will obviously hurt some other group that the consultant should be concerned about. If I am asked to help a manager to win a political battle over another manager, I must ask myself what will ultimately be best for the entire department or organization. Only if I can justify in my own mind that the ultimate client will be better off in terms of my own values can I justify helping this manager.

The distinction here between unwitting and ultimate clients is mostly a matter of degree. The unwitting client is the peer, boss, or subordinate of the primary client I am working with, so the consequences of what we do must be considered immediately because of their proximity. The ultimate client is better thought of as the whole organization, community, or even society in the sense that we would not be providing consultation help to potential criminals or terrorists. At the extreme, the value issues are simple. But for the proximal unwitting client, the situation may be more ambiguous and complex. For example, in the previous case, my colleague and I never considered seriously the possibility that the director was an unwitting client and that an unfavorable survey might lead to his being punished. Nor did we consider what the director might do vis-a-vis his technical staff if he was upset over the negative comments about his management style. We did keep the interviews anonymous so at some level we were thinking about protecting the employees, but they were not the only unwitting clients in the situation.

Primary clients pay for the services directly. Ultimate clients are affected by the outcomes, but may not even know that anything is going on. Unwitting and ultimate clients, therefore, must be defined by the consultant in terms of her own professional criteria. The issue is sharper if we consider the manager in a consulting role. Should a second-level manager help a subordinate manager to exploit the workers under that subordinate, for example? Should a sales manager help her sales representatives to get better deals at the expense of the customers? Should a consultant help a company close a plant in a community that will clearly be harmed by such an action?

There are never easy answers to such questions, but it is important in all helping relationships to recognize the questions. That is, anytime we help someone we are, in effect, allying ourselves with the goals and values *they* represent. We cannot later abdicate responsibility for the help we may have provided if that help turns out to have bad effects on another part of the organization or other groups.

These issues came up frequently in my own managerial role as department chairman in regard to the interests of the faculty and the students. If faculty members asked me to help them to organize projects, teaching schedules, or consulting trips that would be, in my opinion, harmful to student interests, I had to decide when the students as ultimate clients were more important than the faculty colleagues who were the primary clients. If questions about such issues arose in my mind, I found that the best intervention was always to share the question immediately so that the client had to own the issue as well. We could then work out together how to meet the needs of the primary client as well as the unwitting and ultimate clients.

Targets of Influence as Clients and the Impact of Nonclients

In many consultation projects a major dilemma arises when an individual, group, or department is identified as a target of change but the members of that unit do not perceive themselves to be in need of any help. Indeed, they may be unwitting clients in that they do not even know they are the object of someone's attention. This situation usually comes about when the inquiry process with intermediate, primary, and even contact clients reveals that the problem appears to be person A or department B to whom we have no immediate access.

If those targets are hierarchically lower than the client, it is often expected that the consultant will willingly go to them and somehow get access. For example, in the previous case, we never questioned how it came to be that the technical staff was willing to meet with us, nor did we consider that they should become clients if we involved them in the survey. If the target is higher up or geographically unavailable we are often stuck and decide that the project is not workable. Internal consultants are sometimes very creative in dealing with this situation as illustrated in the following case of a large bank.

Frank, the Director of Organization Development (OD) in the Apex Bank wanted to introduce a new team-building program that was very successful in several other banks. The CEO of the Apex Bank was, however, very conservative and very aloof, leading Frank to conclude that a direct proposal to bring in the program would not work. On the other hand, there was no point in starting the program without the CEO's approval and support.

The problem, then, was how to get the CEO, as a target of change, to get on board and to become a client. Frank studied the CEO's behavior over a period of time and observed that he was very conscious of benchmarking the activities of Apex against other banks. Frank also knew Mary, the OD Director in the Beta Bank, where the team-building program was well under way. He also knew that the CEOs of Apex and Beta often got together, so Frank arranged with Mary that at one of the future lunches of the two presidents, the CEO of Beta would bring up the Beta team-building program and report how successful it had been. Several such lunches took place, and in due course the Apex CEO called Frank and requested that the team-building program be instituted in the Apex Bank.

If the situation does not lend itself to this kind of management or benign manipulation, the consultant and the immediate client with whom he is working must share their dilemma and together figure out how to turn a target into a client. From the point of view of the PC philosophy, this can be done only by becoming helpful in some way to the target person or persons, and that in turn requires an inquiry process that will reveal what if any help the target needs. To establish the initial contact that will allow such an inquiry process to begin, the consultant must often begin by seeking help from the client. For example, the internal consultant can approach a given manager who is ultimately a target and inquire what if anything that manager would like the consultant to work on. Offering to work on the target's problems creates the opportunity to build a relationship that will later allow inquiry into other areas that the target may initially have been unaware of or unwilling to delve into.

What of nonclients, those in the organization who perceive what is going on but choose to oppose it? The commonest version of this dilemma occurs when consultants are brought in to help implement a technological or cultural change, but it is perceived by some members of the organization as a disguised way to disempower them or even to cause them to lose their jobs. In these cases the consultant may be productively and happily helping one group to design and implement a program that makes complete sense to them, only to discover resistance and opposition from another group. A productivity program that proposes the involvement of employees in the design of the work may be opposed by the union because it is perceived as an effort to get more work out of the employees for the same pay. Many programs of "job enlargement" are opposed by employees because they are happy with their routine jobs. Many surveys or team-building efforts are opposed because they appear to be vehicles for exploiting rather than helping employees.

In all such cases the consultant must sort out what will ultimately be helpful and deal with the nonclient group in a constructive way. That may mean being a better communication link, encouraging more dialogue and understanding between opposing parties, clarifying the issues, and insuring that the current primary client fully understand the implications of the opposition. Once it is clearly understood, a joint decision on how to proceed can then be made by the consultant and the primary client.

The consultant's knowledge of and experience with organizational dynamics plays a large role in the resolution of such issues because opposition groups can often be anticipated and identified before major interventions are made. One of the most important roles I find myself playing is when managers propose major changes, to "force" them to think through who would benefit, who might be threatened, and who would oppose the changes. Based on such analysis we can then plan interventions that will take all such constituencies into account.

Conclusion and Implications

The most important point to be made about clients is that the consultant must always be clear who the client is at any given moment in time and must distinguish clearly among contact, intermediate, primary, unwitting, ultimate, and nonclients. It is easy to forget who the client is, especially when the consultant has been working in an organization for some time or with different units.

Second, the consultant must always be aware that particularly the unwitting, ultimate, and nonclients may shift according to the level of problem being addressed. For instance, working with the CEO one-on-one can either be counseling on a personal matter with few ramifications for others or can be helping with a major strategic issue that has implications for everyone in the organization and in the outside community.

Third, in either case, if the consultant feels that the next steps taken have implications for others that the client may not have considered, it is important to surface those implications and insure that the primary client is fully aware of them and willing to own them. It is entirely appropriate to raise the question of "Who is *really* the client here?" with contact, intermediate, and primary clients. It is ultimately helpful to them as well as the consultant if they can think clearly about this question.

Case Examples

Case 4.1: Client Complexity in the Multi Company

Client complexities in an evolving project can best be illustrated by reviewing some aspects of my work with the Multi Company, a European multidivisional chemical company in which I ended up doing a variety of consultation activities over a period of several years (Schein, 1985). This case illustrates not only the client issues but the multiple roles that the consultant must play and the way in which a consultation evolves from individual to group to organizational issues.

I was initially called by the director of management development, Dr. Peter Stern, and invited to consider giving a seminar to the top forty-five managers of Multi at their annual meeting in six months. I tentatively agreed because I had met Stern at a previous seminar where he had heard me talk. He convinced me that a similar presentation would be very relevant to their company, and I became interested because of the opportunity to make contact with a top management group of a large multinational organization.

Before the assignment was finalized, however, I had to meet the president, Richard Maier, to see if we could agree on the purpose of the presentations and to test whether Maier would be satisfied with my approach to the meeting. A special trip was set up to meet Maier, who now became the intermediate client. We met, reached agreement on goals, established that we could be comfortable with each other, and, therefore, both agreed to go ahead. Maier now became the primary client.

The next step was to meet a month later with the director of training, Otto Kunz, who designs and manages the annual meetings. He also became a primary client for purposes of developing a detailed plan of when and how I would give my presentations and how this would fit into the structure of the annual meeting. His requirements, however, had to be aligned with what the president, Maier, had indicated to me as his basic purpose in having me give the presentations. At the same time, Kunz became a consultant to me in helping me design my sessions to insure that they would be relevant to the issues that were salient in Multi at the time and to design a presentation that would fit into the culture of Multi.

At the annual meeting itself I met many other managers. The members of the executive committee were clearly potential primary clients, as were some of the division heads and region heads. In each of these relationships the twin goals of inquiring and simultaneously being helpful were my criteria for how to interact with each new person I met. During the meeting a planning group led by Stern, which included the president and several other members of the executive committee, monitored the meeting and replanned events as needed. They asked me to sit in with them and help them in this process, so they as a group became a primary client for that purpose.

In terms of my actual presentation, the whole group of forty-five were my primary clients in the sense that they owned the problems that my seminar addressed. Individual members sought me out during the meeting and subsequently became primary clients concerning particular issues. After the meeting, Maier asked me to continue to consult with the company to make it more innovative. He defined himself, the executive committee, and Stern as primary clients and asked Stern to manage my time during the visits. Once again Stern became the contact client.

As this scenario developed, I ended up working with the senior group, various individuals in the executive committee, and the participants at the next two annual meetings. The company as a whole was clearly one level of the ultimate client, and various departments that were impacted by specific projects were unwitting clients—especially as the company began a process of downsizing in various of its divisions. Stern and Kunz continued in the dual roles of contact clients and primary clients in that management development and training issues became one of the prime foci for the later consultation efforts. Various other managers also became contact and primary clients, in that they began to communicate with me directly about attending meetings or getting help with specific problems.

As a result of the annual meeting, a steering committee was created to design a process for turning the company around, which involved simultaneously reducing the size of some divisions while increasing the profitability of other divisions. This committee assigned projects to twenty-five different task forces, some of whose chairmen sought my help in organizing their projects. In these relationships the client focus was clearly the entire company, even though I was working with individual task force chairmen.

Stern also wanted to redesign the career-development system and sought my help in an expert capacity to help him design a research project to study the careers of the top 200 executives in order to determine what patterns of international and cross-functional movement seemed to be most successful. Careful documentation of these cases led to some striking insights about the importance of international movement that led to a major redesign of how executives were moved.

The lesson of this case for me was to constantly reassess what my relationship was to each of the people I met in Multi and to remain aware of how interventions in one part of the client system could have impact on other parts of the client system. If I was not sure of such impacts, I fell back on "sharing the problem" by involving insiders in the questions or issues rather than trying to make decisions by myself.

I also learned that I had to play many roles vis-a-vis the many clients I was dealing with. It was in this organization that I encountered the norm that to be seen with the consultant was a loss of status. I also learned how strong the norm can be that the consultant must be the expert–doctor, in that throughout the years that I worked with them, they always preferred me to give them my opinion and recommendation. Only after many experiences with me in the PC mode did they begin to recognize the value of process interventions, joint inquiry, and joint diagnosis.

Case 4.2: Consulting with Consultants— The Jackson Strategy Consultants

An interesting example of the ultimate client issue came up in a project where I was part of a faculty group helping a strategy consulting firm to become more effective as consultants by participating in developmental seminars for the consultants. A number of faculty members worked with several senior consultants in the company on issues of marketing, finance, human resources, and consulting technique. The role of the faculty members was to provide research information and to help the consulting group to use this information to improve the tools they used in analyzing their clients' problems.

I was to come in as an expert on consulting method and process. In my individual sessions with members of this company and in group seminars, we discussed issues such as how to decipher what the client really wants, what the client organization's culture is, and how the consultant can optimally manage the relationships. I provided conceptual maps and they provided case materials, which we then used to discuss new analytical tools to be developed for their work with clients.

The ground rules were clear—that faculty members would not get directly involved with clients unless there was some very specific reason to do so. As a result, whatever help was provided to ultimate clients (the companies that Jackson works with) was provided through the intermediates, the Jackson consultants. On the surface this appeared to be a clear-cut case, but the unresolved dilemma was whether the faculty who was training the consultants had any say whatever over the kinds of clients who were ultimately taken on by Jackson, and whether we should have had such say. I found myself monitoring this process by examining my own reactions to the cases presented by the Jackson consultants. Their cases and the approach they took generally fitted my own criteria of valid help, so the issue was resolved without conflict.

This case differed from the more common situation of functioning as a training consultant or a "shadow consultant" in that the faculty group contracted to help the entire consulting firm to become more effective. If the firm then hired people whose values we did not share or took on clients that we would not have approved of, such actions were entirely out of our control. What I found myself doing was monitoring this process moment to moment through getting the Jackson consultants to provide enough case material about their clients to make assessment possible.

Exercise 4.1: Who Is the Client? (One to two hours)

1. Arrange to get together with one or more others who are either fellow consultants, or, if you are a manager, fellow managers.
2. Think back over the past year or two and each group member in turn identify one or two situations where you found yourself providing help to others.
3. Take one case at a time and try to reconstruct it in terms of who was the contact, who were the intermediates, who was the primary, and who were the unwitting and ultimate clients (or targets). If you have trouble deciding who fits into what category, explore the implications of those ambiguities.
4. For each case, review the degree to which you took into account the needs of the unwitting and ultimate clients (or targets), and how this did or did not influence your behavior.
5. What lessons do you draw from an analysis of the cases?

Part II

Deciphering Hidden Forces and Processes

Becoming an effective helper requires a philosophy of the kind described in Part 1, a great deal of practice, and a working *theory*. By theory, I mean mental models of how the world works that help us perceive, understand, simplify, explain, predict, and control what is going on. Good intentions and motivation are not enough. The competent helper/consultant must have some understanding of the psychological, interpersonal, group, organizational, and interorganizational dynamics that influence human affairs. One such model was provided in Chapter 2, where we reviewed some of the psychodynamics of the helping relationship. Understanding comes about from a combination of such "theory" and practice, from learning concepts and learning how those concepts play out in the actual experiences of helping individuals, groups, and larger organizational units or communities. But practice alone will not do it.

Many of the forces that influence the outcome of relationships are hidden and/or hard to decipher. To become a more effective helper requires not only a greater ability to see and hear what is going on in order to detect and decipher these hidden forces, but also a greater personal flexibility in responding to them. One of the most important functions of process consultation is to make visible that which is invisible. But the process of making things visible is not simple or obvious. Just telling the client what is going on rarely works because our cultural assumptions, our defenses, and our perceptual biases keep us from seeing what is out there and what is operating within us. The expert or the doctor can provide a brilliant diagnosis laying out everything that is going on, yet the client can completely misunderstand it because there is neither the ability nor the motivation to decipher it.

The first step in making things visible, therefore, is (1) to create the conditions that will *motivate* the client to see more deeply and (2) to help the client to *learn how to see*. Just as artists must learn how to see what they wish to render, so must we as problem solvers learn to see what we wish to create, enhance, or fix. We all need the feeling that we are in control of our lives, yet we often feel out of control, victims of other people's actions or social conditions we cannot influence. If we cannot get a feeling of control, we often blame ourselves instead of realizing that much of what happens to us is the result of forces and structures we are not aware of. Some of these forces are the result of cultural assumptions that we have learned and that now structure our thinking, but we have forgotten that they were *learned,* not embedded in nature. Some of these forces are the result of the social structures and systems in which we are embedded. Also, some of them come from the structural complexity of our minds and personalities, from our unconscious, and from the way our brains and bodies are put together.

In the next two chapters I will review a number of concepts and models that have been helpful to me in trying to understand what goes on beneath the surface when two or more people are in some kind of relationship. These "hidden forces" become especially relevant when one person is trying to help another person. In Chapter 5 we focus first on what goes on *inside the head.* Then in Chapter 6 I analyze the *cultural forces* that determine the essential patterns and rules that govern face-to-face relationships and explain some of the psychodynamics of the helping relationship that were reviewed in Chapter 2.

5

Intrapsychic Processes: ORJI

The most important thing to understand in any relationship is what goes on *inside the head, especially one's own head.* If the actors in a relationship cannot observe and assess their own feelings, biases, perceptual distortions, and impulses, they cannot tell whether their actions and interventions are based on perceptions of reality or only on their own needs to express or defend themselves. To understand what goes on inside the head and how this affects our overt behavior, we need a simplifying model of processes that are, in fact, extremely complex. The complexity of intra-psychic processes derives from the fact that our nervous system is simultaneously a data-gathering system, a processing system, and a proactive managing system. That is, we observe (O), we react emotionally to what we have observed (R), we analyze, process, and make judgments based on observations and feelings (J), and we behave overtly in order to make something happen—we intervene (I).[1]

In its simplest form we can lay this out as a sequential circular model as shown in Fig. 5.1. Although real intrapsychic processes do not occur in such a simple, logical sequence, the model permits us to analyze in more detail the complexity of what happens inside the mind, what kinds of traps we fall into, and how this makes our interventions more or less effective.

Observation (O)

Observation should be the accurate registering through all of our senses of what is actually occurring in the environment. In fact, the nervous system is proactive, programmed through many prior experi-

[1]There are many models of this kind dealing variously with the learning cycle or with problem-solving cycles. The model presented here includes what many leave out: the role of emotions in the total process.

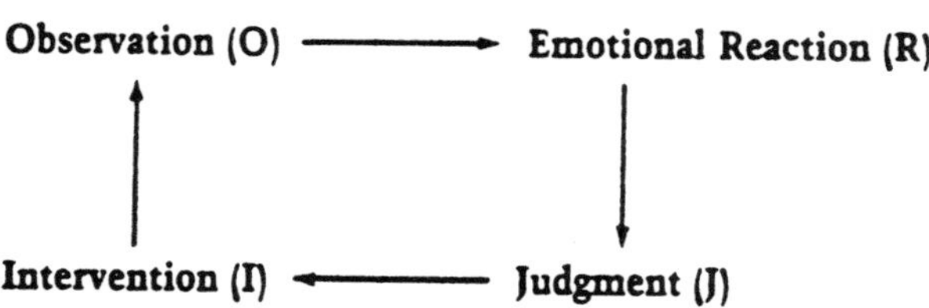

Figure 5.1
THE BASIC ORJI CYCLE

ences to filter data that come in. We see and hear more or less what we "expect" or "anticipate" based on prior experience, and we block out a great deal of information that is potentially available if it does not fit our expectations, preconceptions, and prejudgments. We do not passively register information; we select out from the available data what we are capable of registering and classifying, based on our language and culturally learned concepts as well as what we want and need. To put it more dramatically, we do not think and talk about what we see; we see what we are able to think and talk about.

Psychoanalytic and cognitive theory has shown us how extensive perceptual distortion can be. The defensive mechanisms of *denial* (refusing to see certain categories of information as they apply to ourselves) and *projection* (seeing in others what is actually operating in ourselves) are perhaps the clearest examples. But it has also been shown that our needs distort our perceptions, such as when our thirst makes us see anything in the desert as an oasis. To deal with "reality," to strive for objectivity, to attempt to see how things really are (as artists attempt to do when they want to draw or paint realistically), we must understand and attempt to reduce the initial distortions that the perceptual system is capable of and likely to use.

Some psychologists relate this "ability to see" to right brain versus left brain functions, arguing that it is the left "critical" brain that causes many kinds of misperception. That theory is consistent with what many art teachers argue, that we cannot draw better because we do not actually see what we are drawing; we are drawing what we think things should look like.[2] Similarly, some sports psychologists

[2]Good descriptions of "learning to see" can be found in Frank, 1973 and Edwards, 1979.

argue that our critical brain interferes with our "natural" ability to do things, as when the tennis player convinces himself that he cannot make a certain shot and consequently misses it.[3] To learn to observe, then, is to learn about and overcome the traps to which a history of experience and learning has exposed us. The consultant cannot deal with reality if he or she cannot learn to perceive accurately what is going on, and that means getting in touch with one's own history to identify one's own predispositions, stereotypes, and preconceptions.

Reaction (R)

The most difficult aspect of learning about our emotional reactions is that we often do not notice them at all. We deny feelings or take them so for granted that we, in effect, short-circuit them and move straight into judgments and actions. We may be feeling anxious, angry, guilty, embarrassed, joyful, aggressive, or happy, yet we do not realize we are feeling this way until someone asks us how we are feeling or we take the time to reflect on what is going on inside us.

Feelings are very much a part of every moment of living, but we learn early in life that there are many situations where feelings should be controlled, suppressed, overcome, and in various other ways deleted or denied. As we learn sex roles and occupational roles and as we become socialized into a particular culture, we learn which feelings are acceptable and which ones are not, when it is appropriate to express feelings and when it is not, when feelings are "good" and when they are "bad."

In our culture we also learn that feelings should not influence judgments; that feelings are a source of distortion, and we are told not to act impulsively on our feelings. But, paradoxically, we often end up acting *most* on our feelings when we are least aware of them, all the while deluding ourselves that we are carefully acting only on judgments. And we are often quite oblivious to the influences that our feelings have on our judgments.

Forces we are unaware of cannot be controlled or managed. If we can learn to identify our true feelings and what triggers them, we have a choice of whether or not to give in to those feelings. If we do not know what they are or what causes them, we are de facto victims of them. It is not impulsiveness per se that causes difficulty, it is act-

[3]For example, Gallway (1974).

ing on impulses that are not consciously understood and hence not evaluated prior to the action that gets us into trouble. The major issue around feelings, then, is to find ways of getting in touch with them so that we can increase our areas of choice. It is essential for consultants to be able to know what they are feeling, both to avoid bias in responding and to use those feelings as a diagnostic indicator of what may be happening in the client relationship.

Judgment (J)

We are constantly processing data, analyzing information, evaluating, and making judgments. This ability to analyze prior to action is what makes humans capable of planning sophisticated behavior to achieve complex goals and sustain action chains that take us years into the future. The capacity to plan ahead and to organize our actions according to plan is one of the most critical aspects of human intelligence.[4]

Being able to reason logically is, of course, essential. But all of the analyses and judgments we engage in are worth only as much as the data on which they are based. If the data we operate on is misperceived or our feelings distorted it, then our analysis and judgments will be flawed. So it does little good to go through sophisticated planning and analysis exercises if we do not pay attention to the manner in which the information we use is acquired and what biases may exist in it. Nor does analysis help us if we unconsciously bias our reasoning toward our emotional reactions. It has been shown that even under the best of conditions we are only capable of limited rationality and make systematic cognitive errors, so we should at least try to minimize the distortions in the initial information input.[5] The most important implication for consultants is to recognize from the outset that our capacity to reason is limited and that it is only as good as the data on which it is based.

---

[4]Elliot Jaques (1976, 1982) has noted that one of the ways that different levels of management can be distinguished is by the time horizon that they consider when they plan and by the length of the time units over which they are given discretion. Thus, workers on the shop floor may have autonomy over minutes, hours, or days. Low-level managers may have autonomy for days or weeks. Senior managers plan for and have autonomy over months or years.

[5]Simon, 1960; Tversky and Kahneman, 1974; Nisbett and Ross, 1980; Carroll, J. and Payne, J.W. (eds.) 1976.

Intervention (I)

Once we have made some kind of judgment, we act. The judgment may be no more than the "decision" to act on emotional impulse, but that is a judgment nevertheless and it is dangerous to be unaware of it. In other words, when we act impulsively, when we exhibit what are called knee-jerk reactions, it seems like we are short-circuiting the rational judgment process. In fact, what we are doing is not short-circuiting but giving too much credence to an initial observation and our emotional response to it. Knee-jerk reactions that get us into trouble are interventions that are judgments based on incorrect data, not necessarily bad judgments. If someone is attacking me and I react with instant counterattack, that may be a very valid and appropriate intervention. But if I have misperceived and the person was not attacking me at all, then my counterattack makes me look like the aggressor and may lead to a serious communication breakdown. As a consultant I have to remind myself repeatedly that everything I say or do is an intervention with consequences.

Let us examine a typical example that frequently occurs in group meetings.

I find myself at a group meeting with one member, Steve, who has consistently undermined me or disagreed with me in past meetings. I make a particular point, and it is followed immediately by Steve saying some words pertaining to my point. The cycle now may unfold as follows:

Observation—*Steve is attacking me by disagreeing with my point. What I may be unaware of is that I am perceiving what Steve said as disagreement because I expected it, and I am seeing disagreement as attack because I also expected to be attacked.*

Reaction—*I am anxious and consequently angry at always being disagreed with and attacked. I feel like really fighting back to make my position very clear. What I may be unaware of is that my emotional reaction is now based on the motives I attributed to Steve, not on what Steve's motives may actually have been. What I may also be unaware of is that my anxiety reaction to the perception of being attacked is valid but that there are other possible ways of dealing with the anxiety besides getting angry and counterattacking. I may not be aware that, in a sense, the anger is a feeling that I have* chosen*. It is not automatic.*

Judgment—*I make the judgment that Steve must be competing with me for status in this group and I can not let him get away with putting me down. I have to assert myself to protect my position. What I am probably unaware of at this point is how this entire seemingly logical conclusion is premised on my initial interpretation of what I thought I saw and my particular emotional response. If I now act on this judgment, I may or may not be acting appropriately because I do not in fact know whether or not my initial observation was correct.*

Intervention—*I vigorously put down Steve's point, leaving him puzzled and having to deal with his own ORJI cycle. If his response is in turn unpredictable, I will not be able to figure out what happened because I am unaware of how my own preconception has led to an intervention that may have nothing to do with Steve's intentions.*

Reflective reconstruction of the ORJI cycle often reveals that one's judgment is logical but is based on "facts" that may not be accurate, hence the outcome may not be logical at all. It follows, therefore, that the most dangerous part of the cycle is the first step, where we make attributions and prejudgments rather than focusing as much as possible on what really happened. When we say that someone acted "emotionally" instead of logically, we usually mean that he acted inappropriately to the situation as we perceive it. We could not see the data that would warrant the kind of behavior we observed in the person. When we later interview the "emotional" person we often find that the behavior was rational and logical from that person's point-of-view, that the person "observed" something that made him react appropriately to what was observed. If the behavior was inappropriate, it was not because it was not rational but because it was based on incorrect initial observation.

A poignant example of this process was recently reported by an executive in one of our intensive executive development programs. Dave (the executive) was deeply involved in studying for a finance examination to be taken the next morning. He isolated himself in his den at home and asked his six-year-old child not to disturb him. Half an hour later, the child appeared at the door, thereby interrupting what Dave was doing. Dave immediately got angry because he had asked not to be disturbed, and he "observed" the child's entry as doing something he had been forbidden to do. Dave considered his anger entirely appropriate (judgment) and punished the child by yelling that he was not to be disturbed (intervention).

Later on, Dave noticed that the child was very upset, aloof, and in other ways reacting more strongly than Dave thought was warranted. This new observation triggered a new feeling of tension, concern, and worry about the child, leading to the judgment that he should find out what was going on. Dave decided to ask his wife some questions (intervention). These questions complete a second cycle.

Dave now learned that the child had come down at his wife's request to ask him if he wanted to have a cup of coffee and to say goodnight (new observation). Listening to this explanation made Dave feel guilty and ashamed for blowing up (reaction). He made the judgment that he was wrong to have acted so hastily before so he now decided to attempt to apologize and make-up with his child (intervention).

In this case, Dave had the opportunity to make up for his earlier error and, as he became aware of how he misperceived the situation and how this led to an inappropriate intervention, he could train himself to check on what he was observing before allowing himself to respond "emotionally" in future situations. He discovered that emotions are not automatic, that they are based on what we perceive, and that if we can check our perceptions, we can also control our emotions by this process. Note, however, that often we do not have second chances as Dave did. We do not discover our misperceptions and possibly *never* learn why our actions did not produce the responses we desired. The bigger lesson is to have a more realistic view of the ORJI cycle in the first place and to develop our ability to "see" and reflect on what we are seeing before we make judgments and leap into action. Not only do consultants have to become aware of this dynamic within their own minds, but they must help clients understand how these processes may have led them to inappropriate behavior and how to think more realistically about the relationship of perception and thought to feelings and behavior.

The More Realistic ORJI Cycle

If we were now to redraw what we have been talking about it would look more like Fig. 5.2.

This figure permits us to summarize the traps involved in the ORJI cycle as follows:

Trap 1. Misperception. Due to prejudgments, expectations, defenses, or false attributions, we do not accurately perceive what happened or why.

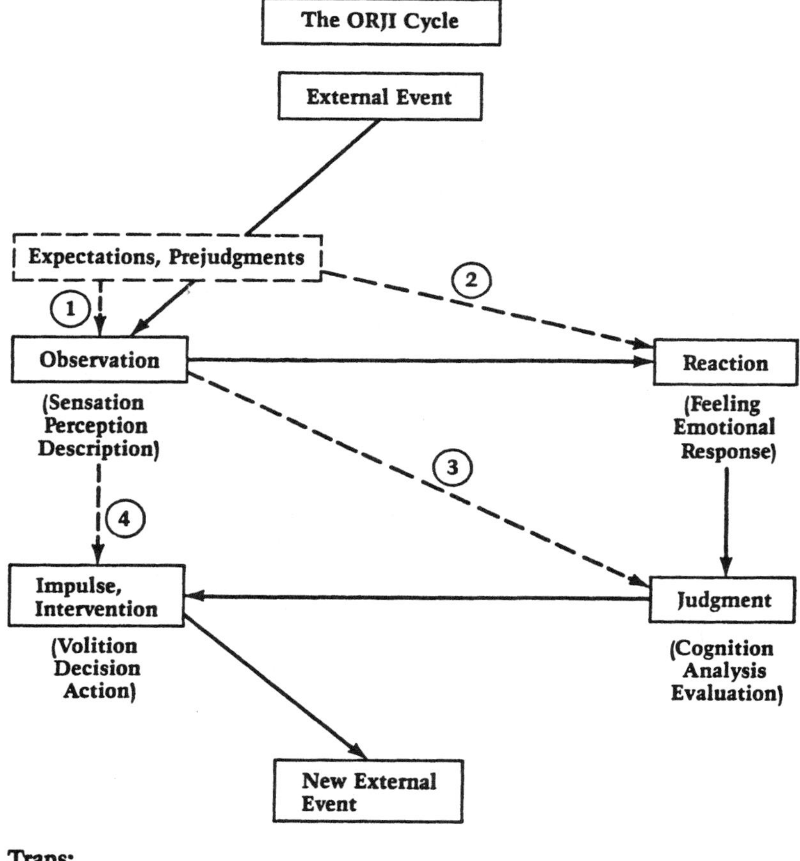

Traps:

1. Misperception
2. Inappropriate emotional response
3. Rational analysis based on incorrect data
4. Intervention based on incorrect data

Figure 5.2
A MORE REALISTIC DEPICTION OF THE ORJI CYCLE

Trap 2. Inappropriate Emotional Response. An inappropriate response could occur for one of two reasons: (1) misperception of what happened or why it happened (Trap 1) and "allowing" ourselves to respond emotionally to our interpretation without being aware that it is based on incorrect data, or, (2) we may have learned to overreact emotionally to valid data or to have an emotional response that is itself inappropriate such as reacting to a loving gesture with anxiety or anger.

Trap 3. Analysis and Judgment Based on Incorrect Data or Faulty Logic. Again there are two versions of this trap. (1) Once we accept our observation and emotional response as correct (Trap 1 and/or 2), we can reason appropriately but still come out with the wrong conclusion if the input was incorrect. Alternatively, (2) we may reason incorrectly or illogically if we are not aware of our cognitive biases or reasoning disabilities.

Trap 4. Intervening on Seemingly Correct Judgments that are In Fact Incorrect. If we allow ourselves to intervene without rechecking and reflecting on the whole cycle—checking whether our observation and emotional reaction were correct and appropriate—we may act rationally but make the situation worse.

Notice that the traps are cumulative and that if we have fallen into the first trap, the others follow naturally. But we must learn to reflect on and dissect our own decision making and action sufficiently to begin to be able to see the whole cycle and diagnose where remedial action is necessary. Again, it is the consultant's job to understand these dynamics in his own head, and to help clients identify such traps in their own mental processes.

How to Avoid Traps

Communication breakdowns, hurt feelings, and destroyed relationships result more often from falling into the traps identified previously than from malice or intention. The manager dealing with subordinates, the consultant dealing with clients, and the group member dealing with colleagues all need to become highly aware of the pitfalls of intrapsychic processes, and all need to learn some routines for avoiding or correcting these pitfalls.

Identify Possible Bases of Misperception

There are at least three distinguishable bases of misperception that need to be sorted out:

1. Taken-for-Granted Cultural Assumptions. The same behavior in different cultural settings can mean different things. In one organization it may be culturally appropriate to argue all points; in another organization it may be culturally appropriate to always agree with a senior member of the group in public. If I, as the consultant, interpret either behavior in terms of my own cultural assumptions instead of theirs, I will misinterpret the meaning, react inappropriately, and make inappropriate interventions. Case 5.1 at the end of this chapter gives a further illustration.

2. Personal Defensive Filters or Biases. Certain kinds of behavior in others may always be perceived by me as having a certain meaning because of my own defense mechanisms and biases, based on my own past experience. I may perceive all disagreement as attacks, or may perceive any silence as agreement because I "need" to see it that way. As a consultant, I have to observe myself in action over a period of time and try to get corrective feedback from others in order to identify the systematic biases in how I perceive things. Once I know what those biases are, I can take greater care in checking things out before reacting to them.

3. Situational Expectations Based on Past Experience. If I have encountered a given situation or person many times before, I may come to believe that I know what to expect. In this case the potential source of misperception is primarily one's past learning, and this is perhaps the hardest to correct for because it requires one to "undo" or ignore one's own prior "knowledge." If I am trying to be a helpful consultant, it is essential to be as objective as possible and to allow for the fact that situations and people do change. Hence I have to remain as observant as possible, even in situations in which I already "know" what to expect. *I have to learn to access my ignorance.*

Identify Own Emotional Response Biases

If I have a systematic bias to respond to certain kinds of data with certain kinds of emotions, I need to know what that bias is in order to judge its appropriateness to any given situation. For example, if I tend to respond defensively and get angry whenever a client challenges me or tells me that I am wrong, I need to recognize this as a bias and learn to control or compensate for that feeling, especially if my judgment tells me that it would not be helpful to the consultation process to get into an argument with the client. However, getting defensive and angry is not always wrong. Sometimes it is the appropriate response. But in order to make choices and decide what will be most facilitative in a given situation, we need to know our biases.

Identify Cultural Assumptions in Judgment and Reason

Reasoning and making judgments is not a culture-free process. Culture provides us with assumptions that tell us how to reason and what conclusions to draw from what data. If we do not know what our assumptions are, we may reason correctly from our point-of-view and still make errors from the point-of-view of others. Such errors often occur because of tacit assumptions about time and space.[6] For example, I might wish to have a "private" meeting with the client. In my cultural setting, privacy might be assured if we can find a quiet corner of a large office complex, but my client might define privacy as being behind closed doors and out of anyone's sight. If I do not understand his definition of privacy, I might not understand why he is ill at ease when I try to talk to him in the open office setting, even though no one can hear us.

As another example, if in my culture being on time is a mark of efficiency and respect for the busy schedule of others, I might be offended if my client keeps me waiting for fifteen minutes past the appointed time. In my client's culture, however, being fifteen minutes late might be appropriate. He might assume that both of us would keep others with subsequent appointments waiting for as long as we wished, and this is how he would show his respect for the importance of our meeting. These kinds of cross-cultural traps are so pervasive and difficult to identify that one must be careful in any helping process to be working with others who understand the local culture.

For example, I once did a seminar in Mexico for two groups in a bank. One of the managers was my client. Partway into the seminar he asked me to describe various kinds of organization development interventions. After I described an intergroup exercise in which each group meets to develop its own self-image as well as its image of the other group, both my client and one of his colleagues asked me to show them how to actually go through it. I reasoned that they wanted a clearer illustration by trying it out and was not aware that they wanted this exercise to help them resolve a major issue between them.

---

[6]Good examples can be found in Hall (1959, 1966, 1976, and 1983) and Schein (1992).

The exercise revealed that my client's group was quite dissatisfied with his leadership, and when this was publicly revealed, it led the other manager to propose that many of the functions that my client had been performing now be taken over by him. A big argument broke out, and I lost control of the meeting because both groups suddenly broke into Spanish and refused to honor their original agreement to keep the conversation in English. My client ended up losing both face and political power as a result of the exercise, and I realized too late that I had completely misunderstood their motives when they proposed to go through the exercise.

What is logical and rational depends very much on the deep tacit assumptions we make, and those assumptions are so embedded in us that we take them for granted. It is therefore quite necessary and appropriate to develop reflective procedures that invite us to examine and even challenge the things we take for granted.

Institute Systematic Checking Procedures

Explicit Questioning. The most important way to avoid traps is to test as best one can whether one's observations, reactions, and reasoning are correct or not. This can be done by more questioning, more observation before intervening, crossreferencing with the observations of others, and playing back to the client what has been observed. Though it may at times be awkward to say "Let me see if I understand. You are saying . . . ." or "I am hearing you say . . . . Have I understood you correctly?" it is at times absolutely necessary.

Silence as an Intervention. One of the most important interventions one can decide to make is to remain silent and continue to observe what is going on. Remaining silent but in an active listening mode may not seem like an intervention, but in fact it may be crucial in order to minimize the risks of misperception, inappropriate emotional reactions, and biased judgments. Often what we see and hear while we are struggling with ourselves to stay quiet reveals the further data we need to make a more helpful response. The interrupted father in the earlier example need only have waited a few seconds in order to have found out that the child wanted to say goodnight and offer coffee.

Silence is often appropriate even when a direct question has been asked. I have often found that if I pondered my answer or "played with my pipe," the other person continued, sometimes even answering her own question or going ahead with her story in a way that suggests she did not really want or expect an answer from me.

Maintaining a Spirit of Inquiry. The best overall protection to avoid the traps is a spirit of inquiry, a desire to decipher what is really going on, a commitment to listening and helping instead of actively displaying one's own impulses and feelings before knowing whether or not they are appropriate. One of the important differences between the three models of consultation is that in the expert and doctor–patient model less emphasis falls on being in an inquiring mode and more temptations exist to assume that one has the answer. The PC model argues that since only the client can solve the problem anyway, the consultant or manager practicing this model can and should comfortably stay in an inquiry role, knowing that, in the long run, this role will produce the best solution.

Conclusion

If consultants are to be helpful, they must intervene in situations. And one cannot *not* intervene, because silence is itself an intervention. If those interventions are to be appropriate and helpful, they must be based on accurate observation, appropriate emotional responses, and a reasoning process that mirrors (or at least takes into account to some degree) what the client observes and how the client reasons. All of this requires some self-insight, and such self-insight is best acquired by maintaining a genuine spirit of inquiry toward oneself and others. Self-insight does not come about automatically. It requires conceptual tools such as the ORJI model, a spirit of inquiry, and reflection and analysis time by oneself and with helpful others.

To build observational and reflection skills one must discipline oneself to take the time to learn to see and to think about what one is seeing. Just as the artist must study the characteristics of what she is going to draw or paint, the helper must study the clients, the situation, and her own responses to it in order to form as clear a picture as possible of the realities. Careful listening and actively picturing things in one's mind are important elements of this active inquiry process, in that it focuses our vision and controls irrelevant distractions. Accessing one's ignorance by *actively* figuring out what one does not know is, in the end, one of the most important process tools available.

Case Example 5.1 Management Selection in Esso Chem Europe

I have chosen to name the company in this example because no individuals will be harmed and the events to be described occurred over twenty years ago. This case brings out some of the dramatic consequences of an inability to "see" one's own cultural biases and how they affect management decisions.

An internal consultant asked me to help him with a project to decipher why the performance ratings of older managers seemed to show a systematic decline with age. In preparing for this project, I was to attend the monthly meeting of the top management committee of the company to review their high potential candidates and discuss future career plans for them. (In a later discussion I will review the age-related findings. The case discussion here is focused on how this executive committee dealt with the problem of locating high-potential managers to be put on their internal board.)

Specifically, at several meetings the focus was on the problem of not being able to locate European managers to promote to the board. This situation was embarrassing in view of the fact that the subsidiary was doing all of its business in Europe. The executive committee, in effect the internal board to which they wanted to add some Europeans, consisted of the twelve top managers, all of them Americans. In reviewing candidates the group had a systematic procedure that included a detailed discussion of each high-potential manager. My role was to listen so that I could learn how the process worked.

A number of the candidates were Americans, and the discussion proceeded in a routine fashion. My insight occurred when the first European candidate was brought up. This candidate was the manager of the Italian subsidiary of the company. The group discussed his performance ratings and his potential ranking which was very high, yet they hesitated to label him a good candidate. In struggling with their own hesitancy, one person brought up the fact that this manager, though very competent, was "too emotional." He allowed his emotions to influence some decisions and he displayed emotions too often in management meetings. The implication was that because he was "emotional" he would not be sufficiently "objective" in the more senior management role. The Americans in the group prized their own "unemotional objectivity" and viewed it as a prime competence.

It never occurred to the group to examine the assumption that the job required someone unemotional, nor did it occur to the group that their inability to find Europeans to promote to this level was a direct consequence of the way they defined the requirements of the job. The group was trapped in two cultural assumptions that they could not bring to consciousness: (1) that to be a senior manager requires you to be unemotional, and (2) that European managers who were more emotional were less competent than their unemotional American counterparts.

I was not expected to intervene in this process, so I could only observe what was going on. It is interesting to speculate, however, what I might or should have said if the group had asked me to make an observation on their process. What would have been a helpful intervention in this situation?

Exercise 5.1 Identifying the Traps in One's Own ORJI Cycle

1. Think back and identify a recent incident where your own behavior led to an outcome that was either undesirable or unpredicted.
2. Reconstruct in detail the observation that you made just before your own intervention, the emotional response you had, the judgments you made, and the logic that led you to the intervention you chose (what you actually did). Write down each step, to force yourself to be concrete.
3. Try to identify where in the cycle you may have erred.
4. If you cannot find any errors, ask a colleague to listen to you as you reconstruct the event step by step and see if the colleague spots any errors in what you saw, felt, thought, and did.
5. Do this for several behavioral incidents to identify systematic biases in your perception, emotion, judgment, and intervention.

6

Face-to-Face Dynamics: Cultural Rules of Interaction and Communication

In this chapter we will explore another category of hidden forces, those that arise between people when they interact and attempt to communicate and build relationships with each other. On the surface we think of this as the exchange of information and opinion. In reality what transpires between people when they communicate in a face-to-face situation is an enormously complex interactive dance in which multiple meanings are conveyed over multiple channels with multiple purposes. Some aspects of this complexity were explored in Chapter 2, where we analyzed the psychodynamics of the helping process. But the helping process is only one form of interaction and communication, so we must now explore and try to understand the broader aspects of the communication process and the hidden cultural forces at play in it.

Why Do People Communicate in the First Place?

We take communication and human interaction for granted, and we consider people who do not care to communicate or interact to be hermits who are strange and even threatening. Why, then, do we communicate and why do we treat it as a normal part of human affairs? Several distinct functions of communication are summarized in Table 6.1.

1. *To make ourselves and our needs known to others so that those needs and aspirations can be satisfied.* From early childhood, we recognize that we are dependent on others and that we must learn to communicate with them if we are to get our needs met.

Table 6.1
SIX FUNCTIONS OF HUMAN COMMUNICATION

1. To get our needs met
2. To figure others out
3. To make sense of ambiguous situations
4. To gain advantage
5. To build collaborative relationships
6. To express and understand ourselves

---

2. *To figure out what others are all about, to get to know them.* We also learn early in childhood that others are a source of satisfaction and threat, and, perhaps most of all, a mystery. We try to establish communication in order to demystify them, to understand them, and to determine from that understanding how we should react. This theme is heavily used in stories about visiting aliens and the intrinsic difficulties of communicating with them.
3. *To make sense of ambiguous situations by sharing perceptions and thoughts.* Life presents us with a constant flow of new data that require deciphering. Once we have a shared language with others, we use that language to collectively figure out or make sense of what is happening. Is it going to rain today? Who should I vote for? Is that department threatening us or not? What did Jane mean when she said what she said? What do the falling sales figures mean? If we analyze the talk between people we find that a great percentage of it is devoted to joint sense-making, to a joint process of figuring out and defining the situation so that we know how to operate in it.
4. *To gain advantage by structuring situations to our own needs, to persuade, sell, convince, teach.* We communicate not only to make sense but to structure situations to our own advantage. We often know what we want so we communicate to make it happen as best we can. We may use formal processes of rhetoric or manipulate the situation in various ways to achieve hidden agendas, but in all cases we are using communication of some sort to achieve our goals.

5. *To enable us to do more than we could by ourselves by establishing cooperative, helpful relationships with others.* We communicate to build collaborative relationships, to seek help, to offer help, and to build teams because we realize that to get a task accomplished that meets our own needs, we have to work with others. If we are just meeting our own needs, we communicate by making them known or making demands; if we are trying to gain advantage, we persuade, seduce, or manipulate; if we are trying to build collaborative relationships or, as in process consultation "helping relationships," we communicate in such a way as to facilitate mutual understanding.
6. *To fully express ourselves and get to know ourselves through self-expression and listening to ourselves.* Some communication is purely expressive and we do it because it is fun and enlightening to see what comes out of our mouths. As some would put it, "I do not know what I think or feel until I hear what I say." For purely expressive communication, we can be our own audience, though the achievement of self-knowledge is enhanced through observing the reactions of others to our self-expression and in getting "feedback" from them.

To fulfill any of these functions (except the most basic expression of need in infancy) requires some form of language, a basic set of symbols whose meaning is shared by the participants in the situation.

The Role of Language

One of the most powerful achievements of the human species is the evolution of shared language that makes abstract communication possible. Some of the functions of communication can be met with grunts and gestures, but to really make sense of ambiguous situations, gain advantage, seek help, build collaborative relationships, and express oneself requires initially a common system of symbols so that situations can be analyzed abstractly. Language enabled human societies to live together in harmony and gain advantage from living communally. With language came abstract thought patterns and symbols, which enabled groups to develop norms and assumptions about the nature of the world. With language also comes what we think of as culture, the accumulated learning of a group as it achieves its external goals and internal harmony. Language ends up being culture's most important artifact in that it both represents the external reality that a group has experienced historically and, at the same time, perpetuates that reality through training newcomers in how to think about and perceive their environment.

All cultures have found that in order for its members to be able to relate safely to each other, some rules and norms have to evolve that govern face-to-face relations. For example, some rules and norms must be observed on how to manage the needs and drives that derive from our biological nature. In particular, we need rules that govern the management of aggressive feeling and the management of sexual feelings and love. Societies not only evolved various kinds of family units that define whom it is OK or not OK to love and whom it is OK or not OK to be aggressive toward, but also evolved a subtler set of rules to govern *all face-to-face relationships* and make life safe and predictable. These rules are so well learned in most societies that we are quite unconscious of their operation except when they are violated. Such rules are often labeled "good manners," "etiquette," or "tact," but behind such labels lie much deeper issues of how to make the social environment safe for all of us. Fortunately, a number of sociologists have deconstructed some of these rules and made them available for our analysis.[1]

Cultural Rules of Face-to-Face Interaction

To appreciate the cultural rules of interaction in our own society, we need to reflect on how our language gives us clues about what is "really" going on in face-to-face relationships. For example, what do we mean by terms such as good manners, tact, poise, deference, demeanor, humiliation, embarrassment, and saving or losing face? Why are etiquette and diplomacy important in human affairs? Why do we describe social events or situations as "scenes," and talk of playing or not playing our "roles" properly? Why do we talk of feeling "cheated" in social relations or say that we need to "pay" attention when someone is talking to us? Why do we say that we "invest" in relationships and/or that we need to give people their "due"?

[1]Excellent reviews of these rules of interaction can be found in the writings of Erving Goffman (1959, 1967) and John Van Maanen (1979).

What our language tells us is that the models that best explain a great deal of what goes on between people focus on (1) *social economics* and *social justice*, and (2) *social theater or drama*. As we learn to perform on various life stages, we learn what is an appropriate actor and audience behavior and we learn what kinds of exchanges are fair or unfair. Our emotional responses are very much determined by what we regard to be situationally appropriate and what we regard to be "equitable" or "just" social exchanges.

The relevance of all of this to the consultant or manager derives from the fact that help must be provided within the constraints imposed by these cultural rules. Even the definition of what is helpful is culturally determined, so the helper cannot function unless she knows a good deal about the culture in which she is working. Recall the seminar in Mexico (pp. 96) in which my primary client was hurt because I did not understand the rules by which he and his colleagues were operating and, once they switched to Spanish, I could not even observe what was going on. Of necessity then, the discussion in this chapter focuses on Western and U.S. culture.

Social Justice: Basic Communication Must Be a Fair Exchange

We all learn early in life that human interaction is reciprocal. If someone is talking to you, you are paying attention; if someone gives you something, you say thank you; if someone insults you, you defend yourself in some manner or another. We also learn what kind of reciprocating action is appropriate and when it is expected, and we have a quantitative sense about this. If we are saying something that we feel is important and we communicate that through our body language, tone of voice, and introductory remarks, we expect more attention and get annoyed when the listener seems to pay too little attention. If we give an important gift or throw a great party, we expect an appropriate level of thanks and feel upset if it seems the recipients or guests take it for granted. If someone insults us and we are unable to defend ourselves appropriately, we feel bad and vengeful. We expect an apology that is commensurate with the degree of insult or hurt. If we have "invested" a lot in a relationship and the other party casually breaks it off, we feel cheated, angry, and hurt. We expect some kind of restitution if the relationship is to continue.

Reactions like these tell us that we have a strong, learned sense of what is an appropriate and fair exchange and that this calculation happens automatically and silently. We only "feel" the results in the sense that when things have gone equitably we feel the situation is normal and we are satisfied; when they have been perceived as not equitable we feel that something is wrong and we are dissatisfied; and if we have intended to "profit" from the relationship and succeed, we feel elated.

If interaction crosses status or rank levels, we have additional learned rules. These rules tell us what are the appropriate ways of showing the right amount of *deference* to someone superior to us, as well as how to display the right kind of *demeanor* to someone below us. The subordinate shows deference by standing up when the superior enters a room, asking questions rather than making assertions, taking the appropriate submissive body posture, following orders, and making various gestures of deference such as not interrupting the superior, listening intently, not disagreeing openly, and supporting the superior in public situations.

The superior, in exchange, displays the appropriate demeanor by being in control of the situation, communicating clearly so that instructions or orders can be followed, acting secure, not getting inappropriately anxious or defensive, maintaining the appropriate bearing and not doing things that would be embarrassing to the followers who are identifying with the superior. Subordinates can lose their cool; superiors must remain composed. Subordinates can give in to human foibles and be tactless; superiors must avoid tactlessness in public situations. The higher the rank of the superior, the more the image must fit the stereotype in terms of bearing, dress, and other aspects of public behavior. Thus, high-ranking leaders have to manage their public images very carefully, lest they "disappoint" their subordinates and leave them feeling cheated. We think of private bathrooms for executives as prerequisites of status and forget that one of their more important functions is to provide leaders some space "backstage" to compose themselves for their public appearances and to maintain the mythic image of being superhuman; i.e. not having ordinary bodily needs.

In other words, any time we enter a situation in which we are interacting and communicating with others, we immediately and unconsciously play by the rules that we perceive to govern that particular situation. These are scripts that we have learned from early childhood on by observation, from formal instruction by parents and teachers, from coaching and feedback, and from our own painful learning to decipher what went wrong in situations where our needs were not met or we created offense and made others angry. In summary, one of the major hidden forces that governs human interaction is our tacit sense of what is a just and fair exchange.

Human Exchange as Drama

The rules of interaction and what we regard as fair and equitable do not apply in the same way across all situations and relationships. Rather, we learn early in life to play a variety of roles in a variety of scenes. The particular rules of appropriateness and equity are linked to those roles and scenes. One of the most amazing human capacities is the ability to remember the multiple sets of scripts that apply to the many human dramas we play out. We know how to be a child, a friend, a teacher, a spouse, a subordinate, a boss, a customer, a leader, a parent, a host, a guest, and on and on; our brain sorts these roles instantly as we move among social situations.

Helping as Drama

One of the complexities of consulting and helping derives from the fact that the idea of "helping" is not well defined or scripted in our society. There are many definitions and concepts of what it means to "help." To make matters even more ambiguous, helping is one of those dramas that is defined more by audience response than by the script-writer or lead actor (i.e. the consultant). In other words, help is defined by whether or not the client feels helped, not by whether or not the helper asserts that he or she has provided help. Aspiring helpers must therefore vary their own behavior according to the stream of feedback signals they get from their audiences, the clients, and they must be prepared to rewrite their scripts constantly. Helping involves "audience participation," and the helper needs help from the audience, the client, to figure out how to be helpful.

Managers and consultants may have general principles in mind when they intend to be helpful, but they have to be innovative in applying these principles in a particular situation. Helping is a performance art more akin to improvisational theater than to formal drama; but as in all arts, the aesthetic elements introduced by the individual artist still have to be consistent with basic principles of design, color, and harmony. To pursue the analogy, helping as theater of improvisation requires not only the basic skills of acting and knowing something about audience response but also improvisational skills and spontaneity. As pointed out earlier, the consultant must "go with the flow" but, at the same time, be prepared to "seize targets of opportunity."

If we go beyond these general social definitions and examine what goes on between client and helper over time, we see that the helping process is a complex reciprocal play in which the person seeking help is initially the actor and the potential helper is initially the audience. The client takes the stage and spells out her problem, often in painful detail, while the potential helper listens attentively. Once the client's lines have been delivered, it is expected that the helper will take the stage and deliver some dramatic lines of her own. This is the "role suction" previously identified, which so often tempts us to become instant experts and doctors. The trap is that the client does not know what to expect when we play expert or doctor, and she often does not like the lines we deliver, so she rejects what we have to offer and no help is delivered.

If the helper stays in the process-consultant mode, a different scenario results. Staying in the PC mode is tantamount to refusing to take the stage, assuming instead an off-stage coaching role. The process consultant keeps the client center stage and helps him to continue, thereby "forcing" him or benignly manipulating him into starting to work on his own problem; i.e. write his own script. The helper stays in the audience/coach role, watching with interest and supporting the efforts of the client as actor to solve his own problem. Therefore, one of the critical skills that effective consultants must learn is how to create the right scenes and to manage the dramatic process toward desirable outcomes. And they must do this without violating the cultural rules of interaction described above.[2]

For example, when the client ends her dramatic tale with "What would you do in my situation, Ed?" one of the most helpful things I can say is "Well, that sounds like quite a dilemma; tell me what you have done about it thus far, or what you think you might be able to do." If pressure mounts for me to give new suggestions, I can say, "If I were in your shoes I guess I would consider some of the following alternatives—*x, y, z*—but I am not in your shoes, so how do you think any of those alternatives would work for you?" By giving more than one alternative and reminding the client that what *you* might do might not fit her situation, you keep her on center stage.

---

[2]It is no accident that one of the great consultants of all time, Richard Beckhard, was a stage manager in his early career.

The Sacredness of the Person: The Dynamics of Face Work

One of the most centrally held cultural assumptions is that relationships depend upon mutual cooperation, giving all parties to the relationship as much as possible what they claim to need. Human dramas must come out equitably between actors and audiences, but both parties need some way of measuring "value" in the human interaction so that equity can be judged. Value in the human interaction can be thought of as the amount of status that any given person claims within the boundaries of what externally ascribed social roles and statuses will allow. For example, the manager in a situation can claim more value than the subordinate because society has defined the managerial role as being "superior" to the subordinate role. The manager can therefore interrupt the subordinate and claim attention more easily than the subordinate can interrupt the manager.

Subjectively the claimed value can be thought of as what we mean by self-esteem, the value we put on ourselves in a given situation. When others do not grant us what we claim or when we act in ways that shows others that we claim very little for ourselves, we feel "humiliated" ("they made me feel foolish" or "I made a fool of myself"). Humiliation in sociological terms can be defined as *being shown that one has much less value in a given situation than one had claimed for oneself.* If we humiliate someone, we destroy his sense of his own value, so we should not be surprised at the strong emotional response humiliation generates.

A vivid example of double humiliation resulting from not knowing the local cultural rules occurred when I tried to purchase some stamps at a local small-town post office in Provence. I was patiently standing in line, and just when it was my turn to ask the clerk for stamps, a man came into the post office, walked up to the window, interrupted me, and made a request of his own. I expected the clerk to ignore him and deal with my request, but, to my horror, she gave her complete attention to him and processed his request for several minutes before returning to mine. Needless to say, I felt upset at this seeming violation of the rules, but when I recounted the event to my French colleague later in the day, he smiled and said: "Ed, the situation is even worse than you imagined. By letting this man get the clerk's attention, and by not reasserting your claims, you were demonstrating to everyone in the post office your low sense of self-esteem. If you had put more value on yourself, you would have interrupted the man and forcefully insisted that you be served first." So much for trying to manage a situation effectively in a culture in which the rules of face are slightly different.

The amount of value that can be claimed in any given situation depends upon the institutional conditions, the formal status system, and the motives of the person within a particular role. Audience response then validates or invalidates these claims. "Face" can then be thought of as the social value that an individual implicitly claims in a given situation and role. These claims are communicated early in any given situation through verbal cues. The other persons in the situation, the audience, automatically feel obligated to sustain those claims if at all possible (i.e. help the person "maintain face"). Their willingness and ability to sustain those claims depend upon whether the amount of face claimed falls within the institutionalized limits accorded a given status or role.

To take a common example, if I say to you "Let me tell you a funny thing that happened to me the other day," you will gear yourself up to "pay attention," and you will be prepared to be amused as soon as I let you know through my tone of voice, inflection, or actual words when you are supposed to react. If the incident is interesting and funny, this process plays itself out smoothly and you laugh at the appropriate time. However, if my claim to be able to amuse you is not sustained, if you are in fact bored or offended, then you will find yourself engaged in what Goffman called "face work."

Face work is what we *both* have to do if the claims made cannot be sustained in the short run, because cultural rules dictate that in the larger sense my social self and our relationship must somehow be sustained in spite of the disappointing interaction. Society ultimately depends upon all of us sustaining as much as possible each other's claimed value and minimizing humiliation and the deliberate destruction of self-esteem. The cultural rules therefore dictate that you must pay attention to my boring story anyway and you must smile and laugh appreciatively even when you don't really feel that it is funny. If you were to frown and say out loud that my story was neither interesting nor funny, you have not sustained my claim, and I have, therefore, "lost face." You have told me that at that moment my social value in our relationship was less than I claimed it to be. Cultural rules dictate that you do not do that except under extreme circumstances or if you are deliberately trying to humiliate me. You must pretend to be amused and do your best to help me be what I claim to be. I, on the other hand, will make every effort to be amusing and interesting, to help you sustain my face. Notice that even in situations where I claim much more than is warranted, you will not humiliate me but gradually will learn to avoid me as boring or too arrogant. Deliberate destruction of face is a rare event socially.

Every day we go through literally hundreds of similar situations in which we make claims on one another and sustain claims in our responses to them, even though we may feel that the desired response was not warranted. How often have we said after an encounter that we felt cheated and dishonest, that we did not like something someone did, that they embarrassed themselves and therefore disappointed us, but have carefully concealed these reactions during the encounter. In fact, cultural learning involves the routinization of emotional responses, so that much of face work is automatic for all participants in the social drama—something we call poise, tact, appropriate demeanor, or good manners. What we feel and how we feel is situationally scripted, so that in many situations we do not even feel any conflict between what we are supposed to feel and what we "really" feel.[3]

If people claim more than their status or their ability to deliver warrants (as when we say that someone is "putting on airs" or "presuming too much"), we do not tear them down, destroy their illusions, or in other ways make them lose face. But if someone consistently makes claims that clearly lie outside the boundaries of his status, as does the co-worker who tries to give us orders and "acts as if he is the boss," or the joke teller who is never very funny, we tend to avoid that person and not interact with him at all. We do not usually tell him to his face to "go to hell," at least not in public where his loss of face would be visible and where we would lose face as well, by displaying our own lack of manners or tact. The central point to understand in all of this is that we always try to grant others their claims, and we go to great lengths not only to avoid losing face ourselves but also to keep others from losing face. We are careful not to claim too much in any given situation and to stay within the bounds of our status and roles, so that others will not have to do extreme face work.

The ultimate reason for face work is that unless we can reassure one another daily that our social selves will be acceptable, life

---

[3]A good discussion of these processes can be found in Van Maanen and Kunda (1986).

becomes too unpredictable and dangerous, and society falls apart. The very essence of society is the implicit contract we have with each other to sustain the social selves as best we can. In this sense persons are "sacred objects," and the deliberate destruction of someone's face is equivalent to social murder. If I do that to you, I am licensing you and others to do the same thing to me, and that makes any form of society impossible.

The only condition under which deliberate destruction of face is culturally sanctioned is during the socialization process where selves have to be given up and reconstructed. For example, in moving from one organization to another or one status to another, an individual often suffers deliberate degradation and humiliation in the process of learning a new role.[4] But it is only during the transition that such face destruction occurs, and then usually only at the hands of parents, teachers, coaches, drill sergeants, and other licensed "agents of change." The person being trained to adopt a new role is generally protected during the training period, then some form of "initiation rite" re-establishes the trainee's status and value in the social group. Initiation rites and other formal promotional rituals are society's way of formally and publicly assigning a higher value to an individual.

Face Work in Helping Relationships

What does all of this have to do with consultation and helping? Everything. As pointed out in the chapter on the psychodynamics of the helping relationship, there is nothing more dangerous to the person with a problem than to have a helper humiliate her by signaling in some way or other that the problem is trivial or reflects the person's incompetence or lack of toughness. The person with the problem is exposing her face in admitting a problem. She is saying that she is not as good as she thought she was, and she is thereby making herself vulnerable and claiming less social value than she is actually worth. She feels "one down."

Because of this vulnerability, potential clients often do not reveal their "real" problems, deny that they really have a problem, claim that everything is already under control, and in other ways "test" the willingness of the helper to be really sympathetic and trust-

---

[4]See Schein, 1961, 1978 and Van Maanen & Schein, 1979. Deliberate destruction of self also occurs in certain forms of therapy and in coercive persuasion of the sort experienced by prisoners of war and civilian prisoners during the Chinese communist revolution (Schein, 1961).

worthy in the relationship. As any helper has learned over and over again, only after much listening and being supportive will the real problem surface. From this perspective, the client's response is a normal and expected one, one the helper must be prepared to accept.

If the listener shows impatience, laughs, implies that the client is silly or stupid for not having figured out what to do, or if he gets angry at the client for having the problem, he is, in one way or another, humiliating the client, causing him to lose face. Given the cultural rules of face, he has then given the client license to express the anger caused by his humiliation and loss of face. The client then feels entitled to get back at the helper any way he can. Solving the problem now becomes secondary to gaining revenge and, thereby, re-equilibrating the situation.

None of this is likely to be conscious. Cultural rules are so over-learned and automatically applied that most of the processes described happen outside of awareness. The humiliated client finds the consultant's suggestion silly or off target, or he finds himself telling the consultant all the reasons why the solution will not work, without necessarily recognizing that he is doing this because he is angry at being humiliated and needs to get back at the consultant, not because the recommended solution is wrong.

In the managerial relationship, we have to additionally consider the rules of deference and demeanor. It is easy for superiors to humiliate subordinates, and bosses should not later be surprised at the depth of anger the subordinates may feel toward them. Similarly, subordinates who unwittingly cause their bosses to lose face should not be surprised at the extent of the repercussions in the form of poor assignments, lost promotion opportunities, and verbal abuse to which they may be subjected. One sociological reason why "whistle blowers" are so often punished is that in the process of revealing what may have happened in their organization, they inevitably threaten the face of various superiors. In these cases, the requirements of efficient task performance may run counter to the cultural rules of face maintenance.

Adopting the expert or the doctor role in a helping situation increases the risk that the client will feel humiliated and will lose face. This has happened most in my own experience with diagnoses or prescriptions that turn out to be things the client has already thought of and rejected. The client feels foolish and put down by my suggestions because they imply that the client did not or could not have thought of them himself. It is more helpful to start out in the process consultation mode because it assumes that the client has the capacity to help herself and has probably already thought of some alternatives. If an obvious alternative has not been mentioned, the consultant should ask herself "why not," instead of blurting out that alternative as a possibility. One of the key questions always to ask before offering suggestions or advice is what the client has already tried or thought of herself.

If the helper can get across the message, "Your problem is real, but you can help yourself, and I will help you to help yourself," this is *granting face*, telling the client that he is worth more than he may have claimed. Granting face is sociologically the equivalent of what I called "status equilibration" in Chapter 3. It gets across the message that it is acceptable to have problems. One of the commonest early interventions I find myself using with a new client is to mention some other cases of similar problems that I have encountered, both as a way of testing whether or not I have understood the client and as a way of telling him that his problem is neither unique nor something to be ashamed of. Two case examples illustrate this further.

Face Work in the Allen and Billings Companies

One of the dramatic differences between Ralston, the Allen Company's division manager, and Stone, the Billings Company's founder and president, is their totally different self-presentation. Ralston is a man of great pride. He takes a very paternal role toward his subordinates. He is not easy to confront, because he makes high claims for himself in interpersonal situations and expects considerable amounts of deference. He presents himself as a teacher and communicates this by giving long speeches at department meetings.

If people disagree with him, he goes to great pains to explain his position and to adhere to it. On the surface he espouses participation, but his manner, body language, and style of communication often send signals to his subordinates that his mind is already made up. To challenge him openly, therefore, runs the risk of making him lose face. Consequently, his subordinates "work around him" rather than directly through him, and often are frustrated because they cannot figure out how to get a practical point across when it disagrees with Ralston's position.

The relationship between Ralston and his department heads was viewed by most of them as inequitable and they often felt unfairly treated. They felt that they accepted and met the challenge of Ralston's tough targets but that he did not give them enough credit. Instead of rewarding them and giving them a bit of rest, they felt he kept piling on more new programs. From their point-of-view there was no way to win. They felt that they were always disappointing their leader somehow or other.

Such feelings of inequity and inadequacy are, in the long run, dangerous, so one of the primary goals of the consultation effort in the Allen Co. was to resolve this issue, either by having Ralston demand less or by having him reward success more. I was able to raise these issues with him because he treated me with great respect and deference and frequently asked for help and feedback. Nevertheless, the issues had to be raised in such a way that he always felt valued and appreciated for what he regarded to be his great leadership skill. He only changed his behavior, for example becoming less punitive, when he saw that punitive behavior was not necessary to achieve his goals. He could change some of his behavior if he felt his ego and social worth remained intact, that he was still the great leader he fancied himself to be.

In contrast, Stone, the founder of the Billings Co., presents himself as one of the boys, easy to confront, easy to argue with, ready to get into a scrap with anyone, but always powerful enough by virtue of his position to say, "Enough, I've made my decision." He is able to clearly communicate when he has had enough, though his subordinates sometimes complain that he does not sufficiently explain his decisions once they have been made.

Stone maintains less distance between himself and his subordinates and is willing to spend a lot of time listening to others in meetings. He views himself as a process-oriented manager and always asked me after the meetings whether I had any feedback that would help him to be more effective in that role. Deference rituals were much less visible in the Billings Company, therefore, though there was evidence that there were areas that Stone had declared as undiscussable, so the group never challenged him in those areas.

Because of Stone's self-presentation it was possible to give him quite direct feedback and criticize his behavior. On the other hand, he felt equally free to criticize others, often in public, which changed many of the rules of face work in the meetings. Public humiliation of subordinates was common and became normalized by being rationalized as "not really being humiliation." You could be highly criticized in front of your peers yet not lose status because it meant that Stone cared enough about you to want to improve your performance. It was a much more serious loss of face to be ignored by Stone, to not be valued enough to become a target of criticism!!!

If one attended meetings in both organizations one noticed immediately how much attention was given by group members to the maintenance of each others' face. One mechanism in the Allen Co. was to agree to let disagreements stand. The agreement to disagree rather than to resolve issues became a way to avoid the risk of making someone lose face by forcing him to back down. When the Allen Co.'s department heads met without Ralston they were more confrontive of one another and resolved issues, but they managed face by not going out on a limb. They presented their ideas as trial balloons or asked for recommendations from task forces so that no one's own face was on the line with respect to a given decision. The group had learned how to manage task conflict without its becoming personally threatening to face.

Meetings in the Billings Co., on the other hand, were vivid examples of high human drama, sometimes comedies, sometimes tragedies, but always highly charged. Stone and the key executive vice president were the main actors and the rest of the group was often put into more of an audience role. Confrontation, argument, and putting each other down was the norm, with Stone taking the lead role. Hours would be spent after each meeting trying to decipher the messages and licking wounds. Much of this post-meeting sense making was restoring face that had been lost and rationalizing that the public humiliation was really an attempt by Stone to help them. They didn't like what was going on but did not know how to handle the situation any differently. Stone's strong personality and confrontive style trained the group members as well as me to play by his rules of communication, but the more traditional cultural rules operated in the post-meeting meetings where relationships, face, and status were painstakingly restored.

These two cases illustrate that different groups and organizations may develop quite different mechanisms for maintaining face, but the cultural rules are powerful enough that each group will find some mechanism to survive or they will dissolve. As human actors we cannot survive in scenes in which our claimed value is never sustained. In the end, relationships must be perceived as equitable and just or they will collapse.

Filtering

The cultural rules of interaction explain much of the communality of communication and, in fact, explain how we can communicate with each other at all. They do not, however, explain the variation in communication that we experience all the time. In other words, within the cultural envelope there is room for huge variation in what we say, to whom we say it, the style in which we say it, our accompanying body language, our timing, tone of voice, and our particular choice of words. What accounts for this variation is that each of us has a unique personal history that in effect creates a set of filters for how we communicate to others and how we hear and perceive them. In any given face-to-face encounter both the sender and the receiver automatically and unconsciously use those filters in selecting what they will send and what they will receive. I am not implying conscious censorship, although this occurs also. Rather, I am implying that all of us select what we say, how we say it, and when we say it in terms of a complex set of decision rules that we have learned over a lifetime and that reflect our unique history. Five such filters can be identified.

1. My Self-Image. Both the sender and the receiver have an image or concept of themselves and certain feelings of self-worth or self-esteem. What their self-concept is at any given time and what value they attach to themselves in a given situation will, in part, determine their communication. For example, if I think of myself as an expert in an area and have great confidence in myself (e.g., attach great worth to myself) in a given situation, I am more likely to communicate in the first place, more likely to choose an assertive and telling style of communication rather than a diffident one, less likely to listen to others on that same topic, and more likely to get defensive when someone else contradicts my point. After all, I am the expert. If I am feeling unsure of my status in a given group, I am more likely to remain silent, to ask genuine inquiry questions, and in other ways avoid the possibility of offending someone whose status relative to mine is initially unknown.

2. My Image of the Other Person or Persons. Both the sender and the receiver have an image or concept of the others in the situation and attach certain values to these others as people. These images of the others and the value we are willing to grant them will also, in part, determine our style of communication. For example, if I see the others in the situation as being less expert and of lower status, I am likely to talk "down" to them, to interrupt them when I think they are off target, to listen less for their original points of view and more for whether they are understanding me and/or agreeing with me. If I perceive them to be more expert or of higher status, I will say less, listen harder, and try to figure out how to gain status in the situation. (This, incidentally, may inhibit good listening also, diverting attention from the task to the relationship issue.) Terms such as arrogance or humility as attributes of a person reflect these kinds of self-perceptions and other perceptions.

3. My "Definition of the Situation." Both the sender and the receiver have a certain picture of the situation in which they are jointly operating—the stage, the roles, the nature of the play. Is it a meeting to solve a specific problem? Is it an informal bull session?

Are we here to give the boss a chance to tell us his ideas? Often this process of "defining the situation" is not verbalized until someone raises the question "What are we here for?" or "What is our task?" The definition of the situation goes beyond specifying the goals or task to be achieved. It is the complete set of perceptions pertaining to one's own role and others' roles in the situation, its duration, its boundaries, and the norms that will govern it. Obviously, what we say and how we say it will be largely governed by how we define the situation. One major reason why relationships or groups have communication difficulties is that the participants come with different definitions of the situation and do not discover this or remedy it. A common definition of the situation is a prerequisite for almost any kind of effective group action.

4. My Motives, Feelings, Intentions, Attitudes. Another set of filters on the communication process both for sender and listener are the various needs and motives they bring to the situation, their intentions, and their attitudes toward others. If my needs are to sell a proposal or to influence others, I will communicate differently than I would if I am curious about something and need to get information. If I am trying to influence, I will listen differently to what others say than I would if I am gathering information, and I will listen for different things. For example, if I am trying to influence, I will listen harder for agreement or disagreement than for new ideas. Insofar as communication serves many different functions from meeting needs and self-expression to joint sense-making and influencing others, senders and listeners will use different means for different functions.

5. My Expectations. The final category of psychological factors that create filters is our expectations of ourselves and of others in the situation, based either on actual experience or on preconceptions and stereotypes. If I expect my audience to be slow to understand, I will use simpler words; if I expect them to be receptive, I will talk in a more relaxed way; if I expect them to be critical, I will frame my points carefully and precisely. If I as a listener expect a speaker to be very smart, I may read in too much meaning in the message; if I expect him to be inarticulate or unintelligent, I may fail to hear the good points; if I expect disagreement, I may read hostility into what the speaker says; and if I expect support, I may fail to hear disagreement.

Given all the various filters described, it is not surprising that the communication process between people is fraught with so much difficulty. As I argued in the chapter on the internal ORJI process (Chapter 5), it is these prior expectations that distort our observation and listening skills and expose us to faulty reasoning and inappropriate emotional reactions. When we are in the PC mode we are not immune to the psychological factors described. We will have our own set of filters based upon our needs, expectations, images, and intentions. We are more trained to observe and more conscious of the necessity to observe accurately so we may spot the effects of filters sooner than others in the situation, but *we certainly cannot see the truth in any absolute sense any better than other members can.* It is partly for this reason that we must help the client to make a diagnosis, rather than simply providing our own diagnosis as if it were the absolute truth. Only out of the joint efforts of all the members, can we make a diagnosis that is likely to be near enough to the truth to warrant remedial action.

The Circular Process and Self-Fulfilling Prophecies

The various factors described previously under the category of filtering make it possible for communications to break down in a particularly dangerous manner. If expectations are strong on the part of both the sender and the receiver, it is possible for each to interpret the cues from the other in such a way that both confirm their stereotypes and thus lock each other into roles from which it is difficult to escape. For example, on the basis of previous experience, Person A has a positive self-image, is confident, needs to influence others, and expects to be able to do so. Her communications are therefore assertive, confident, and clear. Her listeners respond to this clarity and assertiveness by paying attention to what she has to say, thus confirming A's image of herself as an influential person. She gains confidence from being listened to and assumes an increasingly strong role in the group.

By contrast, on the basis of *his* previous experience, Person B is not sure of himself, feels a lack of confidence in the presence of several others, is not sure he can influence people even though he would like to, and expects that he will have difficulty establishing himself in the group. His communications are, as a result, hesitant, low key, and diffident, although they may be just as clear as A's. His listeners may well respond to the diffidence and hesitancy by assuming that B does not have much to offer; and they may cease to pay attention to him, thus confirming his own initial impression of himself as having little to contribute. B loses confidence, communicates less and less—further confirming for the others his lack of potential contribution—and gradually assumes the role of a noncontributor.

In both cases, the final outcome is the result of initial expectations that produce a certain communication style, which in turn leads to confirmation of the initial expectations. The danger is that the initial expectations may have little to do with the actual potential contribution of A and B to the group product; yet A will be a high contributor and B will be a low contributor. Only by becoming sensitive to this kind of self-fulfilling prophecy, can the group protect itself from getting a mix of contributions that are unrelated to actual ability.

A key role for the process consultant is to ask herself, when she observes different rates of participation and contribution to the group, whether this accurately reflects ability to contribute or is the result of circular processes of the sort described. If the consultant finds evidence for the latter, she must help the group reassess its own operations, reexamine its stereotypes of who can contribute what, and build norms that permit the low-confidence contributor to gain confidence by being listened to by others. For example, she may repeat B's point herself or redirect the group's attention to B when they gloss over it.

Conclusion

Cultural rules of interaction are the most elusive but, at the same time, potentially the most powerful determinants of whether or not a viable helping relationship will be established. Clients seem to feel best when they feel they have been helped without being put down. Their dignity is intact and, in fact, they feel stronger after the helping process than before. When we consider managers as helpers, this point becomes even clearer. Subordinates consistently prefer a boss who makes them feel that they can solve their own problems, who will coach them and help them but not do it for them. A boss who is too smart and skillful and who always displays his superiority with his subordinates will get results, but he will be resented and, in the end, will have a weaker and dependent organization.

Maintaining one another's face is central to societal functioning. If someone loses face in a relationship, not only does that person feel embarrassed, humiliated, and ultimately vengeful, but the person who caused the loss of face shows himself to be unreliable in the human drama. Someone who cannot be relied on to play his proper role eventually gets ostracized and isolated. Consultants and managers must adhere to these rules and even play an active role in helping others to understand how important they are. They must be positive role models of face work.

Within these cultural rules, helpers must be conscious of their own and others' filters as determinants of communication. The process consultant must become aware of his or her own filters and must attempt to be a role model for the client in minimizing the perceptual biases that occur when we communicate. All of these factors come into play particularly when we use communication as a tool for learning, as will be discussed in the next two chapters.

Exercise 6.1: Testing Cultural Rules of Interaction (20 minutes)

This brief exercise should only be attempted when there is sufficient time to analyze what happened after the formal exercise.

Pick a time when you are having a conversation with a friend or colleague, and decide at some arbitrary point to suspend your own audience role:

1. "Freeze" your facial expression, and keep it for as many seconds as you can stand;
2. Freeze your body posture; e.g., stop nodding your head, cease to lean forward.
3. Fall silent; i.e., stop saying "uh huh" or in other ways acknowledging that the other person is speaking.

You will observe that after only ten to twenty seconds or so that you and the other person both begin to feel uncomfortable, that it is hard to maintain steps 1, 2, and 3, and that the other person stops their story and begins to ask questions such as "Is something wrong?" "What is going on?" and "Are you still there?"

Discuss what feelings were generated by your ceasing to be an active audience, and examine how automatic our playing by the rules of cultural interaction actually is.

Reverse roles to know how it feels to have your audience become nonresponsive.

Part III

Intervention in the Service of Learning

One of the central principles of PC is that everything the consultant does is an intervention. As all consultants recognize, however, the interventions that are designed to build the helping relationship and diagnostic interventions have a somewhat different character than interventions whose function is to stimulate, produce insight, and eventually facilitate changes in behavior, beliefs, and underlying assumptions. Thus far I have emphasized the relationship building and diagnostic interventions in focusing on various forms of active inquiry. We move now to those interventions that are deliberately designed to aid the learning process on the part of the client. These interventions fall into two main categories and will be illustrated in the next several chapters.

One category can broadly be labeled "Deliberate Feedback," things the consultant says or does that are intended to give the client some data on how he or she is coming across to another person. We get feedback all the time in our normal daily routine, some of it by just interpreting the reactions we get from others, but feedback processes that are in the service of learning have the character that the person providing the feedback has been explicitly or implicitly given the license by the client to provide it and is presumed to have the professional competence to provide such feedback in a helpful way. Chapter 7 will be devoted to the dynamics of these more deliberate feedback processes including some simplifying models of interpersonal communication and guidelines for making feedback interventions as helpful as possible.

Another category of deliberate interventions in the service of learning can be labeled "Process Interventions," by which I mean observations, questions, comments, and suggestions dealing with the *processes* that an individual or group is exhibiting in their own efforts to learn. Process interventions cover many kinds of group processes dealing with how a group establishes its identity, manages its boundaries, works on its primary task, and manages its internal inter-personal relationships. I will provide simplifying models of how groups work and examples of the kinds of interventions I have found useful in regard to those processes.

In focusing on processes I am giving less attention to two other possible foci of observation—the content of what is being worked on and the relatively more stable structures that are operating. Commenting first on structures, it has always seemed to me that these reveal themselves naturally as one observes and learns to see processes. In a sense structures can be thought of as processes that recur predictably under certain circumstances and exhibit a degree of stability. The most important category of this kind is what we have come to label organizational culture, the taken for granted tacit assumptions about how group members should perceive, think about, and feel about the events they encounter. Organization charts, reporting relationships, lines of authority, and other links that are ordinarily thought of as "structure" are subsumed under the culture category in that they reflect the prior learning of the group and rest on tacit assumptions that are taken for granted. Of course many of these assumptions operate most powerfully around process itself in that our assumptions about how things should be done are often the most stable elements of how groups work.

What of "content?" As I have watched many groups and organizations in action I have been struck by two recurring phenomena: (1) the processes the group uses reveal more about what is going on than the content; and (2) clients need more help in the process arena. Most of us are fairly well trained in communication and negotiation around content issues. When it comes to processes we are babes in the woods. We don't notice them, we underestimate their effects on the quality of the content discussion, and we have no skills in designing more effective processes. So I will advocate that process events should be our primary focus, without, however, losing sight of what is going on at the content level and what structures are revealed by the process events we observe.

For example, at the content level we have learned to listen to each other, sometimes to repeat points to make sure we have understood them, to negotiate and compromise in order to get resolution. We use process tools such as Agenda Setting, Roberts Rules of Order, Brainstorming, and Consensus Testing to make sure that content issues get handled fairly. We have much less experience with process events such as chronic interruptions, some members using up too much air time, members leaving the room at key times or drifting off the topic of discussion, and so on. Typically we just complain about such events with the general statement of "committees are no good." We do not have the intervention and design skills to remedy these situations.

In terms of structure a dramatic example is the automatic reliance on "majority rule," the tacit assumption that a majority's will should prevail and that the minority should be good scouts and go along, even if the vote was 8 to 7. I have also observed a structural assumption in Western groups that everyone should get their fair share of air time and is obligated to participate, reflected in the chairperson's willingness to call on people. The tacit cultural assumptions are that we have the right to equal air time, that people will prepare for meetings, that chairperson's have the right to call on people, and so on. Such assumptions also tend to arise around the timing of meetings, their length, the kinds of decision processes that will be used, and so on.

In the chapters that follow I have incorporated the simplifying models that have been most useful to me in figuring out what goes on when I participate in and observe a group in an organization going about its work. Chapter 8 deals with group *task* processes, how groups tackle problem solving and decision making. Chapter 9 focuses on the *interpersonal* processes in groups and how groups manage their internal relationships in the service of maintenance and growth. Chapter 10 discusses how various of these processes come together in the concept of *dialogue*, and the role that dialogue can play in facilitating learning.

The reader should view all of these models, the principles, and the suggested techniques of focused deliberate interventions as the building blocks for developing helping relationships in ever more complex situations as larger groups, organizational units, or parts of larger systems such as communities become involved as clients. These concepts and models build on each other so it is important to read first about relationships and groups before trying to understand the complex dynamics of larger systems.

7

Communication and Deliberate Feedback

In Chapter 6 I described the hidden forces that derive from tacit cultural assumptions about face-to-face relationships and personal filters. These tacit assumptions guide and constrain the communication process. But within those limits there is an enormous range of choices in when, to whom, and how people will communicate. Those choices have consequences for how relationships and groups evolve and must, therefore, be understood by consultants, managers, and anyone else who is trying to build and manage helping relationships. In particular, helpers must understand the hidden dynamics in trying to develop communication processes that will enhance *learning* processes. One of the most fundamental of these learning processes is to give and receive *deliberate* feedback. Deliberate feedback is a particular form of altering what might be thought of as the "level" or depth of interpersonal communication, so we will begin by presenting the "Johari Window"[1] as a simplifying model of such levels.

Levels of Communication

As most of us know from observing our own behavior, not only do we tend to react to the manifest content of what another person says to us, but we also interpret various other subtle cues to get at the "real" meaning of the message—body language, tone of voice, inflection, emotional intensity, message form, and timing. The same message carries both a manifest and a latent meaning. Occasionally, these meanings contradict each other. One simple example is the person who issues an invitation with "Come over to our house anytime," but

[1]This analysis is based on the model originally proposed by Joe Luft and Harry Ingram, hence the name "Johari Window."

leaves the invitation sufficiently ambiguous through his tone of voice, that you realize he does not really want you to come and is merely being polite. Sometimes a person displays an emotion and verbally denies it at the same time. In work teams it is not unusual for a person to argue against a proposal because she feels she has to be consistent with a previous position or defend a group she represents, but she argues in a way that lets others know she is privately prepared to be convinced and will go along eventually. Often we say one thing to save face while communicating something else. Double messages do not pose unusual difficulties if the sender is aware of them and can clarify misunderstandings. Greater difficulty arises when a double message reflects a part of the person of which he or she is unaware.

To illustrate, it is useful to think of the person as having several parts, as depicted in Fig. 7.1. The right edge of the window, Quadrants 1 and 3, are the parts of ourselves that we expose to others. The top edge of the window, Quadrants 1 and 2, are the parts of ourselves that we know. Thus Quadrant 1 represents our *open self*, those areas we are aware of and which we are willing to share with others, even strangers. Quadrant 2 represents our *concealed or hidden self*, those parts we consciously and deliberately try to conceal from others. If a group is asked to reveal anonymously some of the things they conceal from others typical responses are areas of insecurity that we are ashamed to admit, feelings and impulses we consider to be antisocial or inconsistent with our self-image, memories of events where we failed or performed badly against our own standards, and—most important—feelings and reactions to other people that we judge as impolite or hurtful to reveal. For example, Jill might think that the boss made a terrible presentation at the key meeting, leading to loss of the sale, but feels she must withhold this reaction and compliment the boss "in order not to hurt his feelings or make him mad." Successful mutual face work requires us to conceal most of our immediate interpersonal reactions so that we can sustain our claimed selves. Deliberate feedback, as we will see, is at the outset a violation of those deeply held cultural rules.

Quadrant 3 in Fig. 7.1, our "*blind area*," refers to those things that we unconsciously conceal from ourselves yet are part of us and are communicated to others. "I am not angry," says the boss in loud tones, purple-faced, as he slams his fist on the table. "These meetings are quite relaxing for me," says the executive as her hand trembles, her voice cracks, and she tries unobtrusively to slip a tranquilizer into her mouth. "I do not care about the opinions of others," says the

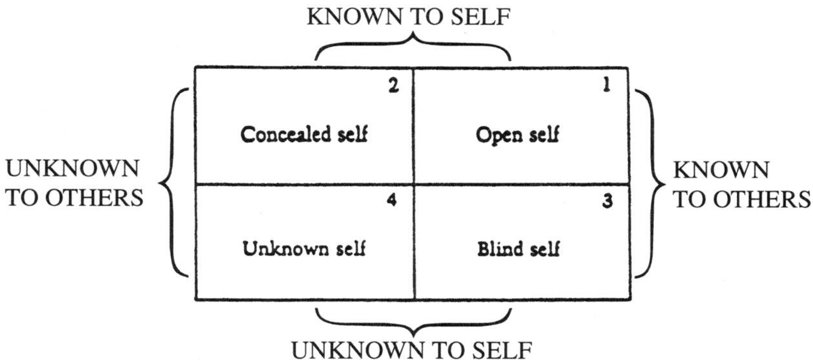

Figure 7.1
THE PARTS OF A PERSON

Adapted from J. Luft, "The Johari Window," *Hum. Rel. Tr. News* 5, 1961, pp. 6–7.

manager, but then gets upset if others do not notice and praise his work.

In the process of growing up, all of us have been rewarded for being certain kinds of people and punished for being other kinds. Much of this learning reflects gender and social class cultural norms. Typically, a young boy learns it is all right to have aggressive feelings but not all right to feel fear or tenderness when with other boys. As a result, the boy begins to reject feelings of tenderness as not being part of himself. He suppresses the feelings or refuses to recognize them as his own when they occur, even though they may be quite visible to other people. How often have we described a gruff, tough man as being really very tender? We see the tender behavior, but the person cannot allow himself to see his own tender side. He must continue to deny it by maintaining a gruff exterior. Some men become aggressive in direct proportion to the amount of tenderness they feel for the people around them.

On the other hand, many young girls learn early in life that certain kinds of aggressive feelings are not appropriate. Even though they experience aggression, they learn to suppress or deny the feeling. If a woman has learned that aggressive behavior is not acceptable, she may become studiously considerate and tender in direct proportion to the amount of aggression she feels but is unwilling to admit to herself. Each of us has feelings and traits that we believe are not part of us; but we are blind to the fact that we communicate many such feelings to others. They may "leak out" and are visible to others.

Quadrant 4 is our truly *unconscious self,* which each of us and others are unaware of. Examples of this self would be deeply repressed feelings and impulses, hidden talents or skills, and untested potentialities. For our purposes, it is important to distinguish three areas of the unconscious self: (1) *repressed knowledge or feelings* based on psychological defenses, (2) *tacit knowledge*, areas of unconsciousness that are easily recovered once we reflect on them (such as cultural assumptions from which we operate); and (3) *hidden potentials*, areas of knowledge, skill, and feeling that are latent because they have never been required or elicited. The presence of this area reveals itself under emotionally extreme circumstances or when we allow ourselves to become genuinely creative. When the consultant attempts to help a client decipher what she is truly after, it is sometimes relevant for the consultant to create conditions where such hidden areas are encouraged to surface. However, when we tamper with the unconscious, we must recognize that we are getting into private areas that we should not explore unless we are clinically trained and the client really wants to get into such matters with the consultant.

The important point to recognize is that the messages we send or do not send reflect the complexity of our psychological make-up. We not only consciously manage our face work, but we leak messages of which we are unaware, and we conceal messages that might be very relevant to others if we chose to reveal them. To examine these dynamics, we can use the Johari Window to illustrate the face-to-face interaction between two people. (Fig. 7.2)

Reciprocal and Interactive Communication Effects

The following model shows four kinds (levels) of communication that occur between two people:

1. Open Communication (Arrow A). Most communication occurs at this first level, between the two open selves. Most popularized analyses of the communication process are confined to this level.

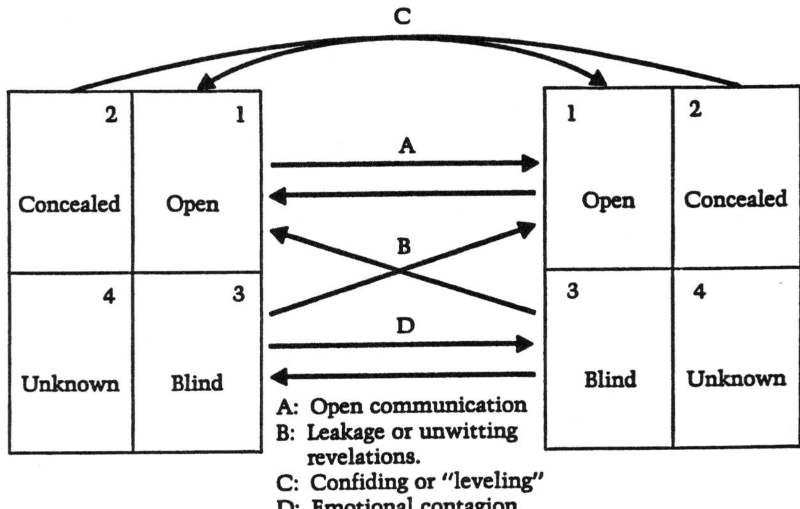

Figure 7.2
TYPES OF MESSAGES IN A TWO-PERSON COMMUNICATION SITUATION

2. Unwitting Communication, Leakage (Arrow B). A second level of communication is the signals or meanings that we pick up from a person's blind self and which he or she is unaware of sending. We can think of this communication as "leakage."

3. Confiding, Leveling (Arrow C). A third level of communication occurs when we deliberately reveal something that we ordinarily conceal. Usually we think of this as "confiding" in someone or "leveling," if we are sharing reactions or feelings generated by immediate events. When we decide to give explicit feedback, we often say "OK, let me *level* with you."

4. Emotional Contagion (Arrow D). This is a less common but no less important level of communication that might best be labeled "emotional contagion." One person influences the feelings of another without either one being consciously aware of the origin of the feeling. Sometimes the feeling aroused in the recipient mirrors that of the sender, as when tension denied by the sender nevertheless makes the receiver tense as well. In other cases, the feeling is different, as when one person's denied but displayed feeling causes tension in the other because he does not know whether he should respond to the manifest level of communication coming from the open self or to the latent level coming from the blind self.

People differ in the degree to which the messages they send from the various parts of their self are consistent and congruent with each other, leading us to judge that some people are more "sincere" than others or more "open." We put a positive value on "congruence" and "openness," and a negative value on "sending mixed signals" or being "closed," such as when we say "I don't like being with Joe because I can never tell what he is thinking." On the other hand, it is the very ambiguity of communication that allows face work to be effective because we can read into the communication what we need to sustain our self. If, as in the story of the emperor's new clothes, we are precise and open in our communication, we would constantly reveal our nakedness to each other, and social life would become impossible.

Deliberate Feedback as a Designed Learning Process

Thus far I have described the status quo, "normal" social relations as dictated by the culture in which we grew up. However, suppose our intention is to learn, to become more congruent, to enlarge our open self, and to become more acquainted with feelings and reactions that we have learned to suppress and deny. The normal process of communication governed by cultural rules of politeness and tact will not provide clear enough feedback to make such learning possible. We may need a more deliberate, designed process of getting feedback on the particular goals we are trying to achieve. That, in turn, involves our blind selves. We need to know whether we are sending signals that might actually be getting in the way of our achieving our goals. We need to know whether, as in the classic Pogo cartoon, "we have met the enemy and he is us." We also need to know more about our unconscious and the tacit assumptions from which we operate. To learn in any of these areas, we need to be able to design processes that make such learning possible, and the consultant plays a critical role in helping to design and create such processes.

Feedback can be thought of as information that informs us of our progress toward some goal that we are trying to achieve. Consequently, *any* information that comes from our physical and interpersonal environment can be feedback. The term has come to mean something more controlled and deliberate, however, as when we say "Give me some feedback" or "Let me give you some feedback." Without this more focused feedback we spend great portions of our lives either guessing at how others perceive us or gossiping behind each others' backs about perceptions and reactions that we will not share with others face to face. Without accurate, focused, deliberate interpersonal feedback, our efforts to learn are reduced to pure trial and error.

Deliberate, focused feedback can be a powerful source of influence between people, especially between superiors and subordinates in a performance appraisal situation or between team members trying to become more effective. The value of the Johari Window as a simplifying model now becomes clear in that it shows how learning through deliberate feedback hinges on a "collusion" between the parties to the learning process. One person cannot get precise feedback on his blind areas without another person being willing to reveal what she ordinarily conceals. As the saying goes, "It takes two to see one." With or without the help of the consultant, two or more people trying to give each other deliberate feedback must first find a way to *suspend the cultural rules of face work* in order to make it possible to reveal *safely* what we ordinarily conceal. Such revelation or "leveling" with each other is a dangerous process. For example, I might hear things that really threaten my self-image. You might unwittingly be hostile or punishing and cause me to want to retaliate, resulting in a damaged relationship. To make it psychologically safe to give each other deliberate feedback, we need to establish new norms that make it OK to say things that ordinarily would not and should not be said. A critical role for the helper in this process is to insure that such norms are created and enforced.

From the point-of-view of the *receiver* of feedback, the critical question is:

"How can I insure that what you will tell me about myself and how I come across will be *truthful*, guided by *sincere motives* to help me, and *relevant* to what I am trying to learn?"

From the point of view of the *giver* of feedback, the critical question is:

"How can I insure that you will *hear me,* will *take seriously* what I have to tell you, and continue to see me as being *helpful* rather than punishing?"

The giver does not want to be the messenger who is shot if the message is not perceived as helpful. In other words, the two parties who engage in a designed feedback process must trust each other; each must believe that the other is trying to be helpful, even if the content of the message is hurtful in the sense of challenging the receiver's self-image. Such trust implies not only that the motives of the giver and receiver are benign, but that the *capacity to observe and communicate clearly is also present.* Feedback from someone who does not accurately perceive how I behave and/or who cannot communicate what he perceives will be of little help to me.

The consultant/helper can play a critical role in facilitating such learning by (1) helping clients to understand the dynamics of the feedback process, (2) training clients to give and receive feedback, and (3) being a role model of how to manage this process so that face is not threatened or lost. The case at the end of this chapter illustrates how delicate this process needs to be.

Setting the Stage for Deliberate Feedback

For deliberate feedback to be possible, a setting has to be created in which the participants can temporarily suspend some of the cultural rules of interaction. Though this can be done by the participants themselves if they have sufficient insight, the more typical situation would require the consultant/helper to play an active role in setting the stage. The first step is to make the participants aware of the Johari Window model and the cultural model that highlights how the rules of interaction are linked to particular situations. Once this is understood in principle, the participants will have to "feel" their way into a trusting situation by taking small steps and evaluating them. The new norms will be built out of a series of small successes.

The next step is for the helper to suggest some guidelines and offer some training to avoid common pitfalls. For our purposes here, it will be useful to analyze such pitfalls primarily in the boss–subordinate relationship because that is the most difficult to manage effectively. It is in the context of performance appraisal that deliberate feedback becomes most delicate, because it is in this setting that the stakes are highest. Not only do we put a high value on our own performance, but the judgment of our performance by others directly impacts our economic well being. If our superiors, peers, or subordinates judge our performance to be lower than expected or needed, it becomes critical to find out what is lacking; i.e., to get valid, useful feedback that would allow us to improve. It falls to the boss in such situations to be the helper/consultant, to set the stage, and to create the climate in which cultural norms can be safely suspended. But equally, it falls to the subordinate to seek deliberate feedback when the routine signals are unclear. If *both* are motivated, there is some possibility of creating a conversation from which learning through deliberate feedback occurs.

Once the stage is set, there are still a number of principles which insure that the threat to face will be minimized and communication clarity will be maximized. Because of the dynamics of the ORJI process and all of the filters that operate in communication, extra care must be taken by both giver and receiver to insure that the right message gets across. The guidelines or principles described below are designed to insure such clarity. They are stated primarily in terms of the superior–subordinate relationship but are applicable in all helping relationships.

Principles and Guidelines for Deliberate Feedback

Principle 1: The Giver and Receiver Must Have Consensus on the Receiver's Goals.

Focused feedback is information that tells the receiver he is on target relative to some *goal* he is trying to achieve. Feedback always implies some goals on the part of the receiver. Therefore, the first and most important pitfall is failing to agree on goals to be achieved and/or performance standards to be met. If the boss and the subordinate disagree on goals and performance standards, or if they are not clear, corrective information from the boss may be perceived as irrelevant criticism by the subordinate.

What this principle implies is that before any deliberate feedback is delivered, the giver and receiver need to have a conversation about the goals the receiver is trying to achieve. As an example, it does me little good to hear from a well-meaning colleague that my lecture was too long and detailed, when my goal was to get through a batch of material that was two lectures compressed into one. To give an example from sports—it does me very little good to have my tennis instructor point out the flaws in my backhand when my goal was to improve my footwork. A good coach will typically ask the trainee "What do you want to work on today?" before launching into corrective feedback.

The same logic applies in the helping relationship between consultant and client. It is very tempting for the consultant to make a unilateral decision to give deliberate feedback to a client. However, this is highly dangerous unless the two parties have agreed on the client's goals. If I feel that I have some crucial feedback to give, I must first broach the question of where the conversation is headed and what the client is trying to achieve. Only if my feedback fits into that scenario should I feel free to offer it.

Principle 2: The Giver Should Emphasize Description and Appreciation.

Feedback can emphasize (1) *positive* things the subordinate did well, (2) *descriptive* and *nonevaluative* information focused only on things the subordinate actually did, or (3) *negative* things the subordinate did not do well. Most learning theory has shown that the consequences of the three types of information are different. Positive feedback is easiest to learn from and most pleasant, in that it guides future behavior directly into more of what is already effective. Positive feedback and appreciation of things well done fits our personal need to maintain a high level of self-esteem.

Descriptive neutral feedback can be effective if the subordinate has her own clear standards and only needs to know *what* she was observed to have done. In areas where people are very sensitive and ego-involved, this may be the only kind of information they can accept. Descriptive feedback also forces the giver to clarify the basis of her evaluations and focus on behavior that may be more malleable.

Negative feedback is often necessary in order to ensure that certain kinds of behavior will not be repeated, but it is also the most problematic because it is likely to arouse defensiveness, be denied or not heard, and rejected in other ways. Furthermore, negative feedback does not offer any guidance on what the person should do and hence does not provide a positive learning direction.

A common pitfall in the feedback process is overreliance on negative feedback and insufficient descriptive and positive appreciative feedback. We tend to link deliberate feedback with the concept of "constructive *criticism*" and forget that it is even more important to learn from what one does well. Appreciation and positive feedback also insure that the receiver can save face. This principle has led to the "sandwich" technique of performance appraisal—say something positive, slip in the constructive criticism as the meat, and finish with something else that is positive. What this technique overlooks is that the positive elements are often more "meaty" than the criticism.

Principle 3: The Giver Should Be Concrete and Specific.

Feedback is a communication process subject to all of the pitfalls of communication previously outlined. Basic lack of clarity in the feedback message or semantic confusion (especially when personality traits are involved) are therefore potential problems. Several examples follow.

"You are too aggressive" (negative, vague, general) vs. "I have observed you shouting other people down when they are trying to express their own views" (descriptive, precise, specific).

"You don't handle your people well" (negative, general) vs. "You don't involve your subordinates in making decisions, and you don't give them a chance to express their own views" (negative, specific) or "I have noticed that your people are more productive when you involve them in decisions and listen to their points-of-view (positive, specific).

"You need to show more initiative" (negative, general) vs. "Instead of waiting for me to discover that your costs are overrunning, why don't you set up your own systems for finding this out and correct it before it goes too far" (neutral, specific).

The key to semantic clarity is specificity. The more general the comment, whether positive or negative, the more likely it is to be misunderstood. The more the feedback can be anchored in behavior *that both the giver and receiver have observed,* the less likely it is to be misunderstood. Another way of saying this is that feedback should deal primarily with *malleable* behavior so that the receiver can do something about what he has been told. On the other hand, if some stable characteristic of the person prevents him from attaining goals he desires, it may on occasion be necessary for someone to tell him this rather than allowing him to live with illusions and unrealistic expectations.

Principle 4: Both Giver and Receiver Must Have Constructive Motives.

Another problem with deliberate feedback has to do with the perceived motivation of the feedback giver and receiver. If the recipient believes that the giver is genuinely interested in helping, she is more likely to listen and pay attention than if she doubts or mistrusts the giver's motives. We have all had the experience of feeling angry with someone and, as a way of expressing the anger, saying, "Let me give you some feedback." Needless to say, the receiver senses that the giver's needs are the ones being served.

Lack of clarity about the receiver's motives is equally a potential problem. What incentive is there for the giver to make the effort if she believes that the receiver is not listening, only wants reassurance, or in some other way signals lack of motivation to learn from the feedback? Again, the following examples will clarify what is involved.

"You should motivate your subordinates to control their costs more because this quarter we have again gone beyond our budget" (the boss wants the subordinate to improve the performance of the next layer down, but the subordinate feels that the boss is only working his own financial needs) vs. "Basically the operation is going well, but I continue to worry about the fact that we are again overrunning our budget. What suggestions do you have for getting your subordinates to be more cost-conscious?" (the boss is appreciative, makes his own feelings clear, and focuses on the specific issue with a specific question).

"I think you need to learn to handle customers better" (the boss may perceive the subordinate to be a person of high potential who has to overcome only one area of weakness, but the subordinate may perceive herself to be generally failing and therefore become defensive) vs. "You are already very effective and could improve that effectiveness even more if you concentrated on learning how to handle customers better" (the boss makes clear her motive to make already good performance even better).

"I could get you only a 2 percent raise this year because things are generally lean in the company" (the boss is trying to be truthful but is vague; the subordinate may conclude that he is being subtly told that he is only an average performer and become demoralized) vs. "Your performance overall was excellent this last year, and I wish I could reward it with money, but the company has had a generally lean year, so no one got more than a 2 percent raise" (the boss is being specific, puts the subordinate performance into the proper context, and expresses appreciation).

Probably the most difficult aspect of operating by this principle is for the two parties to actually be in touch with their own motives and feelings. As the ORJI cycle highlights, it is very easy to go from an observation to a judgment without noticing or reflecting on the feelings involved and the motive such feelings may have triggered.

Principle 5: Don't Withhold Negative Feedback If It Is Relevant.

A major problem in giving feedback is the natural tendency to avoid being critical because criticism so often produces defensiveness and other unpleasant reactions. Critical comments are denied or not heard at all, thus making all of the effort to give negative feedback seemingly a waste of time. But if the boss really has a negative evaluation that influences her handling of the subordinate, she is putting the subordinate into a position of having to guess why there have been no promotions, good raises, or good assignments for him.

The solution here, as in the previous scenarios, is to avoid vague generalities and focus on clear, specific behavioral examples of what led to the negative evaluation. For example, I can accept criticism of some specific behavior in a specific situation, but I find it much harder to accept criticism of my traits and more general characteristics. If my behavior is being criticized, I can assess for myself how much of it is due to the immediate circumstances and learn how to avoid such circumstances, or, if I conclude that it is due to my personal traits, I can decide whether to try to change them or whether I am fundamentally mismatched with the job. But that has to be *my* decision, based on clear feedback.

If the giver of feedback criticizes my traits or personality, my self-image and self-esteem become involved, and I cannot readily change general parts of my personality. Hence I will resist or deny the criticism. On the other hand, if the negative feedback deals with some concrete behavior that both the giver and receiver have witnessed, the giver can express his own feelings about the behavior and his evaluation of it, and the receiver can avoid ego involvement. In other words, if my boss is angry at *me*, this may be a problem for me, but if he is angry at something specific that I *did*, I may get some new insights from that feedback. Some examples of how to give negative criticisms using these guidelines follow.

"We need more team players at higher levels in this company, and your performance so far has made me doubt whether you want to be or can be enough of a team player" (negative, general, and attributes motives and capacities to the receiver) vs. "My problem in seeing you move ahead into higher levels of this company is that whenever you get into a group, you immediately seem to want to take over, like in the XYZ committee. And when you were on the ABC task force, the group never made its best possible contribution because your loyalty to your department made the discussions into win–lose debates. When I see you putting down others that way, it makes me angry, and I worry about whether or not you can learn enough new behaviors to move ahead in the company" (negative and judgmental, but specific so that the basis of the boss's anger is clear).

"You really lack initiative; you are just not aggressive enough for this kind of work" (deals with general traits that may be hard to change and gives no specific data on what the boss means by initiative or aggressiveness) vs. "Several things have concerned me about your performance this past year. When we got stuck on the ABC project, you seemed willing to let matters drift instead of coming up with some proposals for how to confront the problems and move forward. When the other division challenged the direction you were going, you backed off instead of showing them why your solution was the right one. I have seen both of these patterns on other projects and am concerned about the lack of initiative and aggressiveness that is implied by such behavior" (keeps the general attributes, but gives the behavioral data that led to them).

"You really blew it at the last sales meeting; we almost had it sewed up until you stuck in your oar and made the client back off" (evaluates the whole person based on one observation) vs. "When you brought up that XYZ issue at the last sales meeting, I thought you really blew it; we almost had it sewed up until your comments were made, and they seemed to make the client back off" (the emphasis is shifted to the person's behavior, and the giver softens his evaluation by making it his own opinion rather than an absolute judgment).

In the preceding examples, the giver did make evaluative comments, but they were directed at specific behaviors instead of at general traits or the total person. When goals and standards are clear and have been agreed to, such evaluations can be helpful. But if agreement does not exist, descriptive feedback will work better. The giver and receiver can then jointly evaluate the behavior. In either case, specificity is the key. The more general the evaluation, the more likely it is to be misunderstood, resisted, denied, and to trigger defensive behavior.

Principle 6: The Giver Should Own His Observations, Feelings, and Judgments.

There are two important implications of this principle. In terms of the ORJI cycle, the closer the feedback is to the actual observation, the more likely it is to be heard and accepted because the receiver may have observed the same behavior. Furthermore, feedback of the emotional reaction is more likely to be accepted than feedback of the judgment. Saying that your behavior made me angry, anxious, or discouraged is more likely to be heard than the judgment that your behavior was inappropriate or "bad." The same logic applies for positive feedback. Saying that some of your behavior delighted me or made me proud is far more valuable to the learning process than just saying "You did a good job."

The second implication is that the giver should consciously attribute the observations, emotional reactions, and judgments to herself and not allow them to become vague generalizations. The implications are subtle in that they focus on a small difference in feedback behavior. I can say "You are great" (or "You are no good") which makes my judgment a universal statement, or I can say "*I think* you are great" (or "*I think* you are no good"). In trying to be more specific, I can say "When you challenged the client you blew it" or I can say "When you challenged the client *it made me feel angry* because it seemed like he started to back off; *I really felt you had blown it at that point*."

It is important for the giver to own the feedback in order to make it discussible and a source of potential learning. Impersonal generalities are demeaning because they remove the rationalization that it may be just the giver's idiosyncratic reaction. Generalities imply that the giver has committed herself to a final judgment that cannot be challenged or explored. A general judgment also implies that it has been tested with others and is a final conclusion rather than the giver's immediate reaction.

Principle 7: Feedback Should Be Timed to When the Receiver and Giver Are Ready.

I previously articulated the principle "Timing is Crucial" in terms of effective intervention. Timing is also crucial in terms of making deliberate feedback an effective process. By what criteria can we determine when the timing is right for such feedback? By far the most important criterion is the *receiver's readiness or motivation to learn*. If that is present, he can pretty well tell the giver when to have the feedback discussion. If the motivation is not there, the giver is in the awkward (but sometimes necessary) position of having to create a setting so that such deliberate feedback can be given. The boss can say that a feedback discussion on performance is needed within a given period of time, while leaving it up to the subordinate to determine just when and where to have it.

A second criterion is that the *giver* must be ready. That usually means thinking through, at a specific behavioral level, the bases for the giver's reactions, feelings, and judgments, and then preparing psychologically to provide helpful information in a helpful way. Such preparation may involve training in how to give deliberate feedback and carefully thinking through the kinds of principles stated here. It is not likely to be effective to have the subordinate walk in unannounced and demand feedback.

A third criterion is that both parties must have *agreed on the goals* and worked on building some preliminary *norms of trusting each other*. In other words, the timing hinges on proper stage setting, which in turn hinges on some honest reflection by both giver and receiver on their motives and capacities. Even if the boss dictates that a performance review is needed, he can begin the meeting by asking the subordinate to review what her goals have been over the last several weeks or months and then steering the feedback discussion so that it becomes relevant to those goals. If it should happen that the subordinate's goals are out of line with what the boss expected, the two persons must reach consensus on goals before deliberate feedback can be given. Goal consensus is a minimum condition for beginning to build mutual trust.

A fourth criterion of timing is that the feedback must be close enough in time to the relevant events to enable the receiver to remember the events and relate them to himself. If the feedback comes too long after the event, the receiver may not remember the incident and thus deny it. If the feedback comes too soon after the event, the receiver may still be on an emotional high and not be able to hear the feedback if it is negative. For example, my colleagues sometimes want to give me feedback about a class session right after the session, because that is when the behavior is most visible. I usually have a hard time dealing with such feedback, however, because I have not yet processed my own reactions to the event. Until I have assessed whether or not I met my own goals for the session, I cannot really take in new data that reflect someone else's goals for my session.

Summary and Conclusions

In summarizing the seven principles, the most important thing to note is that all seven must be considered together for deliberate feedback to be effective in stimulating and facilitating learning. Goals must be clear and agreed to, the emphasis should be on description and appreciation, the feedback should be as concrete and specific as possible, both giver and receiver must have constructive motives, criticism should not be avoided if it is specific and focused on behavior, the giver should own his own feelings and reactions rather than resorting to impersonal generalities, and both giver and receiver should be psychologically ready for a feedback discussion.

To recapitulate, whether we are considering the boss doing performance appraisal or the consultant inquiring about a client's situation, everything the helper does is de facto an intervention. The consultant is providing feedback all the time, even when she is being silent. The choice, then, is when, how, and in what form to escalate to *deliberate* feedback. When and how is it appropriate to interrupt the "normal" flow of inquiry and set the stage for a different level of communication based on the suspension of some of our norms of face work? Or, to put the question another way in terms of the forms of inquiry discussed in Chapter 3, when is it appropriate to switch from pure or diagnostic inquiry to confrontive inquiry because confrontive inquiry is a form of deliberate feedback, albeit delivered in a very low-key manner?

There is no clear and simple answer to this question. As the relationship between consultant and client evolves, the consultant must be perpetually diagnosing the situation internally and calibrating how "ready" the client is for more confrontive kinds of interventions. Clearly, one cue is when the client asks for direct input. Another cue is when there are enough data on the table, so to speak, to give the consultant confidence that the client can see for herself what may be going on. The more the consultant can link the feedback to behavior that *both* have witnessed, the more likely it is that the feedback will be accepted and learned from. In either case, one must presume that the conversation between consultant and client has reached the level where there is a fairly good mutual understanding of each other's assumptions and goals.

At the beginning of the chapter I summarized a model of two-person communication that reveals why deliberate feedback is necessary and yet difficult. We need such feedback in order to remove some of our blind spots, to learn how we impact others, and to discover what signals we send that we may not even be aware of. At the same time, cultural rules dictate that the other person will conceal reactions to the signals we send. The dilemma of creating a deliberate feedback situation, then, is for the two parties to find a way to suspend the cultural norms of face work sufficiently to allow opening up some of what we conceal. It takes both parties to create such new norms, and it implies a high level of mutual trust. Deliberate feedback is, therefore, a type of communication from which much can be learned, but it must be carefully managed.

Case 7.1: Designed Feedback Processes in the Billings Company

Setting the stage for feedback is not always a carefully planned process. I was meeting with the top management committee of the Billings Company on a regular monthly basis, usually for one or two days at a time to discuss major strategic and operational issues in an "off-site" setting. Stone, the founder and CEO, usually dominated the agenda of these meetings by introducing topics that he wanted to discuss even if they were not on the formal agenda. In the middle of the first day of one of these meetings, he announced that he thought it would be a good idea if the eight members of the group gave each other some feedback on how they were doing their job and how they could improve their situations.

The moment Stone made his suggestion, the tension in the room shot up because of the mutual recognition that he was expecting to get feedback as well. Given his personality and emotionality group members could not calibrate how safe it would be to tell him anything at all, much less anything that was critical. My own tension shot up when Stone turned to me and said: "Ed, with your experience in training groups, why don't you suggest how we should go about giving each other feedback." It was said in a tone that would not have made it easy to suggest postponing the whole exercise, so I felt on the hook to suggest something that would be "safe."

In those moments when the consultant is "on the hook," one hopes one's intuition will come through. My main concern was that the group not get into recriminations about <u>past</u> *behavior so I suggested that the best way to go through the exercise was to take each person at a time and discuss how his particular job could be performed more effectively in the* <u>future</u>, *i.e. in the next 12 months, to fit best into the company's overall strategy. The logic to suggesting "future" behavior was that criticism could be kept implicit, allowing face saving. If the Finance VP was told "Joe, in the next twelve months we think you should work more closely with the product lines to help them manage their inventories," this statement would enable them to avoid saying bluntly what they felt—"Joe, you really screwed us up last year by revealing all those audits of inventory problems before we had a chance to fix them." Joe had been too much of a cop and not enough of a helper and they resented it, but Joe could not have accepted that message directly.*

As each member of the group had his "turn in the barrel," I observed the careful and sensitive way in which negative critical remarks were made through the medium of suggestions for the future. This process was especially crucial in talking to Stone himself. He insisted on his turn in the barrel and listened carefully, especially to comments about being less critical of subordinates in public arenas at future meetings. We managed to get through several hours of what turned into a constructive session of "role negotiation," in which was buried an enormous amount of personal feedback, without having to confront anyone face-to-face with critical comments.

Though it is not applicable to every situation, an important lesson from this experience was how much useful feedback can be gotten across in a "planning" context. It is not necessary to be explicit about the past. Sometimes it is easier to get the message across in planning for the future.

Exercise 7.1: What Is in the Parts of the Johari Window? (30 minutes)

This exercise works best in a group setting where there are at least 15 or more participants.

1. Following a brief presentation of the Johari Window, ask each participant to take out two blank sheets of paper. Do not put names on the paper.
2. On sheet one, write one or more things that you are aware of in yourself but deliberately and consciously conceal from others. Since the sheets are anonymous, feel free to write whatever you feel like. (Concealed self)
3. On the second sheet, write down one or more things that you see in others that you are pretty sure they do not realize that they are communicating. (Blind self)
4. Collect all the sheets, being careful to keep all the sheet one's and sheet two's in separate piles.
5. Shuffle each pile so that the individual sheets cannot be linked to particular people.
6. Read out loud to the entire group a sample of what they typically conceal from others (sheet one). If you have enough examples, you can write them on a board and classify them by type of issue. Encourage the group to analyze with you to get a feel for what we tend to conceal.
7. Read out loud to the entire group a sample of what we typically see in others that they do not realize they are communicating (sheet two). Classify these as well.
8. Analyze the relationship between the two lists. Are they completely different kinds of items? Are there areas where we think we conceal but actually the feeling or information "leaks" out and others see it? What would be the pro's and

con's of being more open in revealing what we conceal or in giving feedback to others on their blind spots?

9. Help the group to see the connection that person 1 cannot remove blind spots unless person 2 reveals something that is ordinarily concealed, i.e. "it takes two to see one."

Exercise 7.2: Practicing Deliberate Feedback

Pair up with one other participant, preferably someone you have not worked with closely. Each of the following parts of the exercise should take no more than 10 to 15 minutes.

Part 1. Freely converse with your partner about some events that you both experienced in the last hour or so. At the end of five minutes, stop the conversation and each take a turn giving deliberate feedback to the other person at a purely *descriptive,* behavioral level. What did each of you observe in the other? Try to be neutral, descriptive, and focus as much as possible on behavioral details (Take no more than five minutes each).

Part 2. Using the last 15 minutes worth of conversation, now shift to giving each other deliberate feedback in terms of the *feelings* which were elicited in you during those last 15 minutes. What feelings did each of you observe in yourself? (Take no more than five minutes each.)

Part 3. Using the last 25 minutes as your conversational base, now shift to giving each other deliberate feedback around the *judgments* and *evaluations* you made during the last 25 minutes (Take no more than five minutes each).

Part 4. Share with each other your observations and reactions during each of the first three parts. In what way did the three parts differ in what you observed in yourself? What have you learned from the experience about deliberate feedback? Were you able to share reactions that you ordinarily conceal? What made it possible to do so? How did the other person react to such revelations? (25 minutes)

8

Facilitative Process Interventions: Task Processes in Groups

This chapter will develop the concept of *facilitative process intervention* to supplement the various diagnostic interventions that were reviewed in the earlier chapters. In this chapter the focus will also shift from the two-person relationship to larger meetings and groups in which the consultant has to deal with larger client systems. The overarching design criterion for interventions remains the same—that any and all interventions should try to be helpful, in other words, should facilitate what the client is trying to do. But the implementation of this principle in meetings and groups becomes more complicated. Diagnostic inquiry and giving deliberate feedback clearly would qualify as potentially facilitative interventions. But there is a whole range of other interventions that occur spontaneously when one is in a conversation or in a meeting. We therefore need a typology and some simplifying models for (1) deciding what to focus on in the plethora of things that one can observe in a meeting, and (2) deciding what kinds of intervention will be more or less facilitative.

The primary focus will be on process. Consultant/helpers must recognize that "process," i.e. *how* things are said and done, is as or more important than content, i.e. *what* is said and done. Yet most of us are not very familiar with process as a concept or focus of attention. We tend to take process for granted instead of thinking of it as something to be managed. And we do not have the conceptual tools for deciding how to use process in the service of helping and learning. In this chapter I will first lay out some general categories for thinking about process, provide some simplifying models for some of the more salient processes that one observes in groups, and then suggest how the helper/consultant can focus her interventions constructively to help clients learn to manage their own processes better.

What Is Process?

In its broadest sense, "process" refers to how things are done rather than what is done. If I am crossing the street, that is *what* I am doing; the process is *how* I am crossing—am I walking, running, dodging cars, or asking someone to help me across because I feel dizzy? If I am talking to another person, that is *what* I am doing, but I may be looking at her, looking at the ground, mumbling or raising my voice, gesturing or standing very still, all of which is *how* I am doing the talking. But because process is everywhere and involves everything we do, how do we become aware of "it" and the consequences of different kinds of processes that we may be using unconsciously? How does a consultant/helper know what to focus on when trying to intervene to improve a situation and to stimulate learning in the client? The earlier chapters on the helping relationship and active inquiry describe a variety of processes that occur in the face-to-face situation. It remains now to extend this analysis to the processes that occur when the consultant is working with two or more people in various kinds of meetings and group events.

Imagine that you have been invited to a staff meeting to see if you can be helpful in making that group more effective. You may have been labeled the "facilitator" but what does that mean in terms of where you should focus your interventions, all the time being mindful of the fact that sitting quietly and observing is also an intervention with consequences? If you are the manager who has called the meeting, imagine yourself trying to make the meeting as effective as possible. What should you be paying attention to and what kinds of interventions should you be considering beyond the traditional focus on the agenda and the content of what members say? Table 8.1 presents a set of general categories of observable events that the consultant could consider as possible foci of attention.

The cells in Table 8.1 overlap and, in reality, the distinctions are not as clear-cut as the descriptions imply, but we need simplifying models if we are to make any sense at all of the complex data that typically confront us in human situations. All groups, and I am including a two-person relationship in this definition, always have three fundamental issues to deal with: (1) How to manage their boundaries, defining who is in and who is out and how to maintain their identity; (2) How to

Table 8.1
POSSIBLE AREAS OF OBSERVATION AND INTERVENTION

	Group boundary management	Group task accomplishment	Interpersonal and group management
Content	(1) Who is in and who is out	(2) Agenda	(3) Member feeling toward each other
Process	(4) Processes of boundary management	(5) Problem solving and decision making	(6) Interpersonal processes
Structure	(7) Recurring processes for maintaining boundaries	(8) Recurring task processes, organization structure	(9) Formal rules in relation to authority and intimacy

survive in their external environment by fulfilling their function or primary task; and (3) How to build and maintain themselves as functioning entities by managing their internal interpersonal relationships. These three basic issues are represented across the top of the table.

If the group or relationship has existed for any length of time, one can observe each of the above issues, how the group functions at three levels: (1) The *content* of what it works on; (2) What kinds of *processes* it uses to conduct its affairs; and (3) What *structures* are in place in the sense of stable, recurring ways or operating. These three foci of observation are represented along the side of the table. The consultant then must decide which process issues to focus on and when to shift to content or structure. In other words, which of the cells are strategically and tactically the optimum place to focus his observations and make interventions? Which intervention focus is likely to be the most facilitative? We will begin with the *task* focus, the middle column, and a *content* focus inasmuch as that is most likely the reason why the consultant was called in initially.

Task Content—Agenda Management (Cell 2)

The most obvious thing to focus on in any meeting or conversation is why the group is there in the first place. What is its primary task or function? What are the goals of the meeting? Why does the group exist at all? Every group or organization has an ultimate function, a reason for existence, a mission, and its goals and tasks derive from that ultimate function. However, a group may not be aware of its ultimate mission or members may not agree on its goals. In fact, one of the main functions of the consultant may be to help the group to understand its task and function.

The most observable aspect of task content is the actual subject matter that the group talks about or works on, what would typically be labeled its formal agenda. If the group has a secretary and keeps minutes, the content of the discussion is what will appear in the minutes. The consultant can keep close tabs on the task content to make sure that it stays "on track." I often find myself at the beginning of a meeting asking "What are we trying to do?" or "What is our goal for today?" or "What do we want to have accomplished by noon today?" (or whenever the group is scheduled to disband). Sometimes the consultant even creates the agenda if she has interviewed the participants and been asked to summarize what is collectively on their mind, or if she has been called in to make an educational intervention, to present some concepts, or conduct a focused exercise.

The potential importance of managing the agenda was revealed to me when I made the unwitting intervention in one of the early meetings of the Billings Co. (see p. 222):

Recall that the group had a written agenda, usually consisting of 10 or more bullet-type items, and would start by going through the agenda one item at a time. By the end of the two-hour meeting, they would typically finish half of the agenda or less and then express frustration that they had not accomplished more. I also noticed that the sequence of items often did not make much sense. My choice was to give feedback to the group on what I was observing or, as I chose to do, to access my ignorance and ask sincerely "How is this agenda produced?"

The first reaction in the group was to look confused, as if no one knew the answer. Then the president said that his administrative secretary produced the agenda and had it ready for each meeting. The group called Martha into the room and learned that people phoned in items or dropped by to request being on the agenda and that she listed them in the order in which they came in.

No sooner had the group heard this than they realized the absurdity of this situation and decided on the spot to keep the system that Martha had, but to process the agenda at the beginning of each meeting in order to cluster items that belonged together and to arrange them in order of priority. This arranging revealed that there were basically two types of items—"fire-fighting"–type immediate decision items, and longer-range planning items. We collectively decided that the fire-fighting items should be placed in priority order by the whole group and that the planning items should not even be attempted in a two-hour Friday afternoon meeting.

Instead, the group decided that once a month the whole group should go off-site and spend a whole day or two wrestling with those longer-range items. Over a period of years these longer off-site meetings became a regular pattern and were institutionalized as a regular part of running the company. I ended up playing an expert role in the design of these longer meetings since I had more experience with that type of meeting. Eventually they evolved into quarterly or semi-annual meetings that lasted two or three days and enabled the group to dig deeply into strategic issues that concerned the growth of the company. All of this resulted from an innocent question about the agenda.

On the surface it appeared that the group was just learning to be more efficient. In reality, all of this agenda processing was forcing the group to confront what its basic primary task really was, and how to design a pattern of meetings that would permit them to fulfill that primary task, namely to set the strategic agenda for the company. They recognized that the Friday afternoon staff meetings could not possibly deal with that issue and, with my help, invented the off-site meetings as the primary vehicle for strategic discourse.

Task Process—Getting the Work Done Effectively (Cell 5)

The arena in which I find myself working most of the time is the cell at the center of Table 8.1—task process. Task process is often mismanaged by clients, and such mismanagement is often the reason why a group feels unproductive. People may not listen to one another or may misunderstand one another; people may interrupt one another, arguments and conflicts may develop, the group may not be able to make a decision, too much time may be spent on what might be regarded as trivial issues, disruptive side conversations may develop, and other behavior may be displayed that gets in the way of effective task work.

If one observes a variety of groups one may also become aware that different groups working on the very same task may approach it very differently. In one group the chair calls on people to give their input; another group's chair invites anyone to speak who cares to. In one group there is angry confrontation and arguing; in another group there is polite, formal questioning. In one group decisions are made by consensus, in another they are made by voting, and in a third they are made by the manager after listening to the discussion for a while.

Task processes are elusive. It is easy to experience and to observe them but hard to define and clearly segregate them from the content that is being worked on. Group members learn that they can partially control the content outcomes by controlling the process, as senators do when they filibuster or as debaters do when they destroy an opponent's argument or composure by ridicule, changing the subject, or in other ways diverting the process from what has been said. One of the toughest tasks for the consultant/helper is not to get seduced by the content, not to get so caught up in the actual problem the group is working on as to cease to pay attention to *how* it is working.

For a group to move forward on its primary task a certain number of process functions must be fulfilled. These functions are often associated with the leadership of the group or are considered to be the duties of the chair, but in well-functioning groups different members will fulfill them at different times, and the main role of the consultant will often be to *identify and fulfill the missing functions*. A simplifying model of the main task functions to be considered is presented in Table 8.2.

In order for the group to make progress on a task, there must be some *initiating*. Someone must state the goal or problem, make proposals as to how to work on it, and set some time limits or targets. Often this function falls to the leader or to whoever called the group together in the first place, but as a group grows and gains confidence, initiating functions will increasingly come from a broader range of members.

In order to make progress, there must be some *opinion seeking and giving* and *information seeking and giving* on various issues related to the task. The kinds of information and opinions a group seeks in pursuing its tasks are often crucial for the quality of the solution. The consultant should help the group to assess for itself whether suf-

Table 8.2
NECESSARY FUNCTIONS FOR TASK FULFILLMENT

Task Functions
Initiating
Information seeking
Information giving
Opinion seeking
Opinion giving
Clarifying
Elaborating
Summarizing
Consensus testing

ficient time was given to the information and opinion-seeking functions. It is also important to distinguish seeking from giving and information from opinion. Groups often have difficulty because too many members give opinions before sufficient information seeking and giving has occurred, leading then to fruitless debate instead of constructive dialogue. The consultant can help by asking what kinds of information might be needed to resolve the issue.

Clarifying and *elaborating* are critical functions in a group in order to test the adequacy of communication and in order to build on the ideas of others toward more creative and complex ideas. If such activities do not occur, the group is not really using its unique strength. One of the most common and powerful interventions that the consultant can make is to ask clarifying questions or test his own listening by elaborating some of the ideas of members.

Summarizing is an important function to ensure that ideas are not lost because of either the size of the group or the length of discussion time. Effective summarizing includes a review of which points the group has already covered and the different ideas that have been stated, so that as decision points are reached, the group is operating with full information. One common problem I have observed in committees, task forces, and executive teams is that they tend to work sequentially and process one idea at a time, never gaining any perspective on the totality of their discussion. What is missing is the summarizing function. It can be fulfilled by having a recorder note ideas on a blackboard as the group proceeds so there is a visible summary before them at all times. Or a group member or the consultant can, from time to time, simply review what she has heard and draw out tentative generalizations from it for the group to consider.

Finally, the group needs someone periodically to test whether it is nearing a decision or should continue to discuss. *Consensus testing* could involve simply asking the question "Are we ready to decide?" or could involve some summarizing: "It seems to me we have expressed these three alternatives and are leaning toward number two; am I right?" The success of this function in moving the group forward will depend largely on the sensitivity of the person in choosing the right time to test, although ill-timed tests are still useful in reminding the group that it has some more discussing to do.

Within this broad structure of task functions we can identify a second simplifying model that focuses specifically on the stages of problem solving. Most meetings have a purpose, a function, a specific problem they are trying to solve.

Group Problem Solving and Decision Making

Problem solving as a process is much discussed and little understood. The simplifying model of this process proposed below resembles many such models in the literature of our field and is chosen because it is particularly amenable to observation and analysis. The steps or stages I will describe and analyze are applicable to any kind of problem-solving process, whether it occurs in an individual manager's head, in a two-person group, in a large committee, or in the total organization. The basic model as presented in Fig. 8.1 is an elaboration of a model originally developed by Richard Wallen for use in sensitivity training programs.

The model distinguishes two basic cycles of activity—one that occurs prior to any decision or action, and one that occurs after a decision to act has been taken. The first cycle consists of three stages: (1) problem formulation, (2) generating proposals for action, (3) forecasting consequences of proposed solutions or testing proposed solutions and evaluating them conceptually before committing to overt action.

This cycle ends when the group has made a formal decision on what to do. The second cycle then involves: (4) action planning,

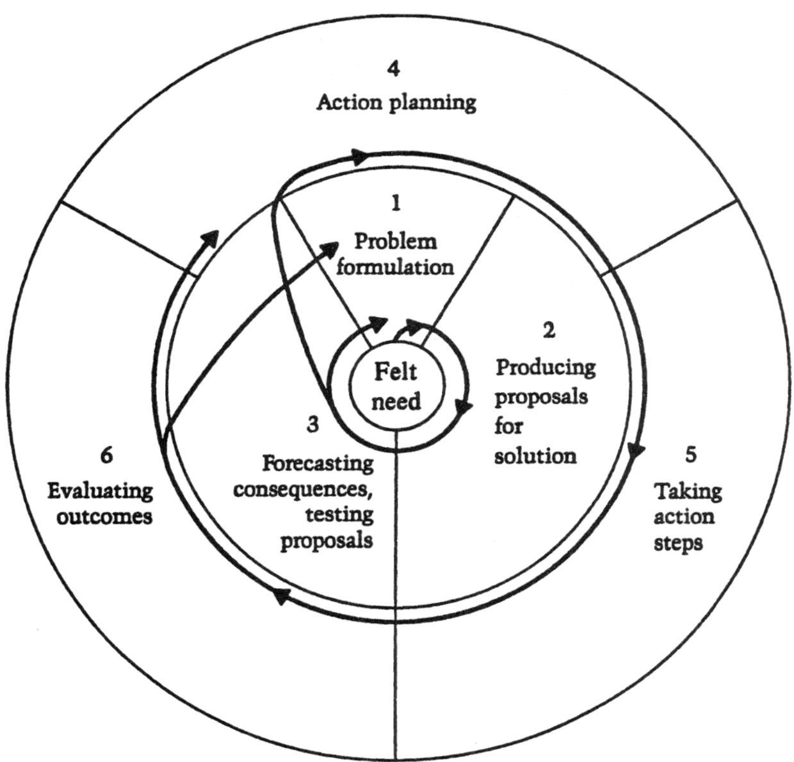

Figure 8.1
A MODEL OF THE STAGES OF PROBLEM SOLVING

(5) action steps, and (6) evaluation of the outcomes of the action steps, often leading back to the first cycle with problem redefinition. The basic reason for breaking the total process into stages is that when problem solving goes awry, it is generally because a given stage is mismanaged or is missing altogether.

In each stage there are characteristic common traps. Awareness of these traps can help the consultant to focus on when and where to intervene. Whether we are focusing on a two-person group, such as a client and me trying to establish a relationship, or a task force meeting that I have been asked to attend as part of getting acquainted with the client organization, there is always a task explicitly or implicitly defined, there are always problems to be solved, decisions to be made, and time and effort to be managed. How, then, should a group tackle and solve problems?

Cycle 1: Deciding What to Do

1. Problem Formulation. The most difficult step by far in problem solving is defining the problem. The difficulty arises in part because of a confusion between *symptoms* and *the problem.* A manager typically starts a problem-solving process when someone brings some difficulty to her attention or she discovers something that is not as it should be. Sales have fallen off, a schedule for delivery has not been met, an angry customer is on the phone, the production line has broken down, a valued subordinate has threatened to resign, or there is a fire in the shop. In a general theory of learning and change, this can be thought of as *disconfirmation.* Something is observed that was not expected and is undesirable.

However, none of the things observed are really "the problem" to be worked on. Rather, they are the symptoms to be removed. Before the manager can begin to solve the problem she must identify the causes of the symptoms, and this is often difficult because it may require further diagnosis. This may reveal not one "root cause" but possibly multiple and systemically interlocked causes that may or may not be accessible or changeable. For example, Manager X has called together his key subordinates to sit down to discuss "the problem" of declining sales. If the manager is not sensitive to the issue raised previously, he may soon be in the midst of a debate over whether to raise the advertising budget or send ten more salespeople into the field. But has he defined his problem? Has he even identified what the various alternative circumstances might be that could cause a reduction in sales and how these might be interrelated?

Falling sales could have any number of causes—erroneous sales forecast, which would imply doing nothing out in the field but something in the marketing department, or a new competitor suddenly entering the market, or a drop in product quality, or the loss of two key salespeople to a competitor, or a change in consumer taste. Without some preliminary diagnosis—which, incidentally, may take time and effort—the manager will not know what he should really be working on. The consultant can often play a key role at this stage because she is less likely to react to the time pressure the manager is under, and therefore is more likely to notice premature shortcuts in reasoning and misdiagnoses. Her role is often to help the group to slow down, to engage in a period of dialogue rather than debate (see Chapter 10), to recognize that it may be acting hastily on an ill-defined problem, and to show that the initial time invested in identifying what is *really* the problem will later pay off in less wasted time and effort.

Problems involving interpersonal relations are especially difficult to diagnose. A manager says he has a "problem" in motivating a subordinate, or coordinating with another department, or influencing his boss, or integrating the efforts of several people, or overcoming "resistance to change." Often these "problems" are felt as frustrations and tensions, with a minimum of clear understanding on the part of the manager of what is actually frustrating him or making him tense. He knows something is not right, but he does not know what the problem really is and therefore what he should do about it.

The most facilitative intervention in such cases is to help the client to be as concrete as possible in identifying the sources of frustration by engaging in a period of *exploratory* inquiry (see Chapter 3). The consultant can ask: "When did you last experience 'this problem'? What was going on? Can you give some additional examples of when you experienced the problem?" Only after a set of examples has been generated should the consultant begin to move toward *diagnostic* inquiry and a joint exploration of what the possible causes were. By carefully going over the incidents in detail and trying to identify which event actually triggered the frustration, the consultant can often help the group to define the real problem. The essential step is to have enough concrete incidents to be able to generalize a sense of the problem from them, and then to seek the patterns that tie them together.

This process, as shown in Fig. 8.2, is a necessary step in any problem formulation and is the one most often skipped, leading to premature closure on what may be an incorrect diagnosis of the problem. In the falling sales example, the group should carefully reconstruct exactly when and where all the instances of falling sales have occurred, and then determine what those instances have in common and how the various factors identified may interact with each other. Using some form of systems diagramming can be very helpful, especially in forcing the problem solvers to consider the interaction of causal factors (Senge, 1990; Senge *et al.,* 1994).

2. Producing Proposals for Solution. Once the problem has been adequately formulated, the group can move on to producing ideas or courses of action that might resolve the problem or improve the situation. At this stage the most likely pitfall is that proposals are

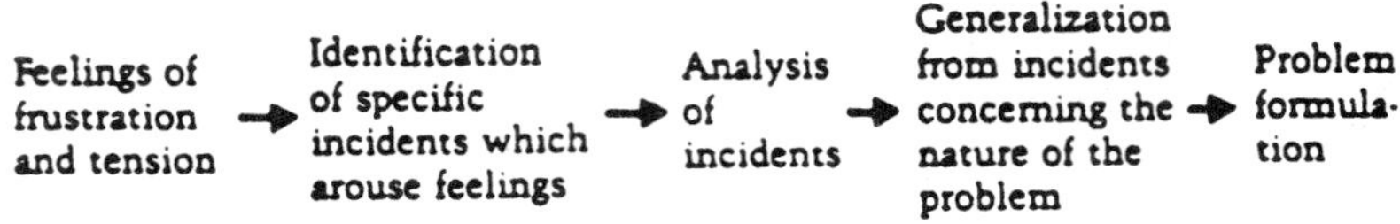

Figure 8.2
NECESSARY STEPS IN INITIALLY FORMULATING THE PROBLEM

evaluated one at a time and that the group lapses into debate instead of developing a dialogue format. If that happens, the group fails to look at a whole array of possible ideas for a solution and never gains a perspective on the problem

The consultant can help here by pointing out the consequences of premature evaluations—there is insufficient opportunity for ideas to be judged in perspective because they cannot be compared to other ideas and the premature evaluation tends to threaten a given idea and the person who proposed it. Members whose ideas have been rejected early may feel less inclined to offer ideas at a later stage. The group should be encouraged to start this stage with some version of brainstorming—producing a number of ideas and keeping them all in front of the group before any of them are evaluated as such. Brainstorming is built on the rule that no evaluation of ideas should be permitted during the idea-production phase to stimulate the creativity that is needed at this point, and ideas should be separated from their proposers so that they can be viewed objectively. I often find myself going to the flipchart in this situation and offering to write down the ideas, thereby also making it easier to say "are there other ideas that we should be getting up here . . . ?"

Once the group has a list of ideas, it can quickly weed out the obviously unworkable ones and explore the two or three ideas that look like they might work. The consultant should encourage systemic thinking at this point and invite the group to examine how the various ideas proposed interact and relate to each other. The consultant should also alert the group to the fact that just getting a number of ideas out does not in any way guarantee that the job of culling them and making a decision on which one to pursue will be easy or quick. In my experience when groups brainstorm they typically fail to allow enough time to evaluate the various ideas that they have produced.

3. Forecasting Consequences and Testing Proposals. Once a number of ideas for a solution have been proposed, it is necessary to forecast the consequences of adopting a particular solution and evaluate those consequences. This process is often difficult because *the criteria the group should be using to do its evaluating are either not clear or there is disagreement on which ones to use.* Such criteria might include (1) personal experience, (2) expert opinion, (3) surveying of existing data or information, and/or (4) planned tests or research. Personal experience and expert opinion are the easiest to fall back on but often the least valid. Surveys, focus groups, interviews, and other more formal research processes are likely to be more valid but also more time consuming and expensive. One of the consultant's key functions at this stage is to provide this range of alternatives and to enable the group to correctly match its validation method to the kind of idea it is trying to test.

For example, if the group is trying to decide between two products to develop, it should probably do some market research and test marketing; if the group is trying to decide whether to put surplus funds into capital expansion or investment programs, it should obtain advice from financial experts; or, if the group is trying to figure out how to overcome resistance to change to a new way of running the organization, it should run focus groups and involve future participants to get an idea of what their reactions will be. All too often a group uses just one validation method, no matter what ideas are being evaluated, and all too often that one method is based on someone's personal experience rather than any kind of formal inquiry.

At each stage of problem solving the discussion may reveal new features that lead to a reformulation of the problem. For example, in testing the idea that a new advertising campaign is needed, examining existing information may reveal that the old advertising campaign was perfectly sound. This discovery then raises the question of whether the initial formulation of the problem as "consumer sales resistance" was correct. The consultant should help the group to recognize that this kind of recycling—from initial formulation through idea production and idea testing to reformulation of the problem—is a very sound way to proceed even though it may take longer and initially appear to be inefficient. Reassurance from the consultant is usually necessary until a group becomes experienced in sensing its own problem-solving cycle because of the tendency to believe that constant reformulation of the problem is merely wasting time.

Cycle 1 ends with the group making a decision to move forward on an action item. That decision may be to gather more information, but it requires going outside the group meeting and doing something beyond considering alternatives. The next issue, then, is how the group actually makes decisions and how well the decision process is aligned with the kind of decision the group is making. A number of alternatives should be considered.

Group Decision-Making Methods

Decisions are involved at every stage of the problem-solving process but are only highly visible in the transition from cycle 1 to cycle 2, where the problem-solving unit commits itself to trying out a proposal for action or decides to gather more information before deciding on a particular proposal for solution. Prior to this step, the group has had to decide when and where to meet, how to organize itself, how to allocate time, by what procedures or rules to run its discussion (for example, with or without a formal chair, with or without Robert's Rules of Order), or how to tell when the problem has been sufficiently well formulated to move on to idea production. Often, group members do not recognize that they have made so many process decisions and that these have real consequences for the climate of the group and the quality of the problem solutions. The consultant must be prepared, therefore, to draw attention to the many available decision-making mechanisms by making an "educational intervention," which lays out the options discussed below.[1]

In reviewing the different decision-making methods listed, it is important not to judge too quickly any one method as better than another. Each has its use at the appropriate time, and each method has certain consequences for future group operations. The important point is for the group to understand these consequences well enough to be able to choose a decision-making method that will be appropriate to the amount of time available, the past history of the group, the kind of task being worked on, and the kind of climate the group wants to establish.

1. Decision by Lack of Response ("Plop"). The most common and perhaps least visible group decision-making method occurs when someone suggests an idea, and, before anyone else has said anything about it, someone else suggests another idea, until the group eventually finds one it will act on. All the ideas that have been bypassed have, in a real sense, been decided on by the group. But the decision has been simply a common decision not to support them, making the proposers feel

---

[1] The "Plop to Consensus" scheme was first developed by Robert Blake and others in NTL workshops in the early 1950s.

that their suggestions have "plopped." The floors of most group meeting rooms are completely covered with plops. Notice that the tacit assumption underlying this method is that "silence means lack of agreement."

2. Decision by Formal Authority. Many groups set up a power structure or start with a power structure that makes it clear that the chair or someone in authority will make the decisions. The group can generate ideas and hold free discussion, but at any time the chair can say that, having heard the discussion, she has decided to do thus and so. This method is highly efficient. Whether it is effective depends a great deal on whether the chair is a sufficiently good listener to have culled the right information on which to base her decision.

Furthermore, if the group must move on to the next stage or implement the decision, the authority-rule method produces a minimum amount of group involvement. Hence it undermines the potential quality of the implementation of the decision. I have often sat in meetings where the chair has decided something after listening to the group for a few minutes, but the action ultimately taken proved to be somehow out of line with what the chair wanted. Upon later reconstruction it turned out that the group either misunderstood the decision or did not agree with it in the first place, and hence was neither able nor motivated to carry it out effectively.

3. Decision by Self-Authorization or Minority. One of the most common complaints of group members is that they feel "railroaded" in reference to some decision. Usually this feeling results from one, two, or three people employing tactics that produce action and therefore must be considered decisions, but which are taken without the consent of the majority. The tacit assumption in this case is that silence means consent.

One version of minority rule is "self-authorization." Self-authorization is where one member makes a proposal for what to do, no other proposals are offered, no one says anything negative, and so the group does what was proposed. The most popular version of this type of decision is what Jerry Harvey called the "Abilene Paradox" (1974) referring to his memory of when his family had an unpleasant drive to Abilene to have lunch only to discover later in the day that no one had wanted to go. One person had suggested it as a possibility, and everyone else had remained silent. The initiator and everyone else assumed that silence meant consent.

In my own experience this form of decision is most common and most dangerously inappropriate when used in choosing the *process* by which the group will work. Someone says "Let's run the meeting by Robert's Rules of Order" and, when no one challenges the suggestion even though they disagree, the group ends up using a method that no one wanted. Or, one person says, "Majority rules, right?" and when no one challenges the statement, the group finds itself making 8-to-7 decisions that get poorly implemented. When a self-authorized proposal is on the table it is often important for the consultant to say "Does the group agree with this? Is this what we want to do?"

A single person can railroad a decision, particularly if he is in some kind of convener role, by not giving opposition an opportunity to build up. The convener says, "I think the way to go at this is to each state our opinion on the topic to see where we all stand. Now my own opinion is . . . ." Once he has given his own opinion, he turns to the person on his right and says, "What do you think, Joan?" When Joan has spoken, the convener points to the next person and the group is off and running, having in effect made a decision about how it is going to go about its work based on the convener's self-authorization. Another similar tactic is to say, "Well, we all seem to be agreed, so let's go ahead with John's idea," even though the careful observer may have detected that only John, the chair, and maybe one other person has spoken favorably about the idea. The others have remained silent. If the initiator is asked how he concluded there was agreement, chances are that he will say, "Silence means consent, doesn't it? Everyone had a chance to voice opposition." If one interviews the group members later, one sometimes discovers that an actual majority was against John's idea but each one hesitated to speak up because he thought that all the other silent ones were for it. They too were trapped by "silence means consent."

Perhaps the commonest form of minority rule is for two or more members to come to a quick and powerful agreement on a course of action, to challenge the group with a quick "Does anyone object?", and, if no one raises her voice in two seconds, to proceed with "Let's go ahead, then." Again the trap is the assumption that silence means consent both on the part of the initiators and on the part of the disagreers who are afraid to be in a minority of opposition. When the group operates this way, one often has a condition of "pluralistic ignorance"—where everyone makes an assumption about the opinions of members that turns out to be wrong, but no one checked. Or, at the extreme, we have "group think" (Janis, 1982) where a decision is made on the presumption of total agreement while a substantial minority (or even majority) may be in disagreement but has been silenced.

The consultant plays an important role with respect to these decision-making methods, primarily because they are rarely recognized and labeled as decision-making methods in the first place. Yet a great many group decisions, particularly pertaining to the important issue of group procedures, rules of order, and the like, are made in these rather rapid ways. For a group member to challenge such proceedings, to say, "We don't really agree," is often seen as blocking; hence there are strong pressures on group members to stay silent and let things take their course, even though they are not in agreement.

The consultant must first make the group aware of decisions it has made and the methods by which it has made them; then she must try to get the group members to assess whether they feel that these methods were appropriate to the situation. For example, the members may agree that the chairperson did railroad the decision, but they may also feel that this was appropriate because time was short and someone needed to make that decision quickly so the group could get on with more important things. On the other hand, the group might decide that a decision such as having each person in turn state his point of view introduces an element of formality and ritual into the group which undermines its ability to build creatively on ideas already advanced. The group might then wish to choose a different method of idea production. The important thing is to legitimize such process discussion and to have some observations available in case the group is finding it difficult to discern what the consultant is talking about.

4. Decision by Majority Rule: Voting and/or Polling. Next we come to more familiar decision-making procedures that are often taken for granted as applying to any group situation because they reflect our political system. One simple version is to poll everyone's opinion following some period of discussion, and, if a majority feels the same way, to assume that that is the decision. The other method is the more formal one of making a motion, getting a second or simply stating a clear alternative, and asking for votes in favor of it, votes against it, and abstentions.

On the surface this method seems completely sound, but surprisingly often decisions made by this method are not well implemented even by the group that made the decision. What is wrong? If one can get the group to discuss its process, or if one interviews members of the minority, it turns out that three psychological barriers to effective implementation exist: (1) the minority members often do not agree that the silent assumption of "majority rule" should apply, but they feel unable to challenge it; (2) the minority members often feel that there was an insufficient period of discussion for them to really get their point of view across; and, (3) the minority members often feel that the voting process has created two camps within the group, that these camps are now in a win-lose competition. Their camp lost the first round but it is just a matter of time until it can regroup, pick up some support, and win the next time a vote comes up.

In other words, voting creates coalitions, and the preoccupation of the losing coalition is not how to implement what the majority wants but how to win the next battle. If voting is to be used, the group must be sure that it has created a climate in which members feel they have had their day in court and where members feel obligated to go along with the majority decision. A key role for the consultant is to highlight for the group the pitfalls of each method and to get enough discussion of group climate to ensure that the group will choose an appropriate decision-making process.

5. Decision by Consensus. One of the most effective but also most time-consuming methods of group decision making is to seek consensus. Consensus, as I will define it, is not the same thing as unanimity. Rather, it is a state of affairs where communications have been sufficiently open, and the group climate has been sufficiently supportive, to make all members of the group feel that they had a fair chance to influence the decision. Someone then tests for the "sense of the meeting," carefully avoiding formal procedures, such as voting. Polling can be effective in reaching consensus provided the group has accepted the principle that it will not go with a simple majority but will seek broader agreement.

If there is a clear alternative that most members subscribe to, and if those who oppose it feel they have had their chance to influence the decision, then a consensus exists. Operationally it would be defined by the fact that those members who do not agree with the extended majority alternative nevertheless understand it clearly and are prepared to support it. It is a psychological state that must be tested for and might be described as follows: "I understand what most of you would like to do. I personally would not do that, but I feel that you understand what my alternative would be. I have had sufficient opportunity to sway you to my point of view but clearly have not been able to do so. Therefore, I will go along with what most of you wish to do and will do my best to implement it."

In order to achieve such a condition, time must be allowed for all group members to state their opposition and to state it fully enough to get the feeling that others really do understand them. This condition is essential if they are later to free themselves of preoccupation with the idea that they could have gotten their point of view across if others had only understood what they really had in mind. Only by careful listening to the opposition can such feelings be forestalled and effective group decisions reached.

The consultant can help the group to determine what kinds of decisions should be made by consensus, i.e. which decisions are important enough to warrant the effort? One guideline he might suggest is that procedural decisions, those which pertain to *how* the group works, are the ones where it is most important that everyone be on board; hence these should probably be made by consensus. The group might decide to give complete authority to the chair, or it might decide to try for very informal discussion procedures, or it might wish to brainstorm some ideas. But whatever is decided, it should be completely clear to everyone and there should not be residual feelings of being misunderstood or desires to sabotage the group procedure.

6. Decision by Unanimous Consent. The logically perfect but least attainable kind of decision is where everyone truly agrees on the course of action to be taken. For certain key kinds of decisions it may be necessary to seek unanimity, but for most important ones consensus is enough, if it is real consensus. The consultant can help the group here by pointing out that the group may be setting too high a standard for itself in some cases. Unanimity is not always necessary and may be a highly inefficient way to make decisions. The important thing is to take some time to agree on which method to use for what kinds of tasks and in what kinds of situations.

A final thought—often the method of decision making is simply announced to the group by the convener or chair. If this is the case, the consultant must try to determine whether the group is comfortable with the method being used, and, if not, find an opportunity to raise with the chair the issue of whether she should permit some discussion by the group of how to handle the decision-making area. In my experience, conveners often tend to feel threatened by such discussion because they fear that they will lose control of the group, resulting in disorder and chaos. One way to reassure them is by pointing out that different ways of making decisions do not necessarily imply a disorderly communication process. If the consultant can provide some viable alternatives, he can often get the chair to experiment with different methods and draw her own conclusions.

Cycle 2. Acting, Evaluating, and Reformulating

All of cycle 1 involves steps that occur in discussion and that do not involve commitment to action unless the group chooses to gather additional data for idea evaluation. As the group reaches some consensus on a proposed solution and makes a decision to act, we go into cycle 2, the action cycle. Making the decision to act is not shown in the diagram but is represented by the act of crossing the boundary between cycle 1 and cycle 2. When a decision has been made on a given proposal or idea for solution, the problem-solving process is far from finished. The group must then still plan a detailed course of action, take action steps, and have some method to determine whether or not the action steps are solving the problem. This last step should be thought out in advance of taking action: "What information should we be looking at to determine whether or not our action steps are achieving the desired results?"

At any of these stages, it is again possible for the group to discover that it had not formulated the problem correctly and must revert back to cycle 1 for some new reformulation, as well as idea proposing and testing. Such recycling is entirely desirable and should not be considered a waste of time. It is far more costly to be working on the wrong problem and discover this only after expensive action steps have been taken, than it is to make a greater effort initially to define the problem correctly.

4. & 5. Taking Action Steps. The action planning stage can be treated as a new problem requiring its own problem formulation, idea production, and idea testing. If these substages are short-circuited or avoided, a good proposal may be carried out inadequately and the group will erroneously conclude that the proposal was deficient, instead of recognizing insufficient action planning as the culprit. Here again, the key role for the consultant may be to slow the group down and encourage them to plan carefully before leaping into action.

One of the major pitfalls of this stage is to make general plans without assigning clear responsibilities to specific members for specific actions. I have sat in many a group meeting where a decision was reached, the meeting was adjourned, and nothing happened because everyone thought that someone else would now do something.

The clear allocation of responsibility for action not only ensures that action will be taken but provides a test of the decision in that the responsible implementer may raise questions about the decision that had not been considered before.

In some cases the whole second cycle is delegated to some other person or group. For example, the original problem-solving group decides "Let's beef up our advertising campaign." Once it has reached this decision, the group orders the advertising department to increase advertising on certain products. The group then relaxes and reverts to watching sales figures. Is this a sound approach? The answer in many cases is "No" because when different people perform cycle 2, they may neither understand clearly nor be particularly committed to the proposal or solution that the cycle 1 person or group has offered. They have not struggled with the problem definition or had a chance to see the reasons why other alternatives that may now occur to them have been rejected. They may also feel that the general proposal given to them is too unclear to permit implementation.

Equally problematic is the case where a management group delegates problem formulation (cycle 1) to a task force or a consulting organization and then waits for a diagnosis and proposal for action in writing. In nine cases out of ten, if the originating group has not involved itself in problem formulation and if the task force has not thought through action implementation (cycle 2), the management group will not like the proposal and will find an excuse to shelve it. Given these kinds of problems, it is desirable to ensure a high degree of overlap (or at least communication) between cycle 1 and cycle 2 members. The ideal situation would, of course, be that they are the same problem-solving unit. If that is not possible, the cycle 1 unit should provide for an interim phase that permits the cycle 2 unit to get completely on board before the two units sever their communication link. One way to do this is to bring the implementer into the problem-solving process at the earliest possible stage, or, at least, to review completely with him all the steps the cycle 1 unit has gone through to arrive at a proposal for solution.

In such a review, the key process would be to permit the implementing unit to satisfy itself completely by asking as many questions as it would like concerning the reasons that certain other alternatives, which might strike it as better ones, were not selected. They should get satisfactory answers, or the cycle 1 group should go back and review the additional alternatives brought up by the implementing unit. The role of the consultant here is to help the group understand how difficult it is to communicate a complex action proposal to an implementer, and then to ensure this understanding early enough in the problem-solving process to institute protective measures against communication breakdown.

6. Evaluating Outcomes. To ensure adequate evaluation, the group should reach consensus on (1) the criteria for evaluation, (2) the timetable—when results should first be expected, and (3) who will be responsible for reporting back information to be evaluated. Once results are in, the group should be psychologically prepared to go back into cycle 1 with an effort to reformulate the problem, not merely to rush in with more solution alternatives. The group should always be prepared to reconsider what it sees as the problem, and the consultant should constantly raise the question "What problem are we working on?"

Summary of Problem Solving and Decision Making

Problem solving can be thought of as consisting of two cycles, one of which involves primarily discussion and the other primarily action taking. The first cycle consists of the phases of problem identification and formulation, idea or proposal generation, and idea or proposal testing through attempting to forecast consequences. The most difficult stage is that of identifying and formulating the real problem, and often this stage requires additional data-gathering efforts before the problem can be clearly identified.

The second cycle involves action planning, action steps, and evaluation of outcomes. The action planning is itself a problem-solving process and should be treated as such. The major difficulty in the total cycle is making the transition from cycle 1 to cycle 2 if different parties are involved. Those who have to implement the decisions should be involved in the earliest possible stage.

The decision process itself can be handled by

1. lack of group response
2. authority rule
3. minority rule
4. majority rule
5. consensus and/or
6. unanimity.

It is important for a group to become aware of these different decision-making methods and to learn to choose an appropriate method for the kind of task or decision it is working on.

Choosing an Intervention Focus

Task issues such as the basic functions, the manner of cycling through the problem-solving process, and the methods of making decisions are so obviously relevant to effective group functioning that it is generally easy for the consultant to get the group to observe and manage them. But, one of the consultant's greatest dilemmas is choosing an intervention focus from among the many categories reviewed previously, i.e., which behavior to bring to the group's attention.

The three key criteria for choosing from the array of possibilities are

1. The degree to which the consultant perceives the process issue to be related to the group's effectiveness;
2. The degree to which the data about the process issue are sufficiently clear so that if attention is drawn to the issue, there is a reasonable probability that the group members will also have perceived what the consultant perceived; and,
3. Whether or not the consultant can think of an intervention that will facilitate moving the process along instead of simply interrupting it.

Obscure references to process issues that are not clearly visible will not enhance group learning, nor is it helpful to get a group preoccupied with how it is working when there is time pressure to make an important decision. The consultant must understand what the group views as its primary task and focus interventions on those task processes that relate clearly to that primary task. My early work with the Action Co. illustrates these issues.

One of the salient features of the Action Co. executive committee meetings was the degree to which members engaged in what amounted to a communications free-for-all. Members interrupted each other constantly, they often got into shouting matches, they drifted off the topic of discussion, and they moved from one agenda point to another without any clear sense of what had been decided. I had a clearly formulated mental model of how an effective group should work, based on my knowledge of group research and my experience with training groups in the National Training Labs, where I had been working as a trainer for 10 years. My early intervention efforts were therefore made from the point of view of an expert consultant. Whenever I saw an opportunity, I would ask the group to consider what the consequences were of constantly interrupting each other, communicating clearly my assumption that interruption is "bad" and interferes with effective group work. I pointed out how important content ideas were lost and how certain potentially good ideas never got fully aired.

The group invariably responded with agreement and a resolution to do better, but within ten minutes we were back to the old pattern. As I reflected on this dysfunctional cycle I became aware that I was imposing an ideal model on a group that was clearly on a different path, best understood in terms of the shared tacit assumptions that were driving this group. As I have detailed elsewhere (Schein, 1985, 1992) the group was trying to arrive at "truth" and operating from the assumption that the only way to achieve truth was to battle ideas to the ground. Only if an idea could survive intense debate was it worth pursuing.

Once I understood this basic premise I asked myself what would in fact be more facilitative and, in that process, came to see the relevance of process consultation versus expert consultation. I had to work within the purposes and assumptions that were driving the group rather than impose my models on them. I had to learn that the primary task of the group as <u>they</u> *saw it was to develop ideas that were so sound that they could afford to bet the company on them. Generating ideas and evaluating them were therefore the two most crucial functions that they worked on in meeting after meeting.*

Two kinds of interventions grew out of this insight. First, I noticed that ideas were in fact being lost because so much information was being processed so rapidly. Partly for my own sake and partly because I thought it might help, I went to the flipchart and wrote down the main ideas as they *came out.*

Incomplete ideas or points (because the presenter had been interrupted) led to the second kind of intervention. Instead of punishing the group for its "bad" behavior, as I had been doing, if someone was interrupted I would look for an opportunity to give that person back the floor by saying something like "John, you were trying to make a point. Did we get all of it?" This created the opportunity to get the idea out without drawing unnecessary attention to the reason why it had not gotten out in the first place. The combination of these two kinds of interventions focused the group on the ideas that were now on the flipchart and helped them navigate through their complex terrain. Ideas that were about to be lost got resurrected and written down.

The lesson was clear. Until I understood what the group was really trying to do I could not focus on the right processes nor did I know how to intervene helpfully. I had to sense what the primary task was and where the group was getting stuck (incomplete idea formulation and too quick evaluation) before I could determine what kind of intervention would be "facilitative."

What about "Task Structure?" (Cell 8)

If one observes a group for some period of time one will perceive that certain patterns recur, that some kinds of events happen regularly, and some kinds of events never happen. For example, one group always uses parliamentary procedure, whereas another refuses to vote on any issue even if they cannot resolve the issue by any other means. One group always has an agenda and follows it slavishly, whereas another waits until the meeting begins before generating a list of topics. Such regularities in the work of the group can best be thought of as the task structure of the group, relatively *stable, recurring* processes that help the group or organization accomplish its tasks.

In large organizations we think of the structure as being the formal hierarchy, the defined chain of command, the systems of information and control, and other stable, recurring processes that are taught to newcomers as "the way we work around here." But it is important to recognize that the concept of structure is only an extension of the concept of process in that it refers to those processes that are stable, recurring, and defined by members in the group as their "structure."

All groups require such regularities and stability to make their environment and working patterns predictable and, thereby, manageable. The assumptions that develop as the underlying premises of those patterns can then be thought of as part of the culture of the group. They become shared and taken for granted, and the structures that we can observe can be viewed as artifacts or manifestations of the culture of the group (Schein, 1985, 1992). The culture itself is not immediately visible because it is best thought of as the shared, taken for granted, underlying and unconscious assumptions that have evolved to deal with the various external and internal issues the group has had to face. But the culture will be reflected in the overt behavior and can be searched out through a joint process of inquiry between the outsider and members of the group. For most purposes it is sufficient to focus on the manifest artifacts, the visible behavior, always bearing in mind that they reflect important underlying assumptions that will eventually have to be taken into account. However, until the group itself is ready to look at its own culture, it is difficult for the consultant to focus on it.

The task structure that evolves in a group is composed of regularities that pertain specifically to the group's survival in its external environment. All groups face at least five, basic, survival problems. By being aware of them, the consultant can focus her observations and create a mental checklist of what to pay attention to.

1. Mission/Primary Task. What is the *fundamental mission* that justifies the group's existence—its *primary task?* The structural elements dealing with this issue are usually company charters, statements of philosophy or mission, formal agenda statements, and other efforts to document members' implicit understanding about the ultimate role of the group.

2. Specific Goals and Strategies. These are usually derived from the mission and are reflected in written goal statements, strategies, formal plans, publicly defined targets, and deadlines.

3. Means to Use to Accomplish the Goals. The structures for accomplishing goals are the defined formal organization, assigned task roles, and recurring procedures for solving problems and making decisions. The organization chart, lines of authority, job descriptions, and formally specified accountabilities all fall into this category.

4. Measuring and Monitoring Systems. Every group needs to know whether or not goals are being achieved. Formal information and control systems are set up, and managerial planning, budgeting, and review processes are formalized.

5. Systems for Fixing Problems and Getting Back on Course. Measurement systems reveal when the group is off target or not accomplishing its goals. The group then needs processes for remedying situations, fixing problems, or getting itself back on course. Often solutions are invented ad hoc, but any group or organization has to be able to regularize remedial and corrective processes, and thus make them part of the structure of the group.

In a young group, the task structures will not be very stable, i.e., the young group is not very "structured." As the group evolves, it keeps those processes that continue to work and comes to share the assumptions about itself that led to its success. The processes then become more visible and may be formally described in organization charts, manuals of procedure, rules of order, and other artifacts of the evolving culture. As these processes become more and more stable we talk of "bureaucracy" and "institutionalization."

Whether or not the consultant can intervene constructively in the task structure depends on the degree to which the group itself is conscious of that structure and needs to change it. In my experience the most powerful interventions in this area are the ones that enable the group to gain insight into its own unconscious assumptions. The visible external structures are easy to observe, but the underlying assumptions that created those structures are much harder to detect. Yet without insight into those assumptions, the group cannot learn how to function more effectively.

The final issue to be addressed, then, is whether the consultant can or should get involved in interventions aimed at structural issues. Observing the group and helping them to confront their own structures is certainly one kind of necessary intervention. More problematic is whether or not to get involved in structure and culture *change*. The main criterion continues to be that the consultant must be facilitative and helpful. If a group really wants me to get involved in working with their structure and culture I will do so, provided we clearly understand that changes in structure may entail change processes that will arouse high levels of anxiety and resistance because the evolved structures provide predictability, meaning, and security for the group members. Culture is embedded in structure hence one cannot change structure without threatening accepted cultural assumptions.

Summary and Conclusion

In this chapter I have first reviewed all the main intervention areas that the consultant can observe and be prepared to intervene on. The focus in this chapter was on the primary task that the group has and on how it defines that task. Within that arena one can focus on the content, the process, or the structure that one finds in relation to the group's task. I reviewed some relevant categories of observation in each area and suggested some of the most helpful kinds of interventions that the consultant can make. The bulk of these will fall into task process, but one cannot ignore content or structure.

In the next chapter I will discuss the interpersonal issues that accompany task issues—how the group defines itself, manages its boundaries, creates workable interpersonal relationships that permit the group to function, grow, develop, and maintain itself. The issue, then, will be when and how to focus interventions on those issues, and how to balance task process and interpersonal process interventions.

I do not provide any specific exercises for task processes here, but the exercises proposed at the end of Chapter 9 cover task processes and group building, as well as interpersonal processes.

9

Facilitative Process Interventions: Interpersonal Processes

In the previous chapter I focused on *task* processes because these are most likely to be the reason why the consultant was brought into the picture in the first place. However, as I have argued throughout, the *interpersonal* processes that are involved in creating relationships and building a group have to be observed and managed in order for effective task performance to occur. In ongoing situations the task and interpersonal processes occur at the same time and are highly interwoven creating a perpetual decision issue about which to focus on and when to intervene on the interpersonal issues.

Interpersonal and group *processes* can be divided into two broad categories: (1) How a group creates itself by defining and maintaining its boundaries (Cells 1, 4, and 7 in Table 8.1), and (2) How a group grows and develops its patterns of internal relationships (Cells 3, 6, and 9 in Table 8.1). In this chapter I will review both areas, provide some simplifying models and suggest how the consultant can best be facilitative and helpful in relation to each area. I will focus primarily on the process issues but also comment on the content and structural issues as appropriate.

Processes of Building and Maintaining a Group

One of the most salient phenomena I encounter in the early contacts with a client organization is that the groups I have to work with are all at different stages of development. The clients who come to me to explore a possible consultation may not have worked with each other before and thus may be a brand-new small group. The exploratory meeting that I am asked to attend or help to design may be a special meeting of a group that has regular meetings every week or, on the other hand, may be a group that has met for the very first time to consider the consulting project. The people that the client may have invited to meet with me may include some who have worked extensively with each other and a few others who are, in effect, strangers to each other at the initial meeting. Given this variety of circumstances, it is essential for the consultant to have a simplifying model of how a group gets started and develops.

The underlying theoretical premise is that when two or more people come together to form a work- or task-oriented group, there will first be a period of essentially *self-oriented* behavior reflecting various concerns that any new member of a group could be expected to experience. As the self-oriented behavior declines, members begin to pay more attention to each other and to the task at hand. The kinds of behavior that help the group to build and maintain itself then occur concurrently with behaviors designed to accomplish the work of the group. I will describe the steps in a chronological sequence because they occur more or less in sequence, although each phase may overlap the others.

Emotional Problems in Entering a New Group—The Causes of Self-Oriented Behavior

The problems that anyone faces when entering a new group stem from certain underlying emotional issues that must be resolved before one can feel comfortable in a new situation. Four of these issues are shown in the left-hand column of Figure 9.1.

Identity and Role. First and foremost is the problem of choosing a role or identity that will be acceptable to oneself and others, and claiming the appropriate value for oneself. In other words, each new member, whether he is aware of it or not, must find an answer to the question "Who and what am I to be in this group?" "How much value should I claim for myself in this group?" "What face will I present to the others in this situation?"

This issue exists in the first place because all of us have a large repertoire of possible roles and behavioral styles to bring to any given situation. Should I be the dominant aggressive leader, a behavior pattern that may have worked for me in some situations; or should I be the humorous tension reliever, which may have worked for me in other situations; or should I be the quiet listener, which has worked in still other situations?

Problems	*Resulting feelings*	*Coping responses (self-oriented)*
1. *Identity* Who am I to be?		1. *"Tough" Responses* Fighting, controlling resisting authority.
2. *Control & Influence* Will I be able to control and influence others?	Frustration	2. *"Tender" Responses* Supporting, helping, forming alliances, dependency.
3. *Needs & Goals* Will the group goals include my own needs?	Tension	3. *Withdrawal or Denial Responses* Passivity, indifference, overuse of "logic and reason"
4. *Acceptance & Intimacy* Will I be liked and accepted by the group? How close a group will we be?	Anxiety	

Figure 9.1
PROBLEMS IN ENTERING A NEW GROUP WHICH CAUSE SELF-ORIENTED BEHAVIOR

In varying degrees, we are different people in different life situations. Therefore, we always have some degree of choice in new situations. In formal committees or work groups, this kind of issue is often partially resolved through the initial mandate. A person is told to join a task force to represent the "personnel point of view," or a strong convener tells members what kinds of roles she wants them to play. Such resolutions are at best only partial, however, in that there is still great latitude for the person to develop a style that will satisfy her and be acceptable to the others in the group. As Fig. 9.1 indicates, as long as the emotional issue is there, whether the person recognizes it consciously or not, it operates as a source of tension, leads the person to be primarily preoccupied with herself, and consequently leads to less listening and concern for others or the group task.

Control, Power, Influence. A second issue that any new member must resolve in any new group is the distribution of power and influence. It can be safely assumed that every member will have some need to control and influence others, but the amount of this need and its form of expression will vary from person-to-person. One person may wish to influence the actual task solution, another may wish to influence the methods or procedures used by the group, a third may wish to achieve an overall position of prominence in the group, and a fourth may only hope to make a modest contribution.

The dilemma for all members early in the group's history is that they do not know each other's needs or styles, and hence cannot easily determine who will be able to influence whom and on what. Consequently, the consultant will frequently observe in early meetings a great deal of fencing, testing each other out, and experimenting with different forms of influence. The consultant must be careful not to misunderstand this behavior. On the surface it seems like a definite flight from whatever task the group is facing. Underneath it represents an important sorting out, getting acquainted, and coming to terms with each other that the members need to do in order to relax their self-concerns and focus on the task.

If a convener insists on a tight formal schedule that prevents some of this getting acquainted and testing, he runs the risk of either producing superficial solutions (because members are not ready to really work on the task), or of forcing them to do their fencing in the context of the task work, thereby slowing down the progress and undermining the potential quality of the solution. In this kind of situation, the consultant must help the convener to understand the functions the initial sorting-out behavior performs for the members, to understand the need for group-building time, and to understand that good communications cannot develop until members' self-preoccupations have been reduced.

Individual Needs and Group Goals. A third issue that faces every group member is the concern that the emerging group goals may not include the individual member's personal goals and needs. Preoccupation with this issue typically leads the person to wait and see how the group develops and not to invest herself too heavily in it until she sees whether things will go her way and include her agenda. The problem for the group as a whole is that if a substantial number of members take the wait-and-see attitude, it is difficult to get any group action started or to develop a coherent group goal. In this situation the group typically turns to any available authority to set the agenda, formulate goals, or suggest a task. If the convener responds to the pressure and sets the goals, she is partially solving the problem, but she still cannot ensure that the goals she sets will involve all the members sufficiently to get them committed to the task.

A sounder procedure would be to face the paradox directly and help group members to understand that until their needs are to some degree exposed and shared, it is not possible to develop valid group goals. Enough meeting time should therefore be allocated at the beginning to permit members to explore what they really want to get out of the group. The role of the consultant in this situation is usually to slow down the group and to reassure members that the early struggles to communicate with each other are a necessary and important part of group growth. It may also be useful to have a formal "check-in" in which each person is invited to state their role or position on any given issue that may be under discussion. As will be seen in the next chapter, in the setting up of Dialogue sessions, a formal check-in during which each person tells a bit about their current situation is an important component of creating a climate of inclusion.

Acceptance and Intimacy. These two issues are lumped together because they deal with the same underlying problem: Will I be liked and accepted by the others in the group, and how close or intimate will we have to be to achieve a comfortable level of mutual respect and acceptance? For every set of people and every situation, norms must be developed by the group that help to resolve these issues. There is no optimal or absolute level of acceptance and intimacy for all groups at all times. It depends on the members, on the group task, on the length of time available to the group, and a host of other factors. But the issue is always there as a source of tension until working norms have been established.

Initially, the issue will appear in terms of forms of address and patterns of politeness. As the group develops, the issue will center on formality or informality of group procedures. At a still later stage, the issue will center on whether group discussion must stick to the formal task or whether more personal exchanges are permissible and desirable. Even if the convener calls for the group exchange to be "open," one will recall that "openness" is itself a highly ambiguous concept and hinges more on the evolved trust level in the group than on what a given convener may call for or desire. The group can attempt to legislate solutions by the adoption of Robert's Rules of Order or similar devices, but such procedures are more likely to sweep the issue under the rug than to resolve it. The consultant's role can be to help the group recognize that the issue is a legitimate one to be worked on.

Types of Coping Responses in New Groups

Each of the underlying emotional problems that confront new members in a group leads to tension, frustration, and self-preoccupation. What does the person typically do in coping with these issues and the resulting tensions? Three basic kinds of coping patterns can be observed as shown in the right-hand column of Fig. 9.1. (1) Basically tough, aggressive coping based on a denial of one's tender affiliative needs; (2) Basically tender, support-seeking coping based on a denial of one's aggressive and assertive needs; and (3) Coping by withdrawal behavior based on denial of any feelings and a falling back on "logic" and "structure."

The *tough, aggressive response* shows up in various kinds of fighting, such as arguing, cutting down other members' points, ridiculing, deliberate ignoring of others, and cutting and hostile humor. Although the behavior may be legitimate within the rules of group discussion under the guise of "debating the point" or "exploring our differences," the consultant should be careful to note whether the underlying feelings expressed are concern for a better task solution or are, in fact, ways of challenging and testing other members in the process of resolving emotional issues.

The aggressive response is also reflected in attempts to control other members through self-authorized setting up of procedures, calling on people, or telling other members what they should be talking about. With respect to any authority figures in the group, such as the chair, this type of emotional coping shows up as counterdependency. Counterdependency refers to feelings of wanting to resist authority: "Let's find out what the chair wants us to do and then *not* do it," or "Let's do it our own way, not the way he wants us to do it."

In most formal groups such behavior is likely to be quite subtle because standards of politeness and formal power differences militate against open expressions of counterdependency. Yet it is not difficult for the consultant to observe such behavior, to help the group to recognize the legitimacy of it, and to help differentiate emotional coping from genuine expression of differences on the task level.

The *tender support-seeking response* is reflected in a variety of ways. Members look for someone with whom they seem to agree and try to form a supportive alliance or subgroup within the larger group. Members attempt to avoid conflict, give support, help each other, and generally try to suppress aggressive, divisive feelings. With respect to authority, such behavior shows up as dependency—looking for someone to lean on, to give guidance, and to solve the problems that the members feel they have.

How can the consultant differentiate this kind of behavior from constructive problem-solving behavior? First, she notes at what point in the group's or member's history the behavior is occurring. The emotionally based self-oriented behavior occurs early in the history when members are trying to establish themselves in the group. Later, the same kind of behavior could simply mean genuine support in reference to the task. A second criterion is whether the consultant feels that the support is based on genuine mutual understanding or is a kind of blind response. The emotionally based behavior I am describing here is often indicated by members forming alliances without really showing evidence of understanding each other's points of view at all. The consultant must help the group to distinguish hasty support seeking, indiscriminate helping, and inappropriate dependency from similar behaviors that may occur later in the process of problem solving and team building.

The *withdrawal or denial response* is characterized by a suppression of tension and feeling, often resulting in a rather passive, indifferent, bland kind of response. It is as if the person were saying, "You people go ahead and fight it out and get this group rolling while I watch; I don't really have any feelings about it, so I'll get on board when things get properly organized." Another version of this emotional behavior is for the person to argue that feelings have no place in group discussion and should be legislated out of existence and suppressed at all costs. When a fight breaks out, the person says, "Fellow members, we are all civilized, mature individuals; we can settle this logically and calmly. Let us not let our feelings get the better of us; let's stick to the facts."

If the person were being truly rational and logical, he would realize that the feelings in the situation are some of the "facts" that must be taken into account. They can be suppressed and legislated off the agenda by formalizing the group's procedures, but they cannot be made to disappear and they cannot be prevented from affecting each member's problem-solving behavior. If a group member has tensions and self-preoccupations, she will not be listening to or concerned about other members and hence will not contribute to effective problem solving.

Each of us, as a human being, is capable of each of these basic types of response in our efforts to cope with the emotional issues of the group. Which style of response we tend to use will depend on our personalities, on our past histories in interpersonal situations, on the behavior of other members in the group, and on the formality and structure of the situation. For example, a formal, tightly controlled group is much more likely to produce withdrawal and denial responses, which in the long run will produce a poorly motivated, alienated group. When such a group tries to solve a difficult problem, there is no guarantee that members will either be motivated enough to direct their energies to the problem or be able to communicate with each other well enough to build a genuine group solution. Permitting the exploration of emotional expressions, on the other hand, will lead to initial discomfort but will, in the long run, produce a higher level of communication and a stronger, more effective group.

Resolution of Emotional Issues and Moving Toward Work

I have described four kinds of emotional issues that every person faces when entering a new group situation—the problem of identity, the problem of influence and power, the problem of needs and goals, and the problem of acceptance and intimacy. In coping with these issues, members will use tough-aggressive, tender-affiliative, or withdrawal kinds of responses in their efforts to get to know each other and to find their own comfort level in the group. Until the members find roles for themselves in the group and until the group develops norms pertaining to goals, influence, and intimacy, they will be tense and will respond in various emotional ways. The price of such behavior for the group is that the members are preoccupied with their own feelings and hence less able to listen to each other and solve problems. Yet every group must go through some growing pains while members work on these issues and find their place. If the formal structure does not permit such growth, the group never becomes a real group capable of group effort. It remains a collection of individuals held together by a formal structure.

Each of us also has a learned preferred style of coping and it is important to gain some insight into what that preferred style is—when I am under interpersonal tension, do I tend to fight, seek affiliation, or withdraw emotionally? What are the consequences of each type of response? Since people differ in their preferred style, one of the dilemmas of a group trying to work on a task is that the different styles can get in each others' way. The very thing the aggressive person wants is what threatens the tender one and vice versa, and both of them threaten the emotional withdrawer. The group cannot work effectively until the members see the differences, acknowledge them, and, most important, accept them as a source of strength in the group. At the end of this chapter there is an exercise to help group members come to terms with these issues.

The consultant can help the group to resolve these emotional issues in a number of ways. First of all, she must be aware of what is going on and not become anxious over the initial communication problems between members. Second, she must help the group to realize that the early fighting, alliances, and withdrawal responses are efforts on the part of members to get to know each other, to test each other out, and to find their own place in the group. She can do this by giving the group perspective on itself through educational interventions, capsules of group theory of the sort given here. She can indicate her belief that members are working on a legitimate group-building task, not just wasting time. Third, she can help the group to appreciate the diversity of emotional styles and to understand that each style has a role to play in the group's life.

In order to be helpful, the consultant must fully understand how groups form and how, as individual self-oriented behavior declines and the group begins to take shape, the group becomes more capable of managing both its external relations and its internal functioning in order to survive and fulfill its primary task. I find myself, as a consultant, having to help client managers to accept the reality of the investments they must make in group functioning. Managers typically expect groups to get right to work, and they do not allow for a period of group formation. If the group does not solve problems quickly, members get angry and disillusioned with group effort, failing to understand the interpersonal emotional reasons why this occurs. The consultant must then encourage those managers to be patient, to allocate enough time to group meetings to permit the group to grow, and to realize that their own anger and impatience are a reflection of the same emotional issues that the other members are facing.

Finally, the consultant must be skillful in giving helpful and useful feedback to members concerning their own behavior. Much of the coping is likely to be occurring without awareness on the part of the group members as to what is happening and why. If they are to gain some insight into this behavior and become more expert in diagnosing it themselves, the consultant must try to help each member to understand his own coping behavior.

As members acquire this insight, as they begin to know how others are feeling and responding, and as they begin to realize that the group can include them and their potential contribution, they gradually relax and their ability to pay attention to others increases. When this happens, there is a change in the climate and mood of the group. There is less urgency, more listening, less running away from tasks to be performed, more willingness to cooperate as a total group, less formality and falling back on arbitrary rules, but more self-discipline and willingness to suppress personal agendas for the sake of the total group performance. The important thing to realize is that such a state can be achieved only if the group is permitted to work out its internal and external problems. It cannot be imposed or legislated.

Group Building and Internal Maintenance Functions

Resolution of the emotional problems of entry does not, unfortunately, guarantee that the group will become an effective working unit. The group, like any complex system, also requires building and maintenance, and it will not evolve to higher levels of functioning unless certain kinds of interpersonal functions are consistently fulfilled. In other words, for the group to survive and grow as an effective instrument of problem solving, members must concern themselves with the building and maintenance of good relationships. Ideally such concerns would be expressed throughout the life cycle of the group, but, as we have already seen when examining the early phases of group life, members do become preoccupied with their own needs and thus may damage their relationships to others.

The problem for the group is how to rebuild damaged relationships and/or minimize initial tendencies for them to become damaged. By a damaged relationship I mean, for example, two members who become angry at each other because they have opposing views on a task issue, or members refusing to help each other because they were outvoted or ignored and thus feel left out, or members failing to implement agreed-on solutions because they feel misunderstood or sidetracked, or members who resent others because they feel they have lost face or been humiliated. In each case, the person is temporarily preoccupied with personal needs and feelings, and is therefore relatively less able to contribute to group effort. If no group maintenance occurs, if the member is not brought back into harmony with the group, she is lost as a resource to the group or, worse, becomes an active saboteur of group effort. To avoid these negative results, the group building and maintenance functions shown in Table 9.1 must be fulfilled by one or more group members.

Harmonizing refers to efforts on the part of members to smooth over disagreements and conflicts by "pouring oil on troubled waters" or defusing a tense situation with humor. However, a real effort to come to agreement and mutual understanding by fully exploring each others' views and the deeper assumptions on which they are

Table 9.1
BUILDING AND MAINTENANCE FUNCTIONS

Harmonizing
Compromising
Gatekeeping
Encouraging
Diagnosing
Standard setting
Standard testing

based is blunted by harmonizing. Conflicts and disagreements that are brushed under the rug or denied may help bring members back into harmony with the group, but such denial may prevent a good task solution. Harmonizing is therefore needed only when conflict and disagreement has become dysfunctional and when members are so self-preoccupied that they can no longer hear each other. Harmonizing should be clearly distinguished from *compromising*, in that the former seeks to deny and avoid conflict while compromising attempts to reduce it by a willingness on the part of one or more members to give in partially for the sake of reaching a workable agreement.

Harmonizing and compromising should be viewed as maintenance functions rather than task functions because they are useful in reducing destructive types of disagreement between individuals, but are definitely of limited usefulness in solving task problems. This is a crucial point because consultants, in being concerned about group effectiveness, are likely to be perceived as favoring harmony and smooth group functioning at all times. In fact, it may be quite necessary for the group to confront and work through tough disagreements to some genuine integrative solution that does not involve any compromising or harmonizing. The consultant often has to help the group to confront and work through a problem when it would rather back-off and compromise. However, if communication has broken down and several members are arguing or taking positions for self-oriented reasons such as maintaining their own status in the group, a maintenance step may be necessary. Such a step will harmonize the conflict and help each member take stock of his own behavior, thereby reestablishing good communication before resuming work on the primary task.

Some member activities can best be thought of as preventive maintenance. For example, the function of *gatekeeping* is to insure that members who have a contribution to make to problem solution have an opportunity to make it. Gatekeeping thus involves both reducing the activity of overactive members and increasing the activity of overly passive members. I have often sat in a group and observed one person repeatedly open his mouth and get one or two words out, only to have a more aggressive person interrupt him, take away the floor, and make her own point. After two or three attempts the person gives up, unless someone notices the problem and provides an opportunity for the person to state his point. The tactics of gatekeeping are complicated, however. One does not want to cut someone off at the risk of making the person lose face, nor invite someone into the conversation for risk of exposing a lack of interest or involvement.

Encouraging serves the function of helping a person to make her point, partly to give the group the benefit of the content, but also to ensure that she and others will feel that the group climate is one of acceptance. Encouraging also serves the important function of helping a person to elaborate and clarify a point that she may not have been able to articulate perfectly. Clarifying is thus more a task-related function, while encouraging is related more to group maintenance and growth.

Diagnosing, standard setting, and standard testing are most relevant as remedial measures when relationships have broken down to some degree. What the group then needs is some period of suspending task operations while it (1) looks at its process, checks out how people are feeling about the group, its norms, and its method of operating; and (2) airs the problems and conflicts that may have arisen. Most groups do not engage in this kind of behavior unless a consultant is present or one of the members takes a real process orientation. Yet such periods of reassessment and catharsis are absolutely necessary for most task groups if they are to remain effective.

In this maintenance area the role of the consultant is often to supply the missing functions. As a group becomes more experienced, its own members will recognize what is needed, and different members will play the necessary roles. At some point, however, the consultant may introduce the whole list of maintenance functions as an educational intervention to alert members to the roles they need to fulfill.

Boundary Management Functions

Every group exists in some kind of organizational or social environment. One of its primary tasks, therefore, is to manage its relationship to that environment (Ancona, 1988). A number of different functions are involved in that process, some having to do with creating the boundaries and some having to do with maintaining them and strengthening them as the group feels the need. Some of the basic functions involved are listed in Table 9.2.

Boundary defining through specifying who is in the group and who is not in is one of the most fundamental of these functions, and the consultant will observe a variety of leader and member behaviors that serve to communicate both to insiders and to outsiders who the group is—membership lists, special uniforms, styles of communication, secret handshakes, names that groups give themselves, and minutes of meetings that communicate who is in and who is out through the distribution of who gets them.

Scouting refers to activities that provide the group with the information it needs about its environment. Such information may refer to what is going on so that the group can forecast its own future, which resources are available, what key people in the environment think of the group, and which sources of support and sources of danger exist. The consultant, by virtue of being in a boundary-spanning role, can be especially helpful in identifying when some of the critical scouting functions are not being performed, and thus prevent the group from being put into jeopardy from unanticipated environmental events.

Negotiating with the environment involves a whole host of activities designed to ensure that the group gets what it needs, manages sources of opportunity or threat, and generally maintains good relations with those people in the environment who can affect the fate of

Table 9.2
BOUNDARY MANAGEMENT FUNCTIONS

Boundary Management Functions
Boundary defining
Scouting
Negotiating
Translating
Technological gatekeeping
Guarding
Managing entry and exit

the group. Thus, from time to time the group will send out information and appoint ambassadors to negotiate with key outsiders if conflicts of interest are involved or to open up communication channels to other groups as these become necessary.

Translating refers to all those functions involved in figuring out what others' messages mean to the group and in formulating the group's own messages to the outside in terms that others will understand. In this process of information exchange with the environment, the group will need to filter, classify, and elaborate information to ensure internal comprehension and external acceptance. Here the consultant again has a special opportunity to raise questions about what different words will mean to others as she listens to the group.

An especially important activity in this arena is *technological gatekeeping,* the activity of bringing to the group whatever special information it needs to perform its task (Allen, 1977). In technically oriented groups, such as product development teams, some members scan the external technical environment for critical information items that bear on their particular task. But every group needs categories of information that need to be brought in for effective work on its primary task, hence someone must fulfill this function.

Guarding or patrolling the border refers to the activities that ensure that the group's sense of integrity will not be violated. Among the activities here are who is invited to meetings, what information is shared with which outsiders, what agreements are made among members about keeping information confidential, how are unwelcome visitors managed, and how are members dealt with who leak information or embarrass the group.

Entry and exit management refers to the processes the group uses to bring in new members (immigrants) and to release present members who leave (emigrants or outcasts). Thus, socialization activities, indoctrination, training, and rites of entry would occur around new members, and various kinds of exit rites would be involved for departing members, depending on the conditions under which they are leaving. Do members leave because they have been promoted out of the group, because they have been sent on a mission by the group, because they do not like the group, because they do not fit into the group, or because they have violated group norms and are being excommunicated? The rites of exit will vary with the reasons.

Other functions can be identified, and the particular lists I have provided are not necessarily the best ways to classify the various activities and roles that members of a group fulfill. The important point for the consultant is to recognize that every group must manage its own creation and its own maintenance both internally and externally. By observing how the group manages these various activities and which ones get over or under managed, the consultant can formulate in his mind where interventions are most necessary.

Group Growth and the Development of Structure and Culture

As a group works together and faces common problems, it gradually builds common assumptions about itself and norms of conduct. In other words, the group as a group learns how to cope with its problems of external survival in its environment and to manage and integrate its internal processes. The sum total of this learning, embodied as a set of shared implicit assumptions that come to be taken for granted, can be thought of as the "*culture*" of that group. In addition, the recurring processes that maintain the culture can be thought of as the interpersonal structure of the group, comparable to the organizational structure that defines task functions on a recurring basis. Thus, there will emerge stable role relationships, stable patterns of status supported by appropriate rituals of deference and demeanor, and stable patterns of who likes whom, who gets together with whom on an informal basis, and so on.

One of the main aspects of the culture will be the norms and rules that guide group members' daily behavior. The process by which norms and, eventually, cultural assumptions develop can be observed if one watches for *critical incidents* in the group's life and how the group deals with them (Schein, 1985, 1992). For example, as a process consultant I often observe that there are moments in the problem-solving process where the manager or someone influential attempts to get his way and one or more other members argue or refuse to go along. Some form of "insubordination" occurs. If the manager reacts punitively and makes it clear that he expects his suggestions to be taken as orders, and if the other group members now cease to argue and accept the punishment, a norm of how to deal with authority has been established. If that pattern is functional in that it leads to success in solving task and interpersonal problems, it gets reinforced until eventually the pattern becomes a shared tacit assumption of how the group works. The test of stability, then, is whether or not a new group member will be told that "this is the way we do things in this group—we follow orders."

To give another example, how do norms pertaining to varying degrees of "openness of communication" come to be formed? One group member suddenly says to another, "I think you did a lousy job of handling that customer." How the other group members, especially people in positions of authority, deal with this comment will begin to build a norm around openness and confrontation. If there is a shocked silence and the boss acts as if nothing had happened and changes the subject, she is sending a clear signal that such openness is not welcome. On the other hand, if she says, "John, I understand how you feel and would like to hear a bit more about what you observed that made you reach this judgment," she is not only accepting such remarks as legitimate, but is furthering the conversation by asking for additional information. She may also be starting to try to build a norm that judgments are legitimate only if they are backed up by examples, facts, and figures.

Norms and cultural assumptions are not easy to define or to identify in group process, yet they are very influential in determining member behavior, perceptions, and feelings. Part of their influence derives from the fact that they operate invisibly, in that they are carried in each member's head as personal guidelines. Even more important is the fact that once norms and assumptions are shared, adhering to them and using them becomes a way of expressing membership in the group. Once a norm or assumption is shared it becomes very difficult to change without involving the entire group because each member will resist change as a way of maintaining his or her membership.

For example, some typical norms in a group might be:

"We should not swear or use foul language in this group."

"We should get to meetings on time."

"We should not challenge or question the statements of the chair of the group."

"We should be informal with each other, use first names."

"Everyone in the group should participate."

"We should reach consensus and not fall back on voting."

"We should not start the meeting until all the members are present."

Those norms that are open, verbalized, or even written down function as the rules and regulations of the group and can for this purpose be called *explicit* norms. Those which are unspoken can be thought of as *implicit* or tacit norms. We know they are there from observing member reactions when they are violated—for example, shocked silences, rebukes, and "Dutch Uncle" talks. If norms are violated repeatedly, members are punished in various ways and ultimately expelled from the group if their behavior does not conform in critical areas.

One important function of the consultant is to attempt to make a group aware of its norms and shared tacit assumptions and, in that process, to check on how much consensus there is in the group on certain issues. In the previous discussion of group functions this activity was identified as the setting and testing of standards. One of the most destructive aspects of group behavior comes about from lack of consensus on critical group processes—when members assume that a norm is operating, but, in fact, none is. Valuable ideas and suggestions are suppressed because members assume that they would not be accepted, sometimes leading to the group doing something that no one really wanted to do, the previously identified Abilene Paradox (p. 159).

The consultant can help the group by observing closely how critical incidents are handled and trying to infer the kinds of norms the group is building for itself, sometimes unwittingly. The consultant can ask what the consequences will be of handling the event in the way the group did, or can help the group to identify and reconstruct some of its norms by recalling critical incidents during periods of reflection and analysis. The group can then test for itself whether the norms are helpful or constitute a barrier to effective action. For example, a group may discover that it has built a norm that people should speak up only when asked directly for an opinion or some information. The group may feel that such a formal mode of operating is getting in the way of producing good ideas. Having identified the norm, the group can then set about changing it by explicitly bringing it into line with their feelings about how the group should operate.

The group may also discover that explicit and implicit norms sometimes counteract each other. For example, there may be an explicit norm to say exactly what is on one's mind, but an implicit norm that one must not contradict the ideas of certain powerful people in the group. Alternatively, there may be an explicit norm that all members of the group are equal and have an equal voice in the discussion, but an implicit norm that higher-status people should speak first and others in the group should go along with their views. Groups often state explicitly that members should be open in their reactions to each other, yet the rules of face work prevent such openness and everyone understands why the explicit dictum is not honored. Norms can be very subtle in their operation, and the consultant must be able to identify concrete examples if the group is to learn to observe the effects of their norms.

As norms develop and become interlocked with each other, one can begin to think of the group's "culture." One of the reasons culture is so difficult to change is that when norms begin to support each other, one must change the whole set of norms instead of just the one or two that may be getting in the way. For example, assume that a group has developed the norm that members should always seek consensus on important decisions and this norm is supported by other norms such as "One must speak up if one disagrees with the decision being made," "One must always be truthful and open in task-oriented discussion," and "One must not try to take an action unless the group has achieved consensus on that action." Suppose that the group has been successful in this open way of operating. A new chairperson is appointed and the group finds itself under pressure to get work done more quickly. The chair decides to make decisions and expects members to obey them. But to change the decision *norm* toward "One must do what the chair asks" is not likely to be possible unless members also change their attitudes toward participation, as well as their deeper assumptions about what constitutes a good decision process and reliable implementation. The consultant must then help the group to see these interconnections so that change processes are undertaken realistically.

Hidden and Undiscussible Agendas. An important group phenomenon that juxtaposes the task and interpersonal issues is "hidden agendas" or a related issue, "undiscussible" agendas. Because the cultural rules of interaction and the mutual protection of "face" are powerful forces, group members often conceal what they might regard as dangerous or inappropriate content for group discussion. One category of such concealed issues is private goals that members may be pursuing which they feel would not be accepted if made public—hence "hidden agendas." Probably the most common version of these is a leader's preconceived idea of where the group should come out on a given agenda item. Members often sense that even though the leader asks for participation, he has already made up his mind and is only looking for ratification.

Another category of agenda items that is undiscussible pertains to things that everyone knows but no one is willing to say out loud because it might cause embarrassment or pain to the group, or because each person believes that the others in the group would not find the item acceptable. The images that this category conjures up tell the story:

"Are we going to throw the dead rat on the table?"

"Are we going to discuss the elephant (horse, moose) that is on the table?"

"Let's throw the dead cat over the wall."

"What is in our left-hand column?"

"What are we brushing under the rug?"

"Don't bring out the dirty linen."

"That might be too hot to handle."

Notice that the undiscussible is always huge, dirty, smelly, too hot or unpleasant to look at. We always know it is there, yet we choose not to look at it or acknowledge it. The role of the consultant vis-a-vis these topics, facts, or issues is tricky inasmuch as the consultant often does not know why the issue is undiscussible or who might be embarrassed if it were acknowledged and brought out into the open (see the case on p. 196). The most I find myself willing to do when I sense this phenomenon is to ask, "Is there something going on that we are not bringing out?" I couch this in a way that permits the group to continue to deny it if they choose to do so. One way of looking at group growth and development is to note that the group gradually builds psychological safety for itself or what Isaacs (1993) would call a "container" that permits things to be handled without spilling over and causing people to be "burned."

What about Interpersonal Content and Structure? (Cells 1, 3, 7, and 9)

Any group or organization needs to develop stable, recurring processes to manage its internal affairs, to enable members to work together, and to feel secure as a group. Recurring and stable processes are necessary to make the internal group environment safe and predictable so that members can relax enough to put their emotional energy into working on the external survival tasks (p. 170). What are the internal problems that require such stability? What is the "content" or the agenda around interpersonal processes? For any group to function it must develop a stable solution for each of the following problems, as shown below. The reader will note that these issues closely parallel the issues identified in entering a new group. But whereas those issues were viewed from the point of view of the process of an individual member entering the group, the issues identified following are more generic issues that apply to any group or organization.

1. Creating a Common Language and Conceptual Categories. The observable structure will be the actual language the group evolves as it works together: special terminology, special meanings attached to certain words and concepts, and special symbols that only insiders will understand.

2. Defining Group Boundaries and Criteria for Inclusion and Exclusion. The observable structure will be the policies and practices of recruitment, who is given symbols of membership such as uniforms or badges, policies about rehiring people who may have left, policies toward temporary members or contract workers, and rules about whom one tells things and from whom one must keep secrets, and so on.

3. Distributing Power and Status. Every group must develop criteria for who can influence whom and on what issues. In this area, what is formally structured and how things work in practice are often different. It is possible to publish organizational charts and to have rules about the chain of command, but observers often note that even on a regular basis some of these rules are ignored and alternate structures develop that often get labeled the "informal" structure. At a deeper level, this set of norms and rules deals with the management of aggression and serves to make it possible for the group to function by channeling destructive aggressive behavior into socially acceptable modes.

4. Developing Norms of Intimacy and Friendship. Every group must develop criteria for openness and intimacy, as well as appropriate levels of cooperation and competition. This area is often the least structured and, therefore, the source of most anxiety for new members until they have learned the implicit rules of the game. In observing indoctrination programs or mentoring discussions, one notes that structure is expressed by remarks such as "Around here teamwork is the name of the game," "Never get caught playing politics," "We always address the boss by his title here," "We are very informal and on a first name basis here," "You always better tell exactly what you think, even if you feel it might get you into trouble," or "You always have to be careful not to contradict the boss in public." Such rules do not get embedded into the visible formal structure as readily as more explicit rules, but they always exist in the culture (Van Maanen, 1979).

At a deeper level, these norms and rules deal with the management of the affiliative and loving feelings. As in the case of aggressive feelings, strong affiliative and sexual feelings have to be channeled into appropriate modes of behavior. When such channels fail to maintain safety for the participants, we see social breakdown such as in cases of sexual harassment.

5. Defining and Allocating Rewards and Punishments. The formal reward system, the performance appraisal system, the discipline system, the ratings of potential, and the actual recurring procedures for promoting and otherwise rewarding and punishing people are usually observable. However, as in item 4, the structures embodied in written policies and procedures do not always match the recurring regularities that may be observed—the informal reward system.

6. Explaining and Dealing with the Unexplainable and Unpredictable. This area is least likely to be formally structured, although every group will evolve rituals and procedures for dealing with unpredictable and stressful events that cannot be easily controlled. It may develop superstitions, myths, or symbolic rituals like "rain dances." Such processes may become stable in that they are passed on and taught to new generations of members.

As it interacts, the group evolves stable perceptions and relationships to deal with each of the previous areas, and these gradually become assumptions about itself and come to constitute a major part of the group's culture. Once again, the underlying assumptions will not be visible in the overt workings of the group, but the consultant will see the effects in the political alliances, in the communication patterns, in the recurring patterns of expressed feelings of members toward each other, and in the deference and demeanor members display toward each other.

The immediate intervention focus should be on the dynamic processes that are visible because then members can see the same things that the observer sees. Eventually, as the group itself becomes more sophisticated in analyzing its own processes, less visible structural and cultural elements can increasingly become the focus of intervention. If the group expresses a need to understand its own culture better, a focused educational intervention geared to culture assessment can be introduced.

Group Maturity

There is no single criterion that can be universally applied to test the degree of maturity of a group, but there are a number of dimensions that a group can use to identify and assess where it has grown and where it may still need further development. These dimensions can be put into a simple self-rating questionnaire that the members can fill out periodically to determine how they feel about each dimension and how these feelings change over time. A sample of such a questionnaire is shown in Exercise 9.2, but there is nothing absolute about the particular dimensions chosen.

The dimensions reflect some of the basic criteria of maturity that have been developed for judging individual personality. Similar criteria can be applied to groups:

1. Does the group have the capacity to deal realistically with its environment, and is it independent of its environment to an optimal degree?
2. Is there basic agreement in the group about mission, goals, and ultimate values?
3. Does the group have a capacity for self-knowledge? Does the group understand why it does what it does?
4. Is there an optimum use of the resources available within the group?
5. Is there an optimum integration of the group's internal processes—communication, decision making, distribution of authority and influence, and norms?
6. Does the group have the capacity to learn from its experience? Can it assimilate new information and respond flexibly to it?

No group is going to achieve some perfect level on all of these dimensions. Their major usefulness is that they permit the group to study its own progress over time and to identify weak spots in how it is operating. This implies a capacity to learn and puts special emphasis on question number 6 in the list.

One can elaborate these criteria further by identifying what can be thought of as a healthy learning or coping cycle for groups and organizations—the steps that have to be successfully negotiated if the group is to learn from its own experience (Schein, 1980):

1. Sensing a change in some part of the environment, either internal or external
2. Importing the relevant information into those parts of the group or organization than can act on it, and digesting the information instead of denying or subverting it
3. Changing internal processes according to the information obtained while, at the same time, reducing or managing the undesirable side effects of the changes made
4. Exporting new behavior or "products" to respond to whatever environmental changes had been sensed
5. Obtaining feedback on the degree to which the new responses successfully deal with the environmental change.

The consultant can play a crucial role in helping the group identify these stages of the coping process and evaluate which steps they handle well and which they handle poorly. It is especially important for the group to identify those areas where they are doing well and have shown real evidence of growth, because so often members see only the dysfunctional aspects of what they do. As a result, they get prematurely discouraged about their work with each other.

Where to Intervene: Task or Interpersonal? Content, Process, or Structure?

In these last two chapters I have reviewed the major elements of what is to be observed when one is in a relationship or in a group setting. The content of what is going on is the most visible and feelable, but not necessarily the most important in terms of the consequences for the group's functioning. The structure is ultimately the most constraining and determinative of what happens but is most difficult to decipher and to change. It is the process dimensions that are most likely to be fruitful for observation, analysis, and intervention. It is in the processes that there is the most potential for helping. But which processes—task processes, boundary management, or interpersonal processes? From my point of view the answer is clearly the processes that concern the group's primary task.

The Primary Task As the Prime Focus for Intervention

The most important criterion for deciding what to observe and where to intervene is the consultant's perception of what the primary task of the group is. By primary task I mean that set of goals that justify the existence of the group; the reason for which it was called together, its basic mission, the perceptions that relate the group to its external environment and that will ultimately determine its survival as a group. The primary task will not always be immediately obvious but can generally be inferred or even asked about. If the timing of the question is premature, one may not get an accurate answer, so further observation and checking may be required, but, in any case, it will be helpful to the group to be forced to be explicit about its primary task.

The focus that is safest and most likely to be productive in a new relationship with an individual client or when managing a new group is the process consultant's own primary task or goal as a helper or manager. What are you and your client or subordinates trying to do? Where do you want to be by when? What next steps make most sense given what you are trying to accomplish? In many consulting models this focus is often identified as "setting a contract with the client." That is usually not the right formulation from my point of view because it requires both client and consultant to guess about an unknown future. It is better to focus on immediate goals in order to be able to intervene effectively from the outset and to try to be helpful to the client or subordinates from the moment of contact.

It is important to *observe* interpersonal process because group outcomes result from a complex interaction of what goes on at the task and interpersonal level, but not necessarily to *intervene* on what you observe unless the group has explicitly decided to deal with interpersonal issues. One of the toughest choices for the consultant is when to intervene around interpersonal processes and when merely to note them and leave them alone. And again, the key criteria are: How much does the interpersonal process actually interfere with task performance, and how visible is the process to all members of the group. Case 9.1 at the end of this chapter illustrates the dilemma.

Summary and Conclusion

In this chapter I have focused on the interpersonal process, content, and structure that one can observe in all relationships and groups. One important focus for observation and understanding is how members enter a group, the interpersonal issues they face, how they cope with the issues, and the different styles they use. Groups have to be built and maintained, and this process is a complex of many functions that have to be fulfilled. Some of these deal with the management of emotions inside the group, and others of them deal with external relations and how the group maintains its boundaries, its identity, and its integrity.

I reviewed the main structural issues that a group faces in managing its internal relations and noted that, as the various processes become routine parts of the group's life, they can be observed as structures for communicating, defining boundaries, distributing power and status, rewarding, controlling, disciplining, defining norms for informal relations, and managing the less predictable and less controllable events that the group faces.

The shared tacit taken-for-granted assumptions that underlie these structures and determine how the group will ultimately relate to its environment, manage its primary task, and manage its internal relationships together constitute the culture of the group.

In choosing an intervention focus, the consultant must be careful not to overreact to the vivid but possibly irrelevant interpersonal events that he may observe. The intervention focus should remain on the task process. Interpersonal events should become a focus for intervention only if there is clear evidence that they are harming the group's effectiveness and if it is clear that the group is ready and able to deal with the interpersonal issues.

Case 9.1: A Dysfunctional Consequence from an Interpersonal Process Intervention

I was asked by the head of a manufacturing group to sit in on the regular biweekly meetings of the eight-person staff. My primary client, the head of manufacturing, wanted me to observe the group and his behavior as its leader in order to make him and the group more effective. I was to sit in on regular work meetings and intervene as I thought appropriate. I met the group as a group, was welcomed, and attended as a regular member.

After about five meetings I noticed a disturbing but recurring pattern.One member, call him Joe, was systematically ignored when he would make a comment. He had a regular assignment in the group and appeared by all visible signs to be a fully functioning member, but the group seemed impolite, almost rude in their treatment of Joe. I observed this interpersonal pattern over enough meetings to conclude that it was really there and that surely other members would have observed it as well, so I decided to point it out. I said "I wonder what is going on in the group around Joe's participation? He seems to be making an effort to contribute but the group is consistently ignoring him."

No sooner were these words out of my mouth than a deadly pall settled over the group and, without any further comment being made on the matter, my client, as chair of the meeting, acted as if I had not said anything and pointedly went on to another agenda item. I realized I had walked into a mine field but had no idea what had happened until after the meeting, when my client took me aside. He explained that Joe was a technical guru who had—early in his career—invented several important products on which this company had made many of its successes, but that as Joe got older he became increasingly "obsolete" and incapable of making a useful contribution. Senior management had decided not to let Joe go or to force him into early retirement, and they had canvassed various groups to see if he could be "parked" somewhere where he would "not do too much harm."

My client had volunteered to take him and had asked his group to be as nice to Joe as feasible under the circumstances; however, everyone knew that Joe's contributions were not very relevant to the group's task accomplishment. In my technical ignorance, I had not been able to observe the irrelevance of Joe's comments. Furthermore, Joe did not seem to mind. He was happy to have a home and a sense of contribution and, as far as anyone could tell, did not notice (or mind) the group's rudeness.

My intervention embarrassed everyone by describing "the elephant on the table," which no one chose to see, and it ran the risk of making Joe aware that he should be offended. I had chosen to discuss an interpersonal event without having enough data on whether it was in fact interfering with group effectiveness. It was the first of many lessons showing that, until you really know what is going on, it is best to stick to task *process issues and only register the interpersonal events for future reference.*

Exercise 9.1: Helping a Group to Learn about Itself

In your role as a convener or member suggest to your next group or meeting that they reserve fifteen minutes before the close of the meeting to "review the decisions and the process they went through to reach them."

The idea is to collect members' feelings about how the meeting has gone. Such feelings can be collected in an open-ended way or with the help of a diagnostic instrument such as that following. This particular set of questions focuses on internal relationships, but it would be equally appropriate to create a set of questions around external-boundary management if you felt that the group needed help in that area.

If a diagnostic questionnaire is used, somewhat more time must be allocated to analysis. If the group is skeptical of the value of any diagnosis, it is better to start with short periods of open-ended discussion, keeping the questionnaire in reserve until the group learns the value of such discussions and is willing to allocate more time to them. You can always start the discussion by focusing on only one or two of the questions where you feel particular issues may have arisen.

Exercise 9.2: Rating Group Effectiveness

Each member should quickly rate the group meeting on each of the following dimensions. Put the dimensions on a flip chart and have each member call out their rating on that dimension. After the group distribution is posted, discuss each dimension, especially exploring cases where one or more members deviated from the central tendency. What events or processes led the members to give the ratings that they gave?

A. Goals

1 2 3 4 5 6 7

Confused, conflicting — Clear, shared

B. Participation

1 2 3 4 5 6 7

Few dominate, poor listening — All get in, good listening

C. Feelings Expression

1 2 3 4 5 6 7

Ignored, not expressed — Freely expressed

D. Diagnosis of Group Problems

1 2 3 4 5 6 7

Jump directly to solutions — Seek basic causes before acting

E. Decision-Making Processes

1 2 3 4 5 6 7

Self-authorization, minority rule — Consensus

F. Leadership

1 2 3 4 5 6 7

Autocratic, centralized — Distributed, widely shared

G. Trust Level

1 2 3 4 5 6 7

Members do not trust each other — Members have high trust

Exercise 9.3: Silent Observation and Feedback

A third and more demanding exercise is to convince the group members that it is useful to assign one member to be a silent observer of process and have him or her provide feedback to the group as appropriate. This role is sometimes combined with the facilitator role. Again, the group should set aside 30 minutes at the end of the meeting to allow the silent observer to make some comments and then analyze their own observations and reactions.

The role of the "consultant" (the silent observer) during the post-meeting diagnostic periods must be carefully managed. The great temptation is to rush in, once the group has opened the door, and report all the meaty observations that the consultant has made over the past several hours. This temptation is often heightened by the group's actually inviting the consultant to tell the group all of the observations. "How do you feel we did during the meeting?" "You've been sitting observing us for a couple of hours; what thoughts do you have?"

At this time the consultant must remind herself of her basic mission: to get the group to share in diagnosis and to help the group to learn to diagnose its own processes. If she succumbs and takes the lead in making observations, there is great danger that the group will abdicate its own responsibility for diagnosis. Furthermore, if the consultant makes observations with which some members disagree, she quickly finds herself in a position of having been neutralized. Finally, if the consultant comes in with her own observations first, she is forgetting that her own filters are operating and that she may be reporting things that are relatively less important or which are a reflection of her own biases.

Once the group has identified an area where members themselves have observations to make, it is entirely appropriate for the consultant to add her own observations and to use the opportunity to deepen members' understanding by offering some group theory as well as observations. But the group must take the lead, and the consultant must work within the areas defined by the group as relevant. If the group urges the consultant to do this job for them, she must politely decline and urge the group to try its own hand at diagnosis.

Exercise 9.4: Measuring a Group's Maturity

In helping a group to assess its "maturity" or growth, it is helpful to supply some dimensions in the form of a questionnaire because it is unlikely that the group would be able to invent these dimensions in an open-ended process analysis period. The questionnaire presented below can serve as a starting point.

A MATURE GROUP POSSESSES (rate each dimension along the scale provided):

1. Adequate mechanisms for getting feedback:

Poor					Excellent
1	2	3	4	5	6

2. Adequate decision-making procedure:

Poor					Very Adequate
1	2	3	4	5	6

3. Optimal cohesion:

Low					Optimal
1	2	3	4	5	6

4. Flexible organization and procedures:

Inflexible					Very Flexible
1	2	3	4	5	6

5. Maximum use of member resources:

Poor					Excellent
1	2	3	4	5	6

6. Clear communications

Unclear					Very Clear
1	2	3	4	5	6

7. Clear goals accepted by members

Clear and accepted					Not clear, not accepted
1	2	3	4	5	6

8. Interdependence with authority figures

Low					High
1	2	3	4	5	6

9. Appropriate sharing of leadership functions

Low					High
1	2	3	4	5	6

10. Capacity for creativity and growth

Low					High
1	2	3	4	5	6

11. Supply additional dimensions that may be relevant

___

___

10

Facilitative Process Interventions: Dialogue

All human relationships evolve around some form of conversation. The consultant establishes a relationship with a client through conversation. Diagnostic inquiry is a form of conversation, as is the delivery of information, persuasion, confrontation, and deliberate feedback. Group interaction during meetings is a series of conversations. From some points of view all of life is a series of structured conversations between various role occupants. It is, in fact, the ability to have conversation that makes us distinctly human.

But, as we all know, some forms of conversation are more satisfactory than others. Some are more likely than others to produce learning and to be helpful to clients in solving their problems and achieving their goals and ideals. Conversation can be totally spontaneous or can be managed according to the intentions of the participants. In Chapter 7, I pointed out how deliberate feedback is one such "managed" form of conversation designed to help clients get a better sense of how they come across to others, how their performance is perceived by others, and what their blind spots may be. Another such form of "managed" conversation is Dialogue.[1]

Dialogue can be thought of as a form of conversation that makes it possible, even likely, for participants to become aware of some of the hidden and tacit assumptions that derive from our cultural learning, our language, and our psychological makeup. Ordinary or spontaneous conversation is governed by all the cultural rules previously described and is subject to all of the psychological biases and filters described in the analysis of the ORJI cycle. In order for us to

[1]There are many versions of Dialogue floating around in the field and world wide. The particular form I will be discussing derives from the work of David Bohm (1989) and is currently being developed by William Isaacs (1993).

function in our daily life we have to assume that we understand each other and that we are operating from similar assumptions. Only when communication breaks down do we question what is going on, and then we often choose to attribute the breakdown to motives or incompetence on the part of others in the conversation. When we get into arguments and conflicts with others we attribute the problem again to motives and intentions and find it difficult to consider the possibility that we are truly operating from different premises and assumptions. One of the most important challenges for negotiation facilitators is getting the parties to accept the possibility that, if they truly understood each other, their goals might not conflict.

Dialogue as a form of conversation starts with the assumptions that every person comes with different assumptions and that mutual understanding is in most cases an illusion. So, before we can even get to the kind of learning that is made possible by deliberate feedback, we need to become more conscious of our own tacit assumptions and to recognize that others in the conversation may be operating from different assumptions. Dialogue makes it possible not only to create a climate for more effective interpersonal learning, but also may be the *only* way to resolve interpersonal conflict when such conflict derives from differing tacit assumptions and different semantic definitions.

In this chapter I will make a more formal analysis of dialogue as a form of conversation, but of course we seek to have meaningful conversations that feel like real dialogues all the time in our normal human affairs. Consultants seek to have meaningful dialogue with their clients without formally labeling their conversations as dialogues. All of us can recall many instances in which we had conversations that were fruitful and filled with a sense of mutual understanding. What we need to understand is what made such mutual understanding possible and how can we structure conversations to increase the probability of dialogue.

Dialogue vs. Sensitivity Training

The best way to explore this concept of Dialogue is to contrast it as a form of conversation and communication with other forms that we are more familiar with, especially the kind of conversation that derives from the concept and practice of Sensitivity Training Groups as evolved in the Bethel Human Relations Training courses (Schein & Bennis, 1965; Bradford *et al.,* 1964). I will describe my own experiences in both kinds of groups in order to demystify both dialogue and sensitivity training. Some proponents have made dialogue sound like a most esoteric experience and sensitivity training as a major personal therapeutic experience. In my view, neither of these stereotypes is correct for the mainstream practice of these learning processes. What links the two methods and, at the same time, sharply differentiates them has more to do with developing particular elements of "listening."

Most communication and human relations workshops emphasize "active" listening, by which is meant that one should pay attention to all of the communication channels—the spoken words, the body language, tone of voice, and emotional content. One should learn to focus initially on what the other person is saying rather than on one's own intended response. In contrast, dialogue focuses initially on listening to oneself and on getting in touch with the underlying assumptions that "automatically" determine when we choose to speak and what we choose to say. Sensitivity training is focused more on hearing others' *feelings* and tuning in on all the levels of communication; dialogue is focused more on the *thinking* process and how our perceptions and cognitions are preformed by our past experiences.

The assumption underlying dialogue is that if we become more conscious of how our thought process works, we will appreciate more the inherent complexity of communication and mutual understanding, and we will gradually build enough common understanding to allow the collective thought process to surmount the individual thought process. An important goal of dialogue is to enable *the group* to reach a higher level of consciousness and creativity through the gradual creation of a shared set of meanings and a "common" thinking process. Though the focus is often on how larger groups achieve this common thinking, the concept applies just as much to the two-person group of consultant and client. Real help can only be delivered when both consultant and client are using a common set of assumptions and have developed some common language.

Active listening to others plays a role in the dialogue process, but is not initially the central focus or purpose. In fact, I discovered that in dialogue groups I spent a lot more time in *self-analysis,* attempting to understand what *my own assumptions* were and was relatively less focused on actively listening to others. Eventually, dialogue participants do "listen actively" to each other, but the path for getting there is quite different.

In the typical sensitivity-training workshop, participants explore relationships through "opening up" and sharing, through giving and receiving deliberate feedback, and through examining all of the *emotional* problems of communication. In dialogue, the participants explore all the complexities of *thinking and language*. We discover how arbitrary our basic categories of thought and perception are and, thereby, become conscious of imperfections or biases in our basic *cognitive* processes. One of my former MIT colleagues, Fred Kofman, provided a good example of such bias by reminding us of the platypus story. When this creature was first discovered, scientists found themselves in a major controversy. Was it a mammal, a bird, or a reptile? The automatic assumption was that the categories "mammals," "birds," and "reptiles" *are the reality* into which this new creature had to be fitted. We tend to forget that these categories were invented to *represent* and *categorize* reality, rather than *being* that reality. Fred reminded us that the platypus was a platypus. It is not necessary to force the platypus into any category, except as a matter of convenience. In fact, when we do force the fit, we reduce opportunities for learning about the reality that is actually out there.

The dialogue process makes us conscious of how the thought process is based on *fragmenting* the world into convenient categories to make perception and discrimination possible. These categories are taught to us early in life, through the language we learn. What we forget is that the categories are arbitrary ones, evolved within cultures for convenience and for ease in dealing with those aspects of external reality that matter to our survival. As we get more reflective in a dialogue group, we begin to see some of the arbitrary ways in which we perceive external reality and realize that others in the group may slice up their external reality differently. We become aware that reality is a continuum and that it is our thought process that fragments it into concepts and categories.

In sensitivity training the goal is to use the group process to develop our *individual* interpersonal skills, whereas dialogue aims to build a group that can think generatively, creatively, and, most importantly *together*. When dialogue works, the group can surmount the creative abilities of its individual members and achieve levels of creative thought that no one would have initially imagined. Dialogue is thus a potential vehicle for creative problem identification and problem solving. In the client/consultant relationship, dialogue can lead to diagnostic insights and ideas for further intervention which surmount what either the consultant or client might have thought of alone.

In sensitivity training, the learning emphasis falls heavily on learning how to give and receive deliberate feedback, a process that is countercultural because of our need to maintain face. Therefore, it elicits high levels of emotion and anxiety. The process promises to give us new insights, to reveal our blind sides to us, and to provide opportunities to see ourselves as others see us. For many, this is not only novel but potentially devastating—even though it may be ultimately necessary for self-improvement. To receive deliberate feedback is to put our illusions about ourselves on the line; to give deliberate feedback is to risk offending and unleashing hostility in the receiver.

In contrast, dialogue emphasizes the natural flow of conversation. It actually (though somewhat implicitly, in my experience) discourages deliberate feedback and direct interpersonal encounters. In dialogue the whole group is the object of learning, and the members share the potential excitement of collectively discovering ideas that none of them might have ever individually thought of. Feedback may occur, especially in relation to individual behavior that undermines the natural flow of conversation, but feedback is not encouraged as a goal of the group process.

Dialogue often works best when the group members sit in a circle and talk to "the campfire" instead of to each other. A general property of the group is what we all have to say, not a set of remarks between specific individuals that others happen to hear as well. Dialogue thus invites violation of some cultural "rules" such as the norm to respond to questions, to look each other in the eye when we address each other, and to give everyone a chance for equal air time. To many, the natural flow of conversation feels like a slowing down, a loss of focus, and an abandonment of concern for getting a task accomplished or reaching a conclusion. One of the most dramatic illustrations of this norm "adjustment" was the comment by a participant at the end of a two-hour dialogue session that this was the first time in many years that he had felt "*empowered* to remain silent."

One of the most important differences between dialogue and other communication enhancers is that the group size is not arbitrarily limited. Whereas sensitivity training only works effectively with groups of ten to fifteen, I have been in dialogue groups as large as sixty and have been told that dialogue has been tried successfully with 100 or more. The notion that such large groups can accomplish anything is counterintuitive. However, large groups are often composed of individuals who have had prior small group experience with dialogue. In the large groups, these people have lower initial expectations and assumptions about the need for everyone to have significant "air time." At the other extreme, dialogue is entirely appropriate for a two-person group and, as I have argued, is necessary as part of the relationship-building process between the consultant and client.

In sensitivity training, everyone is expected to learn and to participate in the learning process. In dialogue, the role of individual contribution is blunted somewhat by the goal of reaching a higher level of communication as a group. Because much of the individual work is internal, examining one's own assumptions, the need to compete for "one's share of the air time" is greatly reduced. In terms of length and frequency of meetings, dialogue meetings can be more flexible, variable, and less intense.

How Does Dialogue Get Started?

In all of the groups that I have participated in, the convener started by arranging the setting to be as nearly as possible a *circle* of chairs and then *describing* the concept of dialogue. In each case, the group could understand the essence sufficiently to begin the conversation. The key to this understanding is to link dialogue to other experiences we have had that felt like real communication. One way to begin is to ask participants to think back to times when they have felt they had really good communication with someone else and then get reports from them to identify the common themes. This process is outlined in Table 10.1.

The theory behind such a startup is entirely consistent with what we know about group dynamics, and it involves several important assumptions about new groups:

1. The group will function best when members feel as equal as possible. (Even if there are actual rank or status differences in the group, everyone should sit in a circle.)
2. The group will function best when all members feel a sense of guaranteed "air time" to establish their identity in the group. Therefore, asking everyone to make some comments in an initial "check-in" guarantees that everyone will have his turn and space. In larger groups not everyone might speak, but the norm is that everyone has an opportunity to speak if he wants to, and that the group will take whatever time is necessary for that to happen. This required "check-in" can also be done by just going around the circle and having each person state his name and make a brief comment. The important point is that everyone will have said something.
3. Early in the group's life, members will be concerned primarily about themselves and their own feelings; hence legitimizing personal experiences and drawing on these experiences is a good way to begin.

Table 10.1
THE ROLE OF THE CONVENER/FACILITATOR IN THE INITIATION OF A DIALOGUE SESSION

- Organize the physical space to be as nearly a circle as possible. Whether or not people are seated at a table or tables is not as important as the sense of equality that comes from sitting in a circle
- Introduce the general concept, then ask everyone to think about an experience of dialogue in the sense of "good communication" in their past
- Ask people to share with their neighbor what the experience was and to think about the characteristics of that experience (this works because people are relating very concrete experiences, not abstract concepts)
- Ask group members to share with the total group what it was in the past experiences that made for good communication and write these characteristics on a flip chart
- Ask the group to reflect on these characteristics by having each person in turn talk about her reactions
- Let the conversation flow naturally once everyone has commented (this requires one and a half to two hours or more)
- Intervene as necessary to clarify or elucidate, using concepts and data that illustrate the problems of communication (some of these concepts are spelled out below)
- Close the session by asking each person to comment in whatever way she chooses.

The length and frequency of meetings depends upon the size of the group, the reasons for getting together, and the constraints operating on members. Most groups with which I have been involved met for one to two hours, but my sense is that the meetings could be shorter or longer. In workshops where I am trying to introduce the idea over several days, I have tried 20-minute sessions each day with good success. If a group is meeting more than once, getting the second and subsequent meetings going is fairly routine, provided each meeting starts with a formal check-in of some sort—even if it is just a one- or two-word statement of feelings of the moment. Again, what is important is to legitimize air time for everyone and to tacitly imply that everyone should make a contribution to starting the meeting, even though the content of that contribution can be virtually anything. Obviously, this process would vary according to the size of the group, but the important principle to communicate is "we are all in this together on an equal basis."

The convener/facilitator has a choice of how much theoretical input to provide, either at the beginning or as the process gets going. Concepts should be provided if the group really needs them, but if their presentation is incorrectly timed, it can disrupt the group process.

Optional Concepts to Introduce Dialogue

If a group is not familiar with the idea of dialogue, some introductory description and conceptual grounding can be helpful. It is especially helpful to show participants how to differentiate dialogue from other kinds of conversation. I have found it helpful to draw the roadmap shown in Fig. 10.1 based on Isaacs' (1993) basic model. By mapping forms of conversation in terms of two basic paths, the model highlights the essential concept underlying dialogue—the discovery of one's own internal process for choice regarding when to speak and what to say.

Suspension. As a conversation develops, there inevitably comes a point where we sense some form of disconfirmation. We perceive that our point was not understood, or we elicit disagreement, challenge, or attack. At that moment we usually respond with anxiety or anger, though we may be barely aware of it. The first issue of choice, then, is whether to trust the feeling and whether to allow the feeling to surface. We typically do not experience these as choices until we have become more reflective and conscious of our own emotions. But we clearly have a choice of whether or not to express the feeling overtly in some form or another.

As we become more aware of these choices, we also become aware of the possibility that the feeling was triggered by our perception of what the others in the group did, *and that these perceptions themselves could be incorrect*. As previously pointed out, the most difficult part of the ORJI cycle is to observe accurately. Before we give in to anxiety and/or anger, we must determine whether the data were accurately perceived and interpreted. Were we, in fact, being challenged or attacked or whatever?

This moment is critical. As we become more observant and reflective, we begin to realize how much our initial perception can be

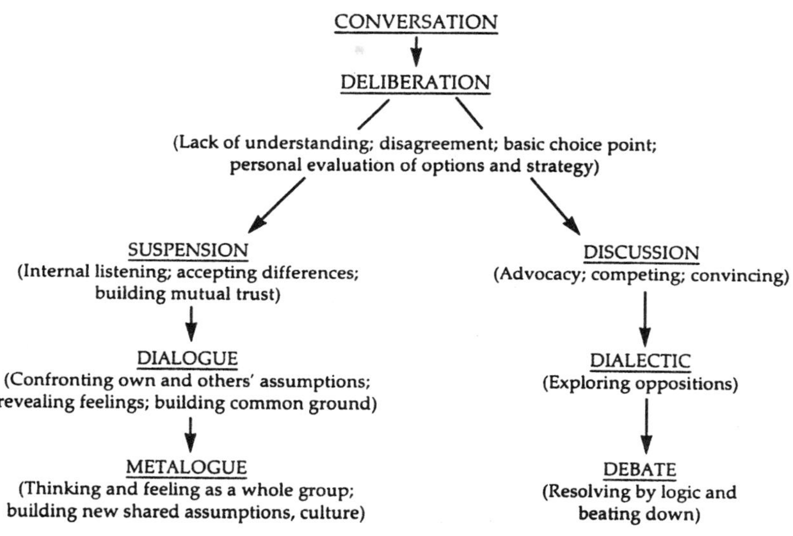

Figure 10.1
WAYS OF TALKING TOGETHER

Source: From "On Dialogue, Culture, and Organizational Learning." *Organizational Dynamics,* Autumn 1993: Volume 22, #2.

colored by expectations based on our cultural learning and our past learning experiences. What we perceive is often based on our needs, our expectations, our projections, our psychological defenses and, most of all, our culturally learned assumptions and thought categories. It is this process of becoming reflective that makes us realize that the first problem of listening to others is to identify the distortions and biases that filter our own cognitive processes. *We have to learn to listen to ourselves before we can really understand others*, and such internal listening is especially difficult when one is in the midst of an active task-oriented discussion. Furthermore, there may be nothing in our cultural learning to support such introspection.

Once we have identified the basic issue that our perception itself may not be accurate, we face a second more fundamental choice—whether or not to actively check the perception by taking up the point, asking what the person really meant, explaining ourselves further, or in some other way focusing specifically on the person who produced the disconfirming event. As we know from observing group process, choosing to confront the situation immediately (for example, asking someone to explain what he or she meant with a specific remark) can quickly polarize the conversation around a few people and a few issues.

An alternative choice is to "suspend." Suspension implies that we let the issue—our perceptions, our feelings, our judgments, and our impulses—rest for a while in a state of suspension to see what more will come up from inside ourselves and from others. What this means operationally in the conversation (and what I have experienced over and over) is that, when I am upset by what someone else says, I have a genuine choice between (1) voicing my reaction and (2) letting the matter go (thereby suspending my own reaction). Suspending is particularly difficult if I perceive that my prior point has been misunderstood or misinterpreted. Nevertheless, I have found repeatedly that if I suspend, I find that further conversation clarifies the issue and that my own interpretation of what may have been going on is validated or changed without my having to actively intervene.

It is when a number of members of the group discover some value in suspending their own reactions that the group begins to go down the dialogue path shown in Fig. 10.1. In contrast, the group goes down the path of discussion and ultimately gets mired in unproductive debate when a number of members choose to react by immediately disagreeing, elaborating, questioning, and in other ways focusing on a particular trigger that set them off. Suspension allows reflection that is very similar to the emphasis in group dynamics training on observing the "here and now." Isaacs (1993) correctly notes, however, that reflective attention is looking at the past. Instead, he suggests that what we need is "proprioception"—attention to and living in the present moment.

Ultimately, dialogue tries to enable us to achieve a state of knowing our thoughts as we are having them. Whether proprioception in this sense is psychologically possible is debatable, but the basic idea is to shorten the internal feedback loop as much as possible. As a result, we can get in touch with what is going on in the here and now and become conscious of how much our thoughts and perceptions are both a function of our past learning and the immediate events that triggered them. This learning is difficult at best, yet it lies at the heart of the ability to enter dialogue.

Dialogue vs. Discussion. How do we know whether discussion and/or debate is more or less desirable than dialogue? Should we always go down the dialogue path? I would argue that discussion/debate is a valid problem-solving and decision-making process *only if one can assume that the group members understand each other well enough to be "talking the same language."* Paradoxically, such a state of sharing categories probably cannot be achieved unless some form of dialogue has taken place sometime in the group's history. The danger in premature discussion is that the group reaches a "false consensus"—members assume that they mean the same thing by certain terms. Only later do they discover that subtle differences in meaning have major consequences for implied action and implementation.

Dialogue, on the other hand, is a basic process for building common understanding, in that it allows one to see the hidden meanings of words in our own communication. By suspending and letting disagreement go, meanings become clearer and the group gradually builds a shared set of meanings that make much higher levels of mutual understanding and creative thinking possible. As we listen to ourselves and others in what may often appear to be a disjointed rather random conversation, we begin to see the biases and subtleties in how each member thinks and expresses meanings. In this process we do not convince each other, but rather we build a common experience base that allows us to learn collectively. The more the group has achieved such collective understanding, the easier it becomes to reach decisions, and the more likely it will be that the decision will be implemented in the way that the group meant it.

Group Dynamics. The dynamics of "building the group" occur in parallel with the process of conducting the dialogue. Issues of identity, role, influence, group goals, norms of openness and intimacy, and questions of authority all have to be worked on, though much of this occurs implicitly rather than explicitly (as in the case of a human relations or group dynamics workshop). The group will display all of the classical issues that occur around authority vis-a-vis the facilitator—Will the facilitator tell us what to do? Will we do it even if we are told? Does the facilitator have the answers and is withholding them, or is she exploring along with the rest of us? At what point can we function without the facilitator?

As issues of group growth and development arise, they have to be dealt with if they interfere with or confuse the dialogue process.

The facilitator should therefore be skilled in group facilitation as well, so that the issues that arise in the group can be properly sorted into two categories: issues that have to do with the development of the dialogue, and issues that have to do with the development of the group as a group. In my own experience, the dialogue process speeds up the development of the group and should therefore be the primary driving process in each meeting. A major reason for this "speed up" is that dialogue creates psychological safety and thus allows individual and group change to occur, assuming that there is already present some motivation to change. Dialogue cannot create the need to change, but it certainly facilitates the process of change.

Some initial motivation to engage in a dialogue must be present. Because the process appears initially to be very "inefficient," a group will not readily volunteer to engage in dialogue unless it is unfrozen in some other respects; i.e., unless group members feel disconfirmed (are hurting), are feeling some guilt or anxiety, and need to overcome such feelings in order to get on with a task. The core task or ultimate problem, then, is likely to be the longer-run reason of why the group will meet in the first place.

The group may initially experience dialogue as a detour or a slowing down of problem solving. But real change does not happen until people feel psychologically safe, and the implicit or explicit norms that are articulated in a dialogue session provide that safety by giving people both a sense of direction and a sense that the dangerous aspects of interaction will be contained. If the group can work on the task or problem using the dialogue format, it should be able to reach a valid level of communication much faster.

Containment. Isaacs speaks articulately of the need to build a *container* for dialogue, to create a climate and a set of explicit or implicit norms that permits people to handle "hot issues" without getting "burned." The consultant/facilitator must contribute to all of this by modeling the behavior—being nonjudgmental and displaying the ability to suspend his own categories and judgments. This skill becomes especially relevant in group situations where conflict heats up to the point that it threatens to spill over or out of the container. At that point, the facilitator can simply legitimize the situation, acknowledging the conflict as real and as something to be viewed by all the members in the here and now without judgment or recrimination, or even without the felt need to do anything about it. Conflict can be suspended as well.

But the most important feature of dialogue that helps contain feelings is that the focus is on the thought process rather than on emotions. Participants can begin to see how emotions come into being as a result of how our thought process works, rather than accepting emotions as the primary reality to be dealt with. Feelings need to be understood, not necessarily expressed. And if expressed, they do not have to be reacted to in a knee-jerk fashion. The group members can attempt to understand where feelings come from and what their consequences are. By intellectualizing emotions, members can contain them.

Task vs. Process: Dialogue about What? A common question that arises when one proposes a dialogue is "What shall we talk about?" In my experience, the answer is situational. Sometimes it is enough to talk about dialogue itself. At other times there are pressing task concerns that need to be talked about, but in a more reflective "dialogue" fashion. Sometimes the facilitator can introduce a topic, but often a topic emerges just from the comments made during the check-in process.

Once a group experiences dialogue, the process tends to feed on itself. I have been in groups that chose to stay in a circle and continue in a dialogue mode even when they tackled other work—concrete tasks with time limits. The insights about the value of a check-in, the growing ability of members to suspend, the common awareness of how our thoughts tend to fragment the external reality in arbitrary ways, and the sensitivity to our own and each others' assumptions carries over into task work.

Dialogue is, by definition, a process that has meaning only in a group. Two or more people have to collaborate for dialogue to occur. But this collaboration rests on an individual choice, based on a certain attitude toward how to get the most out of a conversation and on certain skills of reflection and suspension. Once the group has those attitudes and skills collectively, it is possible to have even highly time sensitive problem-solving meetings in a dialogue format.

As pointed out previously, most people have a general sense of what dialogue is about and have experienced versions of it in their past relationships. Thus, even in a problem-solving meeting, a facilitator may suggest that the group experiment with dialogue. In my own experience it is best to introduce, early on, the idea that behind our comments and perceptions there are always assumptions and that our problem-solving process will be improved if we get in touch with our own and each others' assumptions. Consequently, if the conversation turns into too much of a discussion or debate, I can legitimately raise the question of whether the disagreement is based on different assumptions and then explicitly explore those assumptions. Continually focusing the group on the cognitive categories and assumptions that underlie conversation is, from this point of view, the central role of the consultant.

Conclusions and Implications for Process Consultation

Dialogue can be thought of as "good" communication. We think of dialogue as a conversation in which we have understood each other and have exchanged views in a meaningful way. In this sense, the building of a helping relationship between client and consultant is equivalent to reaching a conversational level that each person experiences as a dialogue, not a discussion or debate. Dialogue is therefore a prerequisite at the face-to-face level for any helping relationship. Analyzing the nature of dialogue at the larger group level helps clarify some of the essential issues that underlie communication, but those issues apply just as much to the two-person situation as to larger groups.

What remains as an issue for process consultation, then, is how to manage conversations to becoming more like dialogues? How can the consultant intervene to improve communication with the client? Obviously the first principle is for the consultant to understand the differences and to know when and how she is making assumptions, how her thought processes fragment the world into arbitrary linguistic categories, and how her assumptions about the nature of reality might differ from those of the client. In her own communication behavior, the consultant must demonstrate the ability to suspend, to check assumptions, and to help the client face his own assumptions.

One of the consultant's best interventions to make this happen is to consciously suspend some answers to some questions. I often find myself pressed by a client to say what I would do or to give advice on what to do next. At this moment, I have a choice that is countercultural but effective. I can remain silent and wait (i.e., suspend my reaction). It is surprising how often the silence is filled by more data from the client, answers of his own, and further and deeper questions. In suspending my own reaction I have also been a role model to show the client that one does not always have to answer questions. Becoming able to suspend is the beginning of developing a skill in reflecting and this is a skill the consultant wants the client to learn because new insights into the client's situation will only come from more skillful observation and reflection.

As the consultant/client relationship develops it will inevitably move toward dialogue, but as both parties get better at it they will also forget what they are doing. It is probably helpful from time to time for them to analyze the nature of their conversation and to assess the degree to which it has become an effective dialogue. Such analysis will help the client to achieve greater insight into conversational dynamics and will enable him to train his colleagues in improving their conversational mode. And, as we will all recognize, the ability to enter into dialogue becomes crucial when the parties to the conversation come from different cultural or subcultural units. The following cases are intended to illustrate some of these general points, and the exercises can help the reader get started in getting a feel for what is involved.

Case Examples

Case 10.1: Countercultural Elements of Dialogue

As part of a five-day training workshop on Process Consultation and Culture I broke the 100 or so participants into groups of eight and asked them to learn how to use dialogue as a form of conversation for thirty minutes each day. I presented the general description and encouraged a more reflective attitude by asking participants to suspend several rules of conversation: (1) pretend that you are sitting around a campfire and make all your remarks to the fire; don't look at each other; (2) do not feel obligated to ask others for clarification even if you have not understood them; and (3) do not feel obligated to answer questions that someone asks you directly.

After the first thirty-minute period I asked for comments and questions. The most powerful reaction was that people found it almost impossible to break the cultural rules of eye contact, clarification, and answering questions. Many participants were acutely uncomfortable and simply ignored the rules, others tried not to look at each other and found it very difficult, and almost everyone agreed that suspension went against the grain. However, by the second or third thirty-minute session, all of the groups were comfortable with suspension of eye contact and were able to converse without getting into polarized clarification or question/answer discussions. In listening to the group, it was striking how the decibel level in the room dropped with successive thirty-minute sessions.

Case 10.2: Challenging the Norm of Equal Participation

As part of a two-day workshop on process consultation I was asked to run a two-hour dialogue session. The twenty people in the group were all professional counselors and consultants so the need to give a lot of guidance was minimal. We began with a check-in that asked people to give their name and one or two sentences of what they hoped to get out of the session. During the two-hour session the conversation flowed relatively comfortably from one topic to another, and I could see group members becoming more reflective.

Toward the end of the session I asked each member to "check-out" by giving one or two sentences of reactions to the previous dialogue session. Among the various comments, the one most striking and revealing was one person's statement that, for the first time in many years, he had during the last two hours "felt empowered to remain silent." He and others noted that in most groups there is a norm that everyone not only should have the right to a certain amount of air time, but that there was a kind of obligation to participate. Being silent is ominous, and chairpersons often call on silent members to see what they are thinking, often on the erroneous assumption that they need help in "getting in." This person reminded us how meaningful silent reflection can be and how important it is to legitimize it in group meetings.

Case 10.3: Introducing Dialogue into a Work Problem

I was working with the Exploration and Production Division of a large oil company to try to identify what the subculture of this particular unit was. They needed to understand their subculture because the company was trying to decide whether or not this division should survive and how its performance should be measured. In the process of doing a cultural analysis with the top forty members of the division, it developed that there were two strong subcultures within it, reflecting the core technologies and primary tasks of Exploration on the one hand and Production on the other hand. The cultural analysis produced a certain amount of insight but did not clarify the question of the division's right to survive and how one would measure its productivity. There were obvious indicators such as the amount of oil/gas discovered and the efficiency of production, but the group could not really agree on anything.

I began to work with the top twelve managers of the E & P group on the task of developing the measurement system and found in several successive meetings that they kept getting into debates about different options. On one of these occasions I had the insight that there were not just two different concepts of measurement reflecting the E & P point of view, but that among the twelve of them there were many more assumptions about the nature of measurement that were tacit. I suggested that for our next meeting we take three or more hours to have a dialogue instead of a meeting.

We picked an evening time, set the room up in a circle, and started with a general orientation. I then suggested that after a short check-in we should systematically go around the room and give each person a chance to talk out in a relaxed way what "measurement" meant to them and how they would like to be measured. The rule was no questions or challenges, just talking out. I recorded each person's concept on a flip chart.

It took over an hour for all twelve concepts to be talked out, but by the end of that hour every member of the group felt a sense of real progress in that they now understood how complex the measurement terrain really was and why they had had difficulty reaching agreement in their previous meetings. In the next hour or so they focused on their task, reached consensus on the need to convince higher management to measure E & P differently, and presented to senior management detailed proposals on each of the systems. In this case the period of dialogue was a necessary detour to reach a working consensus on their task.

What this case highlights is that dialogue as a form of managed conversation was a necessary part of the problem-solving process, but it was very difficult for the group to create such a managed detour without outside help and without some concepts and a method for managing conversations for learning ends. I had to create the container in which it was possible to share their individual views without feeling unsafe in doing so, and dialogue as that container saved face in that this group of active problem solvers could see the detour as an experiment rather than evidence of their failure to reach agreement.

The required process of going around the circle with guaranteed individual air time created safety in that the group was used to a much more challenging debate format. Note that the structure of dialogue requires both periods of required interaction to make sure that everyone shares in the sense that "we are in this together" and other periods in which silence is legitimized so that members can be safely reflective. In the case of the E & P group, once they had gone around with their individual views, the participation changed dramatically but no one was uncomfortable with it.

Exercise 10.1: Quick Exercise in Dialogue (30 minutes)

1. Find six to seven others to work with and sit in a circle.
2. Think of yourselves as a "council" sitting around a campfire.
3. One person starts the check-in process by giving his name and saying one or two sentences of where he is at in terms of perceptions, feelings, thoughts. When that person is done, he says "I'm in" and turns to the person to the right for their check-in until everyone has checked in.
4. When everyone is done, leave a period of silence and then talk to the campfire about whatever comes to mind for about 20 minutes.
5. Go through a period of "check-out" by having each person tell in a sentence or two where they are at the end of this meeting.

Exercise 10.2: Exploring the Conditions for Dialogue

1. Work with one other person.
2. Share with each other one or two times in your past when you felt you had a really good, meaningful conversation with another person.
3. Take turns analyzing the conversation—what were the characteristics of the other person in the conversation, the setting in which it occurred, how long it took, what it focused on, and anything else you consider relevant.
4. Analyze together what the two conversations have in common. How would you generalize the conditions necessary for a good, meaningful conversation? What inferences can you draw about how you would have to set up those conditions in a group?

Part IV
Process Consultation in Action

The basic philosophy of process consultation has now been described and illustrated. The kinds of principles by which consultants must operate and the kinds of interventions that they must make in the conversational process to provide deliberate feedback and to help a group work better or to create more of a dialogue have been detailed. The hidden forces that distort communication and human relationships have been analyzed. Now it remains to illustrate how all of this plays together in the context of some cases that run for a period of time.

What the reader should note is that the three basic roles of (1) giving expert information, (2) diagnosing and prescribing from a "doctor" vantage point, and (3) process consultation are in constant interplay. Any consultant/helper will find it necessary to enter and leave these roles constantly as the reality changes. It is therefore better to think of process consultation as a skill that any helper must have, rather than seeing it as a full-time occupational role, i.e., "Process Consultant." But, paradoxically, in order for the helper to know when to be in which consulting mode, she needs most the skills associated with process consultation—the ability to make instant diagnoses and the ability to vary her own behavior to adapt to reality, go with the flow, and seize targets of opportunity.

Consultation projects evolve in complex ways. One cannot really identify simple sequential patterns such as "scouting," "entry," "contracting," "diagnosis," and "intervention." Instead what happens is that one finds oneself intervening initially with contact clients, then with intermediate clients, then with primary clients who may engage one in a project that involves a whole new set of contact and primary clients, all the while thinking about ultimate and unwitting clients to insure that their needs and issues are not ignored or marginalized. In each relationship the consultant must be perpetually diagnostic and gear her interventions carefully to build and maintain helping relationships. And since conversation is the medium through which most of this happens, maintaining a focus on the dynamics of communication and conversation becomes essential.

How this plays out over a period of time will be illustrated in the next chapter with case material and analytical commentary. In Chapter 12, the final chapter in this volume, I will summarize and recapitulate the essential philosophy of how to build helping relationships in general.

11

Consultation in Action: Entry, Settings, Methods, and the Psychological Contract

Most of the emphasis in building the helping relationship has thus far been focused on the consultant-client relationship in a two person or small group situation. But most consulting takes place in the context of larger organizational learning or change projects. It is the use of process consultation in those larger projects that is the defining characteristic of what has, in those contexts, been labeled "organization development." It is the interplay of process consulting with expert and doctor types of consulting that makes organization development a more relevant process when human factors are involved in organizational change, as they always are. Of course, even the most technical problems involve human factors, so the ability to build helping relationships, to function in the PC mode whenever appropriate is the defining characteristic of any good consultation.

In this chapter I will elaborate this point by focusing more on the organizational context. How does the consultant initially enter an organization, develop a relationship with the various parts of the emerging client system, choose a setting and a method of working with the client, and build viable psychological contracts as the projects evolve?

Much of the case material will be based on the Billings Company.[1] Billings has a special significance for me because I learned the essence of process consultation through my many experiences in that organization. My work as a consultant with this organization lasted from 1966 to 1993, and I was fortunate enough to be invited to

[1]The Billings Company referred to here is the same company identified in my book on culture as the Action Co. (Schein, 1992).

participate in actual work meetings. Though the primary focus will be on Billings, I will provide data on other organizations as well for purposes of contrast and comparison.

First Contact and Entry

Initial contact is made when someone from the client organization telephones or writes me about some problem that he is experiencing or perceives in some part of the organization. The contact client indicates in the initial phone call or letter that he perceives a problem that is not being solved by normal organizational procedures, or sees a lack that cannot be filled by present organizational resources. Often what is requested is an "educational intervention" to come and give a talk to an executive group on a topic that the contact client believes to be related to the problems he perceives in the organization. Such requests usually reflect the topic I am most involved with at the time and about which I have written articles or books—management development, career development, communication and group dynamics, organizational socialization and—most recently—culture, culture change, and organizational learning.

Billings Manufacturing Company

When I first encountered Billings Company in 1966 it was a small, high tech manufacturing company run by a group of three founders who had a technical vision that they wanted to implement. They were basically electrical engineers who had a product idea that they felt they could commercialize, and they had obtained a small amount of seed money from a local venture capital organization. The organization was founded in the late 1950s.

My first contact in 1966 was a phone call from an acquaintance who had worked at MIT and was then a product-line manager one level below the founder/president and also served as the president's administrative assistant. The contact client, Charles, indicated that there were communication problems in the top management group, resulting from a recent reorganization. Because the company expected to grow rapidly in the next decade, the group felt they should work on these kinds of problems in preparation for their growth. Charles knew that I was interested in the human problems of organizations and had had considerable training in group dynamics. Based on this knowledge he convinced the president and primary founder, John Stone, to try bringing a consultant into the top management group. He got approval to call me and to set up a meeting with the president, if I was interested.

Defining the Relationship: The Exploratory Meeting

In the early chapters I explored at length the issue of how to respond to the initial request in a way that will be perceived as helpful. If that initial meeting or phone call is viewed as helpful and if I find that I am interested and able to pursue the issues raised, the contact client and I *jointly* decide on a next step which almost invariably is an *exploratory meeting*. Who attends the exploratory meeting, where it is held, for what length of time, and whether the client will be billed for it has to be worked out jointly with the contact client. The PC philosophy requires that every intervention be jointly owned by the client and the consultant, so the first job is to create a problem-solving process that will lead to a sound decision on the nature of the exploratory meeting. In the exploratory meeting I will probably meet other members of the client system, but I will not know whether they are intermediate clients or the primary client.

The purposes of the exploratory meeting are:

1. To determine more precisely what the problem is
2. To assess whether my further involvement is likely to be of any help to the organization
3. To assess whether the problem will be of interest to me
4. To test the emotional chemistry between me and the clients
5. To formulate next action steps with the client, if the answers to 2, 3, and 4 are positive.

In designing the meeting with the client, the most important question is: Who should be present at such a meeting? If I have a chance to influence this decision, the kind of criteria that I use are as follows:

1. Someone high enough in the organization to be able to influence others if he or she develops new insights
2. Someone who is generally in tune with the idea of bringing in a consultant to work on organizational problems
3. Someone who perceives a specific set of problems or symptoms that require attention or who has some goals and ideals that are not being met
4. Someone who is familiar with behavioral science consultants and the general notion that the client must remain active in the consultation process.

One should avoid having anyone at these early meetings who is hostile, skeptical, or totally ignorant of the kinds of service that can be offered by the consultant. If one or more such people are present and challenge me to *prove* that I can be of help to them, we are no longer *exploring* the problem. Instead I find myself seduced into a *selling* role and, if I permit myself to get into this role, I am already violating the PC model of helping others to help themselves. On the other hand, if the contact starts with members of the client system who are interested in trying a collaborative mode, it is often possible at a later stage to design meetings or settings in which the resistant members of the system can be confronted constructively and conflicts worked through.

The exploratory meeting is usually a long lunch or a half-day meeting. I usually mention to the contact client that the company should be prepared to pay a consultation fee for this meeting because the helping process really starts with the initial contact. The kinds of diagnostic questions I ask, the frame of reference from which I approach the problem, the sorts of things I observe and react to, all constitute initial interventions that, to some degree, influence the client's perceptions of his own problems. After several hours of exploration of his company's problems, the contact client has a new perspective and new insights. At the same time I am sharing my scarcest resource—time.

In Billings Company, an initial exploratory meeting took place with just the contact client. Charles spoke openly about his concerns that the president needed help in handling certain key people, shared his worries that the president and his key subordinates were not in good communication, and indicated that recent company history suggested the need for some stabilizing force in the organization. I asked Charles whether Stone knew he had come to me and what Stone's feelings were about bringing in a consultant. Charles indicated that Stone as well as other key executives were all in favor of bringing someone in to work with them. All saw the need for some outside help.

Our two-person meeting ended with the decision to test the waters further by attending one of the regular executive committee meetings at which time I would also meet Stone, the founder and president, to test whether we would find each other compatible. This step was necessary because Stone had a very strong personality, and I would be working closely with him and his immediate subordinates.

In most cases I cannot tell from the initial contact what the real goal of the consultation is and, therefore, can only agree to discuss it further at an exploratory meeting. If I have some consultation time available, I schedule such a meeting in the near future. If I do not have time or interest, I either ask if the problem can wait or suggest someone else who might be able to help. Occasionally I agree to an exploratory meeting with the understanding that, if anything comes of it, the work will be done at a later time or by someone else. In fact, one of the special services that exploratory meetings can provide is to help the client to sort out what kind of help she needs, with no implication that the initial consultant will be the one to take on further projects. I sometimes suggest to the contact client that their best use of my services might be one or two meetings to decide what the client needs—without any commitment on either part to a longer-range project. At this stage, the consultant functions more like the general medical practitioner helping decide what specialist might be needed in the future.

During the meeting, I ask inquiry questions that are designed to (1) sharpen and highlight aspects of the presented problem, (2) test how open and frank the contact client is willing to be, and (3) reveal as much as possible what my own style will be. If I feel that the client is hedging, unwilling to be critical of her own organization, confused about her motives, and/or confused about my potential role as a consultant, I am cautious. I then suggest that nothing be decided without more exploration, or I terminate the relationship if I am pessimistic about establishing a good relationship. If the contact client seems too certain that she already knows what is wrong, if she miscasts me as an expert in something that I am not expert in, or if she clearly has a misconception of what a consultant with an organizational psychology frame of reference could offer, I am cautious even in suggesting a further meeting, lest we end up wasting time. I am reluctant to proceed if the contact client seems to want merely reassurance for a course of action she has already embarked on or wants a quick solution to a surface problem.

To illustrate an unfavorable outcome, the director of personnel for the Etna Production Co. called me to meet with him and his two key personnel managers to evaluate a new performance appraisal program they were planning to launch across the whole company. I agreed to a one-day exploratory meeting at MIT during which the company representatives planned to outline the proposed program. One half-hour into the presentation I questioned a number of points that seemed internally inconsistent only to discover that the client became openly defensive. The further we went into the discussion, the clearer it became that the client was completely committed to his program and was seeking only reassurance from me. It also became clear from the way in which he reacted to questions and criticisms that he was not willing to reexamine any part of his program. He did not really want an evaluation. I therefore terminated the relationship at the end of the day, saying that I did not think I could be helpful beyond the questions I had already raised.

As can be seen, managing the relationship with the contact client in leading to a joint decision on an exploratory meeting is complex and full of pitfalls if not clearly thought through. My best guideline is to remember that I am trying to be helpful and that everything I do is an intervention. I also find when reviewing cases with colleagues that when things do not seem to work out very well, the "mistakes" that occurred on the part of the consultant almost always occurred *at the very beginning* of the relationship.

Settings and Methods of Work

A major issue to be addressed very early in the relationship, sometimes even before the exploratory meeting, involves the selection of a setting in which to work, the specification of a time schedule, a description of the method of work to be used, and a preliminary statement about goals to be achieved. These decisions are crucial because, by implication, they define the immediate client system to which the consultant will initially relate herself and build the mutual expectations that the client and consultant will have of each other.

Settings. I use a number of general principles for making decisions about the setting:

1. The choice of where and when to make further contact with members of the client system should be worked out collaboratively with the contact and intermediate clients. The consultant must avoid the image of a psychologist with x-ray vision wandering around the organization making observations about anything that strikes him as needing attention. If the client feels most comfortable visiting me, that is a desirable next step. In fact, I avoid visiting the client's organization until I know more about the problem and the political

situation. I have been in the situation more than once where the contact or intermediate clients were "using" me politically by having me make presentations or show up in meetings to demonstrate to their colleagues that they were on top of things. The consultant should only get involved in a setting in which both client and consultant feel comfortable and can explore the problems or issues that motivated the contact in the first place.

2. The setting chosen should involve people at the highest possible level because the higher the level the more likely it is that basic norms, values, and goals can be observed in operation. The higher levels set the tone of the organization and ultimately determine the criteria for effective organizational functioning. If the consultant does not expose herself to these levels, she cannot determine what these ultimate norms, goals, and criteria are, and if she does not become acquainted with them, she is abdicating her own ethical responsibility.

   Only if the consultant can personally accept the norms, goals, and criteria of the organization can she justify helping the organization achieve them. If the consultant feels that the organization's goals are unethical, immoral, or personally unacceptable for some other reason, she can choose to attempt to change them or terminate the relationship, but this choice should be consciously made. The consultant should not operate in ignorance of what the established authority in the organization is trying to do.

   Second, the higher the level the greater the payoff on any changes in process that are achieved. In other words, if the consultant can help the president to learn more about organizational process and to change her behavior accordingly, this change in turn is a force on her immediate subordinates, which sets a chain of influence into motion. The more general way to put this point is to say that the consultant should seek that setting or group of people that she considers to be potentially most influential on the rest of the organization. Usually this turns out to be the top executive group.

3. The setting chosen should be one in which it is easy to observe problem solving, interpersonal, and group processes. Often this turns out to be a weekly or monthly staff meeting,

or some other regularly scheduled activity in which two or more members of the key client group transact business together. It is important to observe processes among the members, not just between individual members and the consultant. For this reason, a survey or interview methodology is only a stopgap measure. Ultimately, the consultant must have access to a situation in which the organization's members are dealing with each other in their usual fashion.

4. The setting chosen should be one in which *real* work is going on. The consultant should avoid the situation where a group initially agrees to meet with him only to discuss their interpersonal relations or only to listen to a presentation. Such a meeting would be appropriate after a relationship had developed between the group and the consultant but would be premature before. The group cannot yet trust the consultant enough to really have an open discussion of interpersonal relations, and the consultant does not yet have enough observational data to be able to help the group in such a discussion. Further, the consultant cannot know whether interpersonal issues are interfering with work issues. Regular committee or work-group meetings are ideal because the consultant not only sees the organization members in a more natural role but learns what sort of work the members are concerned about.

These principles can usually be shared with the contact client in the process of getting joint ownership of the decision on setting. In sharing them, the consultant is also beginning to teach the client something about the process of planned change and how to think about organizational processes and dynamics.

Methods of Work. The method of work chosen should be as congruent as possible with the principles and values underlying process consultation. The consultant should be maximally visible and maximally available for interaction. The method should avoid making the consultant look like a diagnostic expert using mysterious tools to arrive at conclusions that the client would not understand. Thus it is desirable to use *observation*, *informal interviewing*, and *group discussions* to reinforce the presumption that the consultant does not already have pat answers or standard "expert" solutions, and that the consultant is maximally available for questioning and two-way communication. The questions asked should be relevant and make sense within the context of what the client has requested. Often I choose to start a consultation with some low-key inquiry questions to establish a relationship with each of the people in the client system that I will be working with or observing in group meetings. The interview is designed as much to reveal myself as to learn something about the other person.

I do *not* make interviews of everyone in the initial client system a routine part of every project as many consultation models advocate. There are times when the exploratory meeting has made it clear that individuals in the client system do not feel free to speak openly except in private or when a future meeting is designed to reflect agenda inputs from various members of a group. In those instances the contact client and I will plan a series of individual interviews. But the decision to have interviews and the reasons for them should be shared by the contact or intermediate clients. It should not be part of the consultant's routine "method" because it automatically puts the consultant into the expert role by virtue of the information she has collected that no one else has at that point.

If the consultant uses *questionnaires*, *surveys*, or *tests*, or if he uses a lot of jargon, he himself remains an unknown quantity to the respondent and at the same time signals that he has mysterious and esoteric knowledge about gathering data and making diagnoses. As long as he is perceived to be an expert with mysterious skills and remains unknown as a personality, the respondent cannot really trust him and hence cannot answer questions with complete honesty. Hence I prefer not to use any of these tools until they are clearly appropriate and have been agreed to by the client system.

To illustrate the evolution of these processes, I will review several cases that show different aspects of getting involved with the client systems.

In Billings Company, the exploratory meeting was one of the regular meetings of the executive committee. At this time I was to meet Stone, the founder/president, and the other key executives to discuss further what could and should be done. We met in the conference room next to Stone's office and sat around a large kidney shaped table above which hung a mobile that consisted of six separate free floating hands with the index finger pointing straight ahead. As the air moved the hands around, the various fingers would point in various directions making one think of a kind of random "finger-pointing" process that made me wonder about what kind of climate I would encounter in this organization.

At the meeting I found a lively interest in the idea of having an outsider help the group and the organization to become more effective. I also found that the group was willing to enter an open-ended relationship. I explained my philosophy of how to help by observing and making process interventions as appropriate, and suggested that a good way of getting further acquainted would be to eventually set up a series of individual interviews with each member of the group. At the same time, I suggested that I sit in on the regular bi-weekly half-day meetings of the executive committee. The interviews then would occur after several of these meetings. They agreed to this process.

At the initial meeting of the group, I was able to observe a number of key events. For example, Stone was very informal but very powerful. I got the impression initially (and confirmed it subsequently) that the relationships of all the group members to the president would be the key issue, with relationships to each other being relatively less important. I also got the impression that Stone was a confident individual who would tolerate my presence only so long as he saw some value in it. He would have little difficulty in confronting me and terminating the relationship if my presence ceased to have value from his point of view.

It was also impressive, and turned out to be indicative of a managerial style, that Stone did not feel the need to see me alone. He was satisfied from the outset to deal with me inside the group. Near the end of the initial meeting, I requested a private talk with him to satisfy myself that we understood the psychological contract we were entering into. He was surprisingly uncomfortable in this one-to-one relationship, had little that he wished to impart to me, and did not show much interest in my view of the relationship. I wanted the private conversation in order to test his reaction to taking some personal feedback on his own behavior as the consultation progressed. He said he would welcome this and indicated little or no concern over it. As I was to learn later, his reaction reflected a very strong sense of his own power and identity. He felt he knew himself very well and was not a bit threatened by feedback.

Stone also made it quite clear that he expected me to figure out what to do and that he was seeking an improvement in their overall group functioning, not some specific problem solutions. I was surprised and pleased by his openness and his willingness to allow me to attend regular work sessions. In terms of client definition, it was now clear that Stone and his group would be the primary client. I would begin by attending executive committee meetings and would concentrate my efforts on helping that group to function more effectively.

In the Boyd Consumer Goods Company, *the consultation started in essentially the same manner. At the exploratory meeting with the president, I inquired whether there was some regular meeting that he held with his immediate subordinates. There was such a group that met weekly, and since it was a local company it was agreed that I would start by sitting in on its meetings. The president explained to the group that he had asked me to sit in to help the group function more effectively and then asked me to explain how I saw my own role. I described PC and the kinds of things I would be looking for, stated that I would not be very active but preferred the group just to work along as it normally would, and that I would make comments as I saw opportunities to be helpful. It was decided after a few meetings that I would interview each member of the seven-man group individually to learn more about the company and to help define some change targets to make the group more effective.*

In the Central Chemical Company *the pattern was entirely different, since they were geographically far removed and I had agreed to spend only one week with them several months hence. This case also illustrates starting with an educational intervention, in this case a workshop on managing change.*

The contact client was a person in the organization's OD group and was quite knowledgeable about the possible uses he could make of a consultant. Prior to contacting me he had consulted with a colleague of mine, Dick Beckhard, to determine how best to use me. They decided that a workshop devoted to helping line managers improve their diagnoses and action plans for change programs that they wanted to implement was an appropriate workshop goal. Dick then sounded me out about doing such a workshop in the UK, and only after I had agreed, did I hear from the contact client about the details of what was proposed.[2]

Once the workshop had been decided on by correspondence, I worked with my colleague on designing the program for the week. We agreed not to freeze the plan until I was actually on the premises the evening before the workshop. We had, however, made the key decision to invite only managers who had an interest in changing some aspect of their immediate work situation, and to have each manager come to the workshop with a member of the personnel staff reporting to him so that teams *would be looking at the change problems.*

---

[2]Dick Beckhard and I had developed a workshop for the National Training Labs focusing on how to get planned change projects started in an organization. This was to be an adaptation of that workshop. Much of the philosophy underlying this approach to change is derived from Beckhard's work and is presented in detail in three of his books (Beckhard & Harris, 1987, Beckhard & Pritchard, 1992, and Beckhard, 1997).

When I arrived at the Central Chemical Company site some months later, I met with my "inside" consultant contact, his boss (who was personnel director), and one or two other personnel people who were interested in the program. We reviewed the goals and schedule of the week, decided to remain flexible until we could find out more from the participants about their change goals, and agreed that the inside consultant would work with me in implementing the program. The setting for the program was the training center of the company at a remote location in the north of England. All the teams (eighteen men altogether) then met daily at the training center for the actual workshop: All the basic arrangements were made by the contact client, but with input from me.

In Billings and Boyd I went directly into a work group. In the Central Co. I ran a workshop to help managers accomplish some of their tasks better. A third pattern combines these two kinds of settings by organizing a meeting to solve a particular organizational problem. The consultant manages the meeting, but the work done by the participants is real problem solving.

This project was conducted with the Internal Revenue Service *in the 1960s. Some members of the IRS training department had become exposed to sensitivity training several years back, introduced it to their middle and senior manager development programs, and gained a good deal of sophistication in analyzing organizational process. It became clear to a number of them that one of the major difficulties of the organization was conflict between the central headquarters and the various field units—conflicts over how much decentralization of decision-making authority there should be, conflicts concerning how much the system actually reflected earlier agreements to decentralize, and conflicts over lines of authority.*

The organization had strong functional directors in the headquarters organization who often clashed with the regional and district directors who ran IRS operations locally. As HQs developed new financial and marketing programs to improve IRS operations and its image, they tended to bypass the formal line organization going instead directly to the financial and marketing people in the field. This caused discomfort and anger both in the HQs and in regional management.

The central training group knew that there was an annual meeting of all the key executives, including headquarters and field people—15 in all. One member of this group called me to find out if there was a possibility of organizing one of these meetings in such a way as to enable the entire group to work on the organizational problem and if I could help in setting up and running such a meeting.

I had an exploratory meeting with several members of the training group and learned that they were not sure how the Commissioner and his im-

mediate subordinates would respond to the idea, since there was no prior history of exposure of the group to an outside consultant. However, when they polled a number of the regional managers who had attended sensitivity training groups and learned something about the potential of bringing in a "behaviorally oriented consultant" they felt reassured that something like this meeting should be tried.

A core group, consisting of the training director, two of his key staff people, and one enthusiastic regional manager, then met with me for one day to plan further strategy. We decided that for such a program to work, a substantial number of the people who would eventually be at the meeting would also have to become involved in the planning and design of the meeting. A group consisting of equal numbers of HQ and regional managers was formed. The mission of this group was to meet for two days to plan the total meeting. The plan developed by the group was then to be presented for approval to the Commissioner and his key staff.

My role as a consultant was critical at two stages in this enterprise. First, during the two-day meeting of the planning group I had to steer them away from a traditional format in which I would make presentations about headquarters/field-type problems for them to discuss. Second, I had to take some responsibility for the success of the meeting format finally chosen and find a role for myself that would make this format work.

The plan that emerged from the two days of planning had the following elements:

1. *The three-day meeting would be billed as an exploration of organizational problems at the top of the organization, toward the end of improving organizational relationships.*
2. *The meeting would be chaired by me rather than the Commissioner to symbolize that neither HQs nor Field could dominate the discussion.*
3. *The agenda for the meeting would be developed by a procedure suggested by Dick Beckhard in which each member of the fifteen-person group would be asked to write me a letter at my home outlining what he saw to be the major organizational problems facing the group. It was then my job to put together the information from the fifteen letters into major themes and issues. These themes and issues were to be presented by me to the total group at our first session and would constitute the agenda for the three days.*

The first purpose in having such letters written was to provide each person the opportunity to be completely frank without having to expose himself to the possible wrath of the boss or other members of the group. Second, it provided an opportunity to gather data from all the members before the meeting began. Third, it involved each member in helping to set the agenda, a considerable departure from previous meetings where the agenda had been set by the Commissioner or his staff. It could be expected, therefore, that all the members would feel more involved in the meeting from the outset.

The letter writing had two problems connected with it: (1) it seemed a little bit gimmicky, and (2) it was difficult to know how someone would react who had not as yet met me. Would he write a frank letter to a strange professor about rather critical organizational issues? We decided that we would have to run the risk of getting no response or poor response, but that we could minimize this risk by having the members of the planning group talk to others they knew and make a personal appeal to write a frank letter.

The procedure was agreed on, presented to the Commissioner, received enthusiastic approval, and thus became the plan for the meeting. I pointed out to the planning group that the Commissioner and his deputy would have to be careful in how they managed their own role. If they reverted too quickly to their power position and abandoned the role of helping to diagnose organizational problems, the group would retreat into silence and the problems would remain unsolved. I talked to both men and felt that they understood the risks, were willing to take them, and had the kind of personality that would make them accept this somewhat different meeting format.

Having agreed to go ahead, the group then decided that the deputy would send out the letter explaining the meeting format and inviting the diagnostic letters. Members of the planning group were to follow up in the districts to ensure that everyone understood the plan and the fact that the plan had come from organization members themselves, even though I had suggested many of the separate elements.

This rather lengthy procedure was essential to obtain the involvement of the members in a process-oriented meeting. Even though the ideas came originally from the training department and from me, the concept clearly appealed to regional and HQ managers. Had they not become committed, it would not have been possible to hold such a meeting at all.

The letters were full of frank appraisals of the current situation which made it easy to construct an agenda that the group considered highly relevant. My role was to organize these appraisals into a reasonable number of organization issues that the meeting could address. I could sharpen and focus these issues without any member being threatened because only issues that were brought up by several people were put on the agenda. I chaired the meeting and steered it through to various kinds of consensus on how the participants wanted to structure HQs-field relationships in the future. The Commissioner and his deputy blended into the group and fulfilled their role of not dominating the meeting.

By carefully planning the helping process we were able to address difficult issues that had created tensions for years, bring them out into the open, neutralize them, and separate them from particular individuals. Thereby, we created a climate in which the group could deal with difficult issues constructively and confront each other across some tough hierarchical boundaries. I also learned from this experience how much the outcome depended upon collaborative inquiry and intervention between me, the outsider, and various insiders.

I have tried to convey through these cases that the method of work is highly variable and highly dependent on the realities that surface in the initial contacts and exploratory meetings. The key point to emphasize is that I do not bring a "standard method" to the party, but attempt to involve the client in deciding what will work best to move things forward. At the same time, I am prepared to resist if the client suggests a method that I would not be comfortable with. For example, if the client suggested that I give psychological tests to the group members prior to the meeting, I would have to attempt to convince the client that this was not desirable. In that discussion my own principles of process consultation would have to be revealed and tested. If the client persisted, I would have to consider disengaging myself with the strong recommendation that I thought it would be a mistake for the client to pursue that strategy. Notice also that "gimmicks" such as having the participants write me a private letter are always designed to maximize the up-front involvement of the client in the whole problem-solving process. Without such a process, they would arrive at the meeting in a passive, dependent state waiting for a formal leader to state the agenda. All of these considerations have to do with the concept of the "psychological contract."

The Psychological Contract

The psychological contract is the tacit set of expectations on the part of the consultant and client about what each will give and receive in the relationship above and beyond the basics of when to meet, for how long, and for what fee. Many consulting theories argue that such tacit expectations should be made as formally and explicitly as possible at the outset. In my own experience, trying to be explicit up front about all one's hopes and expectations is not very feasible or fruitful because neither party knows enough about the evolving reality of the situation to make a good estimate of what they will give and what they expect to receive. Frequently, even the formal things we have agreed to turn out to be unworkable. It makes sense to be open about expectations at each stage but that openness includes saying that I am not sure where we are going, how things might evolve, and/or what kinds of issues might lie ahead.

In Billings the psychological contract between Stone and me was very vague. We both had good intentions, but neither one of us knew at the outset how my participation in the meetings would work out and how the relationship would develop from that point on. What I did not know then, and Stone could not have told me, is that this willingness to be vague was not just temporary but actually reflected Stone's basic style. As he put it once years later in referring to my contribution to the company's affairs: "When I would see a problem somewhere, like in the engineering department, I would ask Ed Schein to talk to the people and I would expect the problem to go away."

Stone expected me to intervene and fix things and saw no need to intervene himself or even to check-up on what I was doing. In fact, when I sometimes wanted to report to him what I was working on, he often acted bored and obviously had lost interest in the issue. He did not expect to monitor my behavior and would only get involved if I convinced him that his behavior had to change in response to something I observed or found out.

I also learned that one of Stone's strong needs was to have a relationship with a neutral outsider with whom to think out loud. I spent many hours in his office just listening to what was on his mind about the company, his subordinates, his frustrations, his management philosophy, and whatever else was on his mind. We would often have an agenda for the meeting but might abandon it in the first few minutes and just talk for an hour or more about what was on Stone's mind that day. I had to learn to be completely flexible in how to respond, all the way from just listening at one extreme to challenging his thinking at the other extreme. Stone needed others to help him think and often said when challenged to make a decision that "By myself I'm not that smart, but when I talk it out with a bunch of smart others in a group, I get smart very fast."

In the staff meetings I was on my own, as well. Stone and his subordinates were willing to have me attend and do what I could, but there were no discussions of what I would do or when I would do it, unless I volunteered some statement of how I saw my own role. I think the group expected me to be helpful but until I did something specific they had no preconceptions of the form that this help would take. Furthermore, they did not seem to have a need for role clarification, which, it turned out, was an important theme in

Billings culture. Roles and responsibilities were generally vague and the group was comfortable with this vagueness. A more formal contracting process would simply not have worked.

My bills, which detailed where and how I was spending my time, went to the VP of Human Resources, who became one of my inside informants as things evolved. He and I would spend many hours discussing what was going on with Stone and how best to handle the agendas that Stone produced. Similar conversations occurred with other members of the group so that, in a sense, I became simultaneously a counselor to all of them individually as well as to the group as a whole.

A vague psychological contract such as that described previously is often par for the course. In fact, the whole philosophy of PC argues against formalizing consulting arrangements because neither the client nor the consultant can predict the reality that they will face day-to-day. The only things that have to be formalized are the amount of time the client thinks she needs, the amount of time the consultant has available, and the fees to be charged. But even on time planning, I find it more useful to start in an open-ended way allowing for a *maximum* amount of time to be allocated, but not expecting that it will all be used. The overarching criteria should be what makes sense and what will be most helpful given the emerging realities that the client faces.

I will commit to working for a certain number of days per month for a set per-hour and/or per-day fee. But I do not wish the client organization to formally commit itself to a retainer or a predetermined contract of a given size, nor do I wish to promise a continuing relationship. Both parties should be free to terminate the agreement at any time if the relationship is no longer satisfactory or useful. This mutual freedom to terminate is important to ensure that the basis of the relationship is the actual value obtained, not the fulfillment of some obligation.

On the other hand, both the client and the consultant should be prepared to give as much time to the project as is mutually agreed on as desirable. If I have only one day per month available, and the nature of the problem is such that more time may be needed by the client, I obviously should not begin the consultation in the first place. I try to make a reasonably good estimate of how much time any given project might take if it goes well, and ensure that I have at least that much time available. For his part, the client should budget costs in such a way that if more days are needed, he has the resources to pay for them. In no case has anything of this sort ever been formalized beyond a general letter of intention written by the client. Once we agree on the daily rate, I keep records of the amount of time spent and send monthly bills to the client.

I try to figure out as early in the relationship as possible all the expectations that may be deliberately or unwittingly concealed by the client and which may involve actions on my part that I am not willing to take. For example, beyond wanting me to work on the presented problem, the client may expect me to help in a variety of other ways, such as giving her personal evaluations of her subordinates, helping her deal with "problem people" in her organization, providing expert opinions on how certain management problems should be handled, giving support to some of the decisions she has made, helping her to sell her decisions to others, serving as a communication channel to people with whom she has trouble communicating, and mediating conflicts. As many of these expectations as possible must surface early so that they do not later become traps or sources of disappointment if I refuse to go along with something that the client expected of me. On the other hand, if the client wishes to conceal certain motives, all I can do is to be diagnostically sensitive and avoid traps.

On my side, I have to be as clear as I can be about what I expect of the client system and of myself in my role as consultant. For example, I expect a willingness to inquire, to explore problem issues, and to take enough time to find out what is really going on. I expect to be supported in my process orientation and to have organization members be committed to the process of sharing ownership of diagnostic and other interventions. I have to state clearly that I will not function as an expert resource on human relations problems that are unique to the organization and its culture, but that I will try to help the client to solve those problems by providing alternatives and helping to think through the consequences of different alternatives. I need to point out that I will gather information by observing people in action, by interviewing, and by any other method we mutually agree on. Finally, I have to make it plain that when I am participating in meetings, I will not be very active but will comment on what is happening or give feedback only as I feel it will be helpful to the group in accomplishing its task. The fact that I will be relatively inactive is often a problem for the group because of their expectation that once they have hired a consultant they are entitled to sit back and just listen to her tell them things. To have the consultant then spend hours sitting in the group and saying very little not only violates this expectation but also creates some anxiety about what she is observing. The more I can reassure the group early in the game that I am not gathering personal data of a potentially damaging nature, the smoother the subsequent observations will go.

I have to explain fully the idea that my client is not just the contact person or the person of highest rank but the entire group with which I am working and, by implication, the entire organization and the broader community. In other words, I would not support decisions that I believe would harm any given group, such as the employees, customers, or suppliers, even if I never had any contact with such groups. This concept of unwitting and ultimate clients is one of the trickiest, yet most important, aspects of PC. In observing other consultants operating in an organization in which I have been working, I have noticed that many of them essentially take the highest-level manager, typically the president, as their primary client, convince him of what the remedial intervention should be, and then proceed to help him to sell and implement the intervention even though this may be hurtful to others in the organization.

In contrast, I have found myself to be most effective if I can gain the trust of all key parties with whom I am working so that none ever thinks of me as pushing someone else's ideas. The metaphor of being a facilitator or catalyst is more appropriate than change agent for this kind of helping. Once a given level of trust has been established, it is quite possible to work across several levels of the organization.

In Billings, after many months of working with Stone and his six key subordinates, I arrived at a point where all of them saw me as a potentially useful communication link. My primary work was clearly with this group and its meetings, but I interviewed them all individually over the next several months to give each of them a chance to tell me what they hoped to get out of my presence in the meetings. As I got to know them better they asked me quite sincerely to report to each one of them the feelings or reactions of others whenever I learned anything that I felt should be passed on. In particular, they wanted to know how Stone felt about certain things and they wanted me to pass on how they felt about certain things to Stone. They were quite open with me about each other and about Stone, knowing that I might well pass on any opinions or reactions they voiced to me. They did not want me to treat everything they said to me as confidential, because they trusted me and each other enough and saw my linkage to all of them as an additional useful communication channel.

This development was of great interest to me because of my own initial feelings that serving as a carrier of this type of information was not an ideal role for me and reflected an insufficient ability on their part to tell each other things directly. Hence I took two courses of action. First, I tried as much as possible to train each of them to tell others in the group what they felt directly. At the same time, I intervened directly in their process by occasionally passing on information and opinions that they could not share when I thought this would be helpful in accomplishing their work goals.

A simple yet critical event will illustrate what I mean. Two members, Pete and Joe, did not always communicate freely with each other, partly because they felt some rivalry. Pete had completed a study and written a report that was to be discussed by the whole group. Three days before the report was due, I visited the company and stopped at Pete's office to discuss the report with him and to ask how things were going. He said they were fine, but frankly he was puzzled about why Joe had not come to him to look at some of the back-up data pertaining to Joe's function. Pete felt this was just another bit of evidence that Joe did not really respect Pete very much.

An hour or so later I happened to be working with Joe and raised the issue of the report (my unilateral decision to intervene because I thought it might be helpful). Joe and his staff were busy preparing for the meeting, but nothing was said about looking at the back-up data that Pete had available. Joe said that he was sure it was private and would not be released by Pete. Joe wanted badly to see it, but felt sure that Pete had deliberately not offered it.

I decided that it would be helpful to reveal what I knew about Pete's feelings of willingness to share the data. Joe expressed considerable surprise and later in the day went to Pete, who gave him a warm welcome and turned over three volumes of the data that Joe had been wanting to see and that Pete had been wanting to share. I had to judge carefully whether I would hurt either Pete or Joe by revealing Pete's feelings, and decided that the potential gains would clearly outweigh the risks, as proved to be the case.

The psychological contract between me and various members of Billings management had clearly evolved to a state that none of us could have predicted or would have necessarily wanted to achieve. Rather, it evolved in response to the realities of the situation, and those realities would likely be different in every consulting situation.

Summary and Conclusions

The process of contact and entry, the choice of a setting and a method of work, and the evolution of the psychological contract are each highly variable. It is important that both the setting and working procedure be jointly decided on between the contact client group and the consultant. Whatever decisions are made should be congruent with the general assumptions underlying PC so that whatever learning the client system achieves can be self-perpetuating. What the consultant needs to be expert in is the instant design of interventions that will simultaneously be helpful and reveal further realities. How the consultant reacts always has to be viewed both as an intervention and as a source of new data.

The most difficult idea to grasp in all of this is that diagnosis and intervention are one and the same process. I always have to be open to the realities as they reveal themselves and, at the same time, I have to realize that whether I react verbally, just look puzzled, remain silent, argue, or ask another question it is an immediate intervention with consequences. I have to think about all those consequences in the fleeting moment. I cannot take "time out" to think about what to do next. Everything I do is an intervention.

12

Process Consultation and the Helping Relationship in Perspective

In this chapter I want to summarize, comment on, and, reflect on what has come before. Some of the questions I want to address were stimulated by the detailed feedback from my colleague Otto Scharmer and his wife Katryn who read the manuscript carefully and thoughtfully. I am grateful for their suggestions. I also benefited greatly from the reviews of four colleagues—Dick Beckhard, Warner Burke, Michael Brimm, and David Coghlan. Their thoughts and suggestions have been incorporated into this volume and have strengthened it greatly.

What then is to be said in a concluding chapter? First, I want to revisit the ten principles of process consultation because I find them increasingly helpful as a diagnostic of where I have gone wrong when things do not work out as I expected them to. Then, I want to take up some remaining issues, especially pertaining to the teaching of process consultation.

Ten Principles as the Essence of Process Consultation

In reflecting on process consultation and the building of a "helping relationship," the question arises: where is the emphasis or the essence that makes this philosophy of helping "different"? Why bother to learn all of this stuff. In my reflections on some 40 years of practicing "this stuff," I have concluded that the essence is in the word *relationship*. To put it bluntly, I have come to believe that *the decisive factor as to whether or not help will occur in human situations involving personality, group dynamics, and culture is the* ***relationship*** *between the helper and the person, group, or organization that needs help.* From that point of view, every action I take, from the beginning contact with a client, should be an intervention that simultaneously allows both the client and me to diagnose what is going on and that builds a relationship between us. When all is said and done, I measure my success in every contact by whether or not I feel the relationship has been helpful and whether or not the client feels helped.

Furthermore, from that point of view, the principles, guidelines, practical tips, call them what you like, fall-out as the kinds of things I have to constantly remind myself of in my efforts to build that kind of helping relationship. Let us review the principles from that point of view.

1. Always try to be helpful.

Obviously, if I have no intention of being helpful and working at it, it is unlikely to lead to a helping relationship. In general, I have found in all human relationships that the intention to be helpful is the best guarantee of a relationship that is rewarding and leads to mutual learning.

2. Always stay in touch with the current reality.

I cannot be helpful if I cannot decipher what is going on in myself, in the situation, and in the client.

3. Access your ignorance.

The only way I can discover my own inner reality is to learn to distinguish what I know from what I assume I know, from what I truly do not know. And I have learned from experience that it is generally most helpful to work on those areas where I truly do not know. Accessing is the key, in the sense that I have learned that to overcome expectations and assumptions I must make an effort to locate within myself what I really do not know and should be asking about. It is like scanning my own inner data base and gaining access to empty compartments. If I truly do not know the answer I am more likely to sound congruent and sincere when I ask about it.

4. Everything you do is an intervention.

Just as every interaction reveals diagnostic information, so does every interaction have consequences both for the client and for me. I therefore have to own everything I do and assess the consequences to be sure that they fit my goals of creating a helping relationship.

5. It is the client who owns the problem and the solution.

My job is to create a relationship in which the client can get help. It is not my job to take the client's problems onto my own shoulders, nor is it my job to offer advice and solutions in a situation that I do not live in myself.

6. Go with the flow.

Inasmuch as I do not know the client's reality, I must respect as much as possible the natural flow in that reality and not impose my own sense of flow on an unknown situation. Once the relationship reaches a certain level of trust, and once the client and helper have a shared set of insights into what is going on, flow itself becomes a shared process.

7. Timing is crucial.

Over and over I have learned that the introduction of my perspective, the asking of a clarifying question, the suggestion of alternatives, or whatever else I want to introduce from my own point of view has to be timed to those moments when the client's attention is available. The same remark uttered at two different times can have completely different results.

8. Be constructively opportunistic with confrontive interventions.

When the client signals a moment of openness, a moment when his or her attention to a new input appears to be available, I find I seize those moments and try to make the most of them. In listening for those moments, I find it most important to look for areas in which I can build on the client's strengths and positive motivations. Those moments also occur when the client has revealed some data signifying readiness to pay attention to a new point of view.

9. Everything is a source of data; errors are inevitable—learn from them.

No matter how well I observe the previous principles I will say and do things that produce unexpected and undesirable reactions in the client. I must learn from them and at all costs avoid defensiveness, shame, or guilt. I can never know enough of the client's reality to avoid errors, but each error produces reactions from which I can learn a great deal about my own and the client's reality.

10. When in doubt share the problem.

Inevitably, there will be times in the relationship when I run out of gas, don't know what to do next, feel frustrated, and in other ways get paralyzed. In situations like this, I found that the most helpful thing I could do was to share my "problem" with the client. Why should I assume that I always know what to do next? Inasmuch as it is the client's problem and reality we are dealing with, it is entirely appropriate for me to involve the client in my own efforts to be helpful.

These principles do not tell me what to do. Rather, they are reminders of how to think about the situation I am in. They offer guidelines when the situation is a bit ambiguous. Also they remind me of what it is I am trying to do.

Can One Develop a Useful Typology of Interventions?

In previous versions of this book I attempted to categorize interventions. As I reflect on possible ways to do this, I have concluded that such categories are not really useful because they divert one from the more fundamental question of figuring out what will be helpful at any given moment in the evolving relationship. I prefer a general concept of "*Facilitative Intervention*" that implies that the consultant should always select whatever intervention will be most helpful at any given moment, given all one knows about the total situation. Certainly the consultant should be familiar with a variety of questions, exercises, survey-feedback technologies, and other forms of intervention many of which have been illustrated in the previous chapters and well described in other books on organization development.

But knowledge of many different kinds of interventions does not substitute for the knowhow of sensing what is needed "right now" in terms of facilitating forward movement in the relationship. In fact, having a skillset of interventions "at the ready" makes it harder to stay in the current reality because one is always looking for opportunities to use what one believes oneself to be good at. As the saying goes, if all you have is a hammer, everything in the world looks like a nail. What then is the *essential* skill we are talking about?

Formal Knowledge, Skill, or Tacit Know-How?

When I conduct workshops on process consultation, I am often reminded that much of what I suggest to young consultants may work for *me* because of my experience and stature, but it would not work for them. This issue has two components. What exactly do I have that they assume they do not have? And how much of what is relevant to creating a helping relationship is explicit formal knowledge, skill based on formal training, or tacit know-how based on experience? The reader will have noticed that I did not distinguish these three levels of knowledge throughout the previous text. The reason is that all three are relevant to the creation of a helping relationship. Formal knowledge, such as the simplifying models presented in several of the chapters, is essential. It is especially important for the budding consultant to understand as much as possible about psychology, group dynamics, and organizational dynamics. But formal knowledge is clearly not enough. With workshop training, apprenticeships, and actual trial and error one develops the skill and—most important—the know-how that gradually becomes tacit and automatic. It is in the last two categories of knowledge that I clearly have an advantage over the novice, but I always point out that if an essential element of the philosophy is to deal with reality, then the novice must work from his reality, whatever that implies.

Let me illustrate. If I am working with a manager who is familiar with my work, I know that she understands that I am supposedly expert in this form of consultation. I must appreciate that set of perceptions and make my interventions accordingly. If a younger, novice consultant goes to that same manager, he knows that the manager is relatively unfamiliar with the consultant's experience or skill, and he must therefore operate from that reality. Consequently, we would make quite different interventions, but we each would be trying to build a helping relationship, and we each could succeed. The relationship might evolve differently, but there is nothing in each of our experiences that would automatically determine that I would be more successful than the novice.

When I have observed novices in these situations, their lack of success is invariably connected to not sticking to the principles, of trying to be prematurely expert, or of giving advice when none was called for. Of course, those errors themselves are the result of lack of experience; but this does not invalidate the principles. If the novice does stay in the helper role, if he stays focused on what has been described here, he will be just as successful as I would be in the same situation.

I have observed this over and over again in my classes on managing planned change where project groups are from time to time trying to help each other with their projects. If I play the role of consultant, I can help, but—more importantly—when I encourage fellow students to try their hand at being helpful, the ones who operate by these principles are as or more helpful than I could have been. It is their insight that is crucial, not their length of experience. It is their willingness to give up the expert role and deal with current reality that is crucial, not how many hours of practice they have had.

It must also be acknowledged that the helping relationship is a product of two personality styles. Two equally experienced consultants might produce two quite different kinds of relationships, each of which would be helpful. It is not accidental that a number of my clients did not want to proceed only on the basis of what contact clients had told them about me. They wanted to meet me and test the "chemistry" between us for themselves. From that point of view, in any relationship, a novice with the right chemistry could do as well or better than an experienced consultant with the wrong chemistry.

In conclusion, tacit know-how and skill are important, but even the novice consultant has some history of human experiences to draw on. Lack of experience is not nearly as predictive of problems as is not understanding what it means to help someone and not doing one's best to operate by those principles.

A Concluding Personal Note

I sometimes ask myself why I am so passionate about preaching this stuff. My experience has taught me some lessons that I want my readers to understand. In watching my own helping efforts, and especially in observing the helping efforts of others, I keep rediscovering the same simple truths. We have learned much about these truths in related fields—psychotherapy, social work, teaching, coaching. Yet we persist in treating organizational consultation as something different. Consultants tell me over and over how important it is to make a formal diagnosis, to write reports, to make specific recommendations, or they feel they have not done their job. I cannot really figure out why the learning we have acquired in the other helping professions—about client involvement, about people having to learn at their own pace, about helping clients to have insights and solve their own problems—has not generalized more to the field of management and organizational consulting.

If I take a cynical view, I think it is easier to sell products, programs, diagnoses, and sets of recommendations than it is to sell a helping attitude. Consulting firms are businesses and they must survive financially, so there is inevitably a great pressure to have products and services that clients are willing to pay money for. However, once consulting becomes a business, I believe it ceases to be *consulting* in the sense I mean it. It becomes transformed into the sale of some expert services. Consulting firms sell information, ideas, and recommendations. But do they sell help? For me that is the tough question.

Helpers also have to make a living and charge for their services. But therapists and social workers do not define their work at the outset in terms of specific longer-range projects involving formal diagnostic methods and formal programs of therapy. They first build a relationship and only recommend other services as they decide jointly with their client that something else is needed. What I find missing in so much managerial and organizational consulting is that initial relationship-building that would permit clients to own their problems and make sensible decisions about whether or not to do a survey, or have an off-site confrontation meeting, or engage in a two-year formal change program run by the consulting firm.

The strength of my feeling about the need to build a relationship first, derives from the experience of working with organizations that have previously been subjected to expert consultants who had formal programs to implement. All too often I learn that very little of what the client wanted was accomplished, even though a great deal of money was spent. As a result, I have to confront again my own reality that help will not happen until the right kind of relationship has been built with the various levels of clients we may have to deal with, and that the building of such a relationship takes time and requires a certain kind of attitude from the helper. In the end, then, this book is an attempt to articulate what that attitude is all about.

References

Allen, T. J. (1977) *Managing the flow of technology.* Cambridge, MA: MIT Press.

Ancona, D. G. (1988) "Groups in organizations: Extending laboratory models." In C. Hendrick (ed.) *Annual Review of Personality and Social Psychology: Group and Intergroup Processes.* Beverly Hills, CA: Sage.

Argyris, C. & Schon, D. A. (1996) *Organizational Learning II*, Reading, MA: Addison-Wesley. (Original edition 1974)

Barrett, F. J. & Cooperrider, D. L. (1990) Generative metaphor intervention: A new approach for working with systems divided by conflict and caught in defensive perception. *Journal of Applied Behavioral Science*, 26, No. 2, pp. 219–239.

Bateson, G. (1972) *Steps to an ecology of mind.* New York: Ballantine.

Beckhard, R. (1967) The confrontation meeting. *Harvard Business Review,* 45, March-April, pp. 149–155.

Beckhard, R. & Pritchard, W. (1992). *Changing the essence: The art of creating fundamental change in organizations.* San Francisco: Jossey-Bass.

Beckhard, R. (1997) *Agent of change.* San Francisco: Jossey-Bass.

Beckhard, R. & Harris, R. T. (1987) *Organizational transitions: Managing complex change (2d ed.).* Reading, MA: Addison-Wesley.

Blake, R R. & Mouton, J. S. (1969) *Building a dynamic organization through grid organization development.* Reading, MA: Addison-Wesley.

Blake, R. R., Mouton, J. S., & McCanse, A. A. (1989) *Change by design.* Reading, MA: Addison-Wesley.

Bohm, D. (1989) *On Dialogue.* Ojai, CA: Ojai Seminars.

Bradford, L. P, Gibb, J. R. & Benne, K. D. (Eds) (1964) *T-group theory and laboratory method.* New York: Wiley.

Bunker, B. B. & Alban, B. T. (1997) *Large group interventions.* San Francisco: Jossey-Bass.

Carroll, J. S. & Payne, J. W. (Eds) (1976). *Cognition and Social Behavior.* Hillsdale, NJ: Lawrence Erlbaum.

Chisholm, R. F. (1998) *Developing network organizations*. Reading, MA: Addison-Wesley.

Coghlan, D. (1997) *Renewing Apostolic Religious Life*. Dublin: The Columba Press.

Cooperrider, D. L. & Srivastva, S. (1987) "Appreciative inquiry into organizational life." In R. W. Woodman & W. A. Pasmore (eds.) *Research in organizational change and development, Vol. 1.* Greenwich, CN: JAI Press, pp. 129–169.

Cooperrider, D. L. (1990) "Positive image, positive action: The affirmative basis of organizing." In S. Srivastva & D.L. Cooperrider (Eds) *Appreciative management and leadership*. San Francisco: Jossey-Bass. pp. 91–125.

Dyer, W. G. (1995) *Team building: Current issues and new alternatives*. Reading, MA: Addison-Wesley.

Edwards, (1979) *Drawing on the right side of the brain.* Los Angeles, Tarcher.

Eriksson, K. E. & Robert, K. H. (1991) From the big bang to sustainable societies. *Reviews in Oncology,* 4, No. 2, pp. 5–14.

Frank, F. (1973) *The zen of seeing*. Garden City, New York: Doubleday.

Fritz, R. (1991) *Creating*. New York: Fawcett Columbine.

Gallway, W. T. (1974) *The inner game of tennis*. New York: Random House.

Goffman, E. (1959) *The presentation of self in everyday Life*. New York: Doubleday.

Goffman, E. (1967) *Interaction ritual.* New York: Aldine.

Goffman, E. (1961) *Asylums.* New York: Doubleday Anchor Books.

Hall, E. T. (1959) *The silent language.* New York: Doubleday.

Hall, E. T . (1966) *The hidden dimension.* New York: Doubleday.

Hall, E. T. (1976) *Beyond culture.* New York: Doubleday.

Hall, E. T. (1983) *The dance of life*. New York: Doubleday.

Harvey, J. (1974) The Abilene paradox: The management of agreement. *Organization Dynamics*, 17, pp. 16–43.

Heifetz, R. A. (1994) *Leadership without easy answers.* Cambridge, MA: Belknap Press of Harvard Univ. Press.

Heron, J. (1990). *Helping the client.* London: Sage.

Hirschhorn, L. (1988) *The workplace within.* Cambridge, MA: MIT Press.

Hirschhorn, L. (1991) *Managing in the new team environment.* Reading, MA: Addison-Wesley.

Isaacs, W. N. (1993) Taking flight: Dialogue, collective thinking, and organizational learning. *Organizational Dynamics*, Winter, pp. 24–39.

Jaques, E. (1982) *The forms of time.* London: Heinemann.

Janis, I. (1982) *Group think (2d ed. rev.).* Boston: Houghton Mifflin.

Lifton, R. J. 19—(p. 6.15). *Thought Reform and the Psychology of Totalism.* New York: Norton.

Likert, R. (1961) *New patterns of management.* New York: McGraw-Hill.

Luft, J. (1961) The Johari window. *Human Relations Training News*, 5, pp. 6–7.

March, J. & Simon, H. A. (1958). *Organizations.* New York: Wiley.

Marshak, R. J. (1993) Managing the metaphors of change. *Organizational Dynamics*, Summer,

Michael, D. N. (1973) *On learning to plan and planning to learn.* San Francisco: Jossey Bass.

Michael, D. N. (1997) *Learning to plan and planning to learn. (2d ed.)* Alexandria, VA: Miles River Press.

Nadler, D. A. (1977) *Feedback and organization development.* Reading, MA: Addison-Wesley.

Neumann, J. (1994) "Difficult beginnings: Confrontation between client and consultant." in Casemore, R., et al (Eds) *What makes consultancy work: Understanding the dynamics.* London: Southbank Univ. Press, pp. 13–47.

Nevis, E. C. (1987). *Organizational consulting: The Gestalt approach.* Cleveland: The Gestalt Institute Press.

Rashford, N. S. & Coghlan, D. (1994) *The dynamics of organizational levels.* Reading, MA: Addison Wesley.

Schein, E. H. with Inge Schneier and C. H. Barker. (1961a) *Coercive persuasion.* New York: Norton.

Schein, E. H. (1961b) Management development as a process of influence. *Industrial Management Review*, 2, pp. 59–77.

Schein, E. H. (1966) The problem of moral education for the business manager. *Industrial Management Review*, 8, No. 1, pp. 3–14.

Schein, E. H. (1978) *Career dynamics: Matching individual and organizational needs*. Reading, MA: Addison-Wesley.

Schein, E. H. (1980) *Organizational psychology, 3d Ed.* Englewood Cliffs, NJ: Prentice–Hall.

Schein, E. H. (1985) *Organizational culture and leadership*. Jossey-Bass.; Second edition, 1992.

Schein, E. H. (1990) *Career anchors (Rev. Ed.)* San Diego, CA: Pfeiffer, Inc.

Schein, E. H. & Bennis, W. G. (1965) *Personal and organizational change through group methods: The laboratory approach*. New York: Wiley.

Senge, P. (1990) *The fifth discipline*. New York: Doubleday Currency.

Senge, P., Roberts, C., Ross, R.B., Smith, B. J., & Kleiner, A. (1994) *The fifth discipline field book*. New York: Doubleday Currency.

Simon, H. A. (1953). *Models of man*. New York: Wiley.

Simon, H. (1960) *The new science of management decisions*. New York: Harper.

Tversky, A. & Kahneman, D. (1974). Judgment under uncertainty: Heuristics and biases. *Science*, 185, pp. 1124–1131.

Van Maanen, J. (1979) "The self, the situation, and the rules of interpersonal relations." In Bennis, W., Van Maanen, J., Schein, E. H. & Steele, F. (Eds) *Essays in Interpersonal Dynamics*. Homewood, IL: Dorsey.

Van Maanen, J. & Kunda, G. (1989) "Real feelings: Emotional expression and organizational culture." In B. Staw (Ed) *Research in Organizational Behavior, Vol. 11*. Greenwich, CT: JAI Press.

Van Maanen, J. & Schein, E. H. (1979) "Toward a theory of organizational socialization." In M. B. Staw & L. L. Cummings (Eds) *Research in Organizational Behavior, Vol. 1*. Greenwich, CT: JAI Press.

Weisbord, M. R. & Janoff, S. (1995) *Future search*. San Francisco: Berrett-Koehler.

Worley, C. G., Hitchin, D. E. & Ross, W. L. (1996) *Integrated strategic change*. Reading, MA: Addison-Wesley.

Index